Dr Damian O'Connor began researching ~~~~~~~ ~~~~~~
Institute in 2003 as part of his PhD studies at the University of East
Anglia into nineteenth-century British imperial defence policies. A
history teacher by profession, he has travelled widely in Africa, North
America and Asia in pursuit of his lifelong interest in imperial, naval
and military history. He also served as a Territorial Army officer in
the Royal Artillery (Volunteers) in the 1980s.

BETWEEN PEACE AND WAR

British Defence and the Royal United Services Institute, 1831–2010

DAMIAN P O'CONNOR

Published in 2011 by Royal United Services Institute
for Defence and Security Studies (RUSI)
Whitehall, London SW1A 2ET, UK

ISBN 0-85516-173-6

Printed and bound in Great Britain by Stephen Austin and Sons Ltd.

This book is dedicated to Corporal John O'Connor and Private Alexander James McDowell of the Loyal North Lancashire Regiment, veterans of the Somme and Gallipoli, and to Tom who sank the Bismarck, *manned the dockyards and patrolled the streets of Northern Ireland and Afghanistan. They guard us while we sleep.*

CONTENTS

EDITOR'S NOTE

The Royal United Services Institute for Defence and Security Studies has, throughout its history, changed its name on a number of occasions. For the sake of readability it is referred to as RUSI or as the Institute, with a few exceptions. The *RUSI Journal* likewise has changed its name alongside the Institute; the periodical is either referred to by its current name or as the *Journal* throughout the text. RUSI's sister organisation, the United Service Institution of India, is referred to as USI, and its own periodical is referred to as the *USI Journal*.

LIST OF ILLUSTRATIONS

Plates

1. William Henry Smyth, by William Brockedon (black and red chalk, 1838). NPG 2515(85). Reproduced courtesy of the National Portrait Gallery.

2. Letter to the Editor, *United Services Journal and Naval and Military Magazine*, 1829, Part 1, p. 239.

3. The Thatched House Tavern, appears in Walter Thornbury, *Old and New London* (London: Cassell, Petter & Galpin, 1874).

4. Interior of the Thatched House Tavern, St James's Street, London: View showing a dinner meeting of the Dilettanti Society, c1840. RUSI collection.

5. Major General Howard Douglas, unsigned. RUSI collection. Photograph by Adrian Johnson.

6. Henry Hardinge, 1st Viscount Hardinge of Lahore, by and published by Charles Turner, published by Colnaghi, Son & Co, after Eden Upton Eddis (mezzotint), 20 March 1833. NPG D19531. Reproduced courtesy of the National Portrait Gallery.

7. The Royal United Service Institution, Whitehall Yard, 1886, unsigned. RUSI collection.

8. Sir John Charles Ready Colomb, by Sir (John) Benjamin Stone (platinum print in card window mount), 1 June 1898. NPG x15731. Reproduced courtesy of the National Portrait Gallery.

9. 'The New War Game, "Polemos," as played at the Royal United Services Institution', appears in *Illustrated London News*, 3 November 1888, p. 517. RUSI collection.

10. 'The Bazaar at the Royal United Service Institution, Whitehall: The Committee', appears in *Illustrated London News*, 17 June 1893, p. 720. RUSI collection.

11. Illustration in R H Elsdale, 'The Defence of London and of England', *RUSI Journal* (Vol. 30, No. 135, 1886). RUSI collection.

12. 'The King and Queen Return to London from Royal Tour of Canada and the United States: Scenes During Drive to Palace', Topical Press, 22 June 1939. RUSI collection.

13. Appears in David Bolton, 'Has Peace Broken Out?', *RUSI Journal* (Vol. 134, No. 3, 1989).

14. Richard Cobbold and George W Bush at Banqueting House, 27 November 2003. RUSI collection.

15. David Petraeus at Land Warfare Conference, 9 June 2010. RUSI collection.

16. Tony Blair speaks to RUSI onboard HMS *Albion*, by Susan Schulman, 11 January 2007. RUSI collection.

ACRONYMS AND ABBREVIATIONS

ANC	African National Congress
APC	Armoured personnel carrier
BAOR	British Army of the Rhine
BEF	British Expeditionary Force
CDC	Colonial Defence Committee
CENTO	Central Treaty Organization
CIA	Central Intelligence Agency
CND	Campaign for Nuclear Disarmament
COIN	Counter-insurgency
EEC	European Economic Community
FCO	Foreign and Commonwealth Office
FRELIMO	Liberation Front of Mozambique
GDP	Gross domestic product
HQ	Headquarters
ICBM	Intercontinental ballistic missile
IFV	Infantry fighting vehicle
MC	Military Cross
MK	Umkhonto we Sizwe
MLRS	Multiple launch rocket system
MoD	Ministry of Defence (UK)
MP	Member of Parliament
NATO	North Atlantic Treaty Organization
NBC	Nuclear, biological and chemical
NCO	Non-commissioned officer
PR	Press/public relations
RA	Royal Artillery

RAF	Royal Air Force
RAMC	Royal Army Medical Corps
RE	Royal Engineers
RENAMO	Mozambican National Resistance
RFA	Royal Fleet Auxiliary
RN	Royal Navy
RPF	Rwandan Patriotic Front
RSM	Regimental Sergeant Major
RUF	Revolutionary United Front
RUSI	Royal United Services Institute
SADF	South African Defence Force
SDI	Strategic Defense Initiative
SDP	Social Democrat Party
SEATO	South East Asian Treaty Organization
SLBM	Submarine-launched ballistic missile
SWAPO	South West Africa People's Organization
TA	Territorial Army
UK	United Kingdom
UN	United Nations
UNAMIR	United Nations Assistance Mission for Rwanda
UNITA	National Union for the Total Independence of Angola
US	United States
USAAF	United States Army Air Force
USI	United Service Institution of India
USM	United Service Museum
USMC	United States Marine Corps
USSR	Union of Soviet Socialist Republics
VC	Victoria Cross
WAAF	Women's Auxiliary Air Force
WMD	Weapons of mass destruction
ZANU	Zimbabwe African National Union
ZAPU	Zimbabwe African People's Union

I. ORIGINS
1829–60

The Thatched House Tavern, a popular watering hole for the bright lights of London society throughout the eighteenth century and the first decades of the nineteenth, lay on St James's Street, just off Pall Mall. Jonathan Swift had dined there; Charles James Fox and William Pitt had glowered at each other there; Edmund Burke had complained that the pies served there smelled of dead dog, while Lord Canning had discussed poetry with his crony, the poet-diplomat John Hookham Frere, over his Madeira in the bar. Beau Brummel had preened in the dining room and the Prince Regent had caroused there; all sorts of dining clubs met there, including the Dilettanti Society, apparently dedicated to advancing the cause of classical antiquity, but in reality, more dedicated to getting drunk. Freemasons, artists, writers and politicians there were in plenty, but also more charitable institutions, such as the Old Royal Naval Club, which existed to look after old salts beached on hard times, and who dined at the tavern every year on the anniversary of the Battle of the Nile.[1] It was possibly for this reason that the venue was chosen for a meeting at two o'clock on 25 June 1831 of distinguished military and naval officers who had come together to found the 'Naval and Military Museum and Library', parent to the world's first defence think tank – what is today the Royal United Services Institute.[2]

The inspiration for such a foundation no doubt had its roots in the great upsurge of amateur literary, philosophical and scientific interests that occurred in late Georgian Britain,[3] but the background to the calls for a specifically military and naval society lay in the tensions that existed in the military establishment after the end of the Napoleonic wars. On one side of a growing debate was the idea that there had been far too many incidents of failure in the late wars due to the poor training and education of both officers and men and that therefore a more professional approach was needed. For every Waterloo, they felt, there had been a Walcheren and for every Nelsonian band of brothers there had been a hell afloat ruled by a tyrant contemptuous of 'bosun captains'. The other side held that as Napoleon had been driven off by the tried and trusted methods of the eighteenth century, innovations were therefore neither welcome nor necessary and, indeed, might turn out to be dangerous. After all, revolutionary ideas in France had produced not utopia, but more than two decades of war and what the world, military and political, really needed was a rest from change. Warfare, if necessary, would continue to be waged by aristocrats born to command and forelock-tugging lower orders who would follow a 'gentleman' anywhere. After 1815, even though the Duke of York was nominally commander-in-chief, it was an increasingly conservative Duke of Wellington whose influence dominated the military scene; few would challenge him openly, even when he was increasingly distracted by his involvement in parliamentary politics and, during the 1840s, increasingly deaf, increasingly irascible and increasingly indisposed (although not implacably opposed) to consider reforms to the military. He was also disinclined to delegate, even when it was clear that he had not the time to give sufficient attention to the work.

Change had already begun to make itself felt, however, ever since Sir John Moore had rejected the idea that soldiers were merely automata to be shifted around the battlefield by rigid drill and then ordered to point their weapons in the general direction of the enemy. Moore had also held the view that officers should act in a paternalistic way towards their men if they were to become effective instruments of war and not desert as soon as battle approached. His idea that soldiers were more effective when trained to think and act on their own initiative had proved its worth in the Light Infantry during the war and those officers who had served in the Light Infantry took this idea with them when they moved on to other regiments. Other officers, such as the influential Lord Frederick Fitzclarence, had also picked up these ideas. Fitzclarence was an illegitimate son of William IV who from 1824–32 commanded the 11th Foot and then the 7th Royal Fusiliers where he campaigned against drunkenness among the troops, introduced company schools and regimental libraries, and gave rewards to encourage good conduct rather than simply relying on the lash to achieve it. He also believed in regular training and exercises so that both officers and men could learn their *profession* – an outright rejection of the more conservative view that blue blood and moral fibre were the true arbiters of victory.

There was also a shift in the social make-up of the officer corps to reinforce the demand for a more professional approach to warfare. The industrial revolution and the expansion of commerce had produced a class of nabobs, capitalists and lawyers who were only too eager to buy the status that a commission could bring and sent their sons into the army with enthusiasm. In 1831, just under half the officer corps had their social origins in the rising middle class and by 1854, this had risen to nearly two thirds.[4] A belief that competence came before inheritance as a surer guarantee of success was central to their experience.

The inspiration for the United Services Institution came more specifically from an article in the *United Service Journal*, 1829, penned by Captain W H Smyth, 'an old Egyptian campaigner' and naturalist,[5] which called for a society dedicated to the application of 'the tone of Science' to the military art.[6] The suggestion was duly picked up by two men, Commander Henry Downes of the navy and Major General Sir Howard Douglas. Downes was a native of Colchester in Essex who had made his name with the capture of the notorious slaver, *Henriquetta*, in 1829.[7] In the meantime he had acquired a taste for natural history and had built up a collection of 'stuffed birds, Quadrupeds and Fishes ... and a variety of curiosities', which along with Smyth's collections he felt might make the basis of a museum collection.[8] Douglas was an artillery officer who had seen action at Walcheren and in the Peninsular War, but who had risen to fame more particularly while supervising the running of the Royal Military College in High Wycombe. This august institution, which would later become both the Staff College and the Royal Military Academy, Sandhurst, had been founded by a French general who could not bring himself to serve Napoleon; but, given that Britain was then at war with France, it was felt more fitting that a British officer should lead it, and Douglas had been recalled from Spain for the purpose. Douglas was a thinking soldier who published works on military engineering, fortification and logistics before turning himself into an expert on naval gunnery and tactics. Recently returned from a colonial governorship of New Brunswick, Douglas was a Fellow of the Royal Society, and a founder of the Royal Geographical Society, which he helped to establish at the same time as RUSI.

Downes and Douglas were experienced networkers who quickly attracted support for their new venture from the highest echelons of the British political establishment. They knew Lieutenant General Sir Herbert Taylor, aide to King William IV, and as a result he, the Duke of Clarence and the Duke of Wellington, notwithstanding his conservatism, all endorsed the project. When the meeting took place at the Thatched House Tavern, the founding resolution was moved by Major General Sir Henry Hardinge, recently the secretary of state for war, future victor of the Sikh Wars and successor to Wellington as commander-in-chief of the British Army. The seconder was Captain Francis Beaufort RN, head of the Admiralty Hydrographic Office, another co-founder of the Royal Geographical Society and Royal Society council member. The patrons were no less than King William IV and the Duke of Wellington, while the six presidents included the

First Lord of the Admiralty, the Master General of the Ordnance, the Lord Lieutenant of Ireland and the General of Marines.[9] Thirty-two vice-presidents and thirty council members (of whom one third would retire each year) were also chosen from among the military and naval elite, while Douglas, Downes, Lieutenant W S Hall and Charles Downes (treasurer) took over the day-to-day running of the Institute. Those who thought that they might be joining just another dining club were quickly disabused of such notions; the aim of the Institute was to be 'strictly a scientific and professional Society, not a Club',[10] directed towards the acquisition and advancement of professional knowledge, and neither party politics, gambling, eating nor drinking on the premises would be tolerated. Detaching 'our friends from the clubhouse and the billiard table' and directing young officers away from 'idleness and dissipation' were high on Commander Downes's list of priorities.[11] He publicly rebuked a Mr Simpson for allegedly soliciting subscriptions for the Institute from 'an establishment for young ladies in Sloane Street', a charge that Mr Simpson vigorously denied; he was rather soliciting for the British and Foreign Seaman and Soldiers' Friends Society.[12] Such controversies did not stop the more senior officers, however, from meeting at the Thatched House Tavern for the Institute's first annual general meeting in 1832 with Sir John Hobhouse, secretary-at-war, in the chair – Sir James Graham, First Lord of the Admiralty, should have taken the chair, but made his excuses and sent a twenty-guinea donation instead. Once Hobhouse left, 'the greatest conviviality and cordiality prevailed until a late hour', to the great satisfaction of the members who were impervious to irony on this occasion and who continued to use the same venue for the next two decades.[13]

Remarkably for the time, an emphasis was placed on the encouragement of junior officers' involvement and the Institute gained an unofficial reputation as the only place where a younger officer, if he were brave enough, might ask a question of a senior officer without automatic rebuke. Two thousand officers joined within a year for a subscription of ten shillings per annum – cheap enough to be 'a matter of trifling import to the very junior officers of the service' – or six pounds for life membership;[14] by 1835 the membership had doubled to a stable 4,000. 'Nothing, we apprehend', reported *The Times,* 'can prevent an institution, so excellent in its object and patronized by such persons from being attended with very beneficial results'.[15] Here then was a nexus of political, military, naval, geographical, imperial, colonial, scientific and intellectual power harnessed in the serious endeavour that would both define RUSI and, eventually, give it its influence.

A Place to Call Home

However convivial a venue, the Thatched House Tavern was hardly a suitable site for the Institute. After a brief stay in temporary accommodation in Whitehall Yard, an approach was made to the Board of Works, who granted the use of Vanbrugh House – described by Jonathan Swift as resembling a goose pie[16] – close by, necessitating the removal of the Poor Law Commissioners. Conversion works to provide a library, model room and natural history room were carried out by G L Taylor Esq, civil architect to the Admiralty, at a cost of £1,830 and the Institute took up residence in 1833.[17] The original site is now buried beneath the Old War Office buildings – roughly where the statue of a Gurkha now stands – but it was a pleasant and prestigious location (both Robert Peel and Benjamin Disraeli would live at addresses in adjacent Whitehall Gardens). In 1833, the Board of Works made over a further building in Inner Scotland Yard to the Institute, and in 1849 a small house which separated the two buildings was purchased, demolished and a new lecture theatre built; it was in these premises that the Institute remained until 1895.

The increased demand for space resulted from a rather ill-defined appeal for objects of interest for display in the Museum, which meant that rather than specifically military artefacts, a wide array of interesting objects turned up, which, as a later secretary tactfully commented, 'bore witness to the officers of both Services as sportsmen and their industry as naturalists'.[18] Admiral Sir Charles Hamilton's gifts of 'some articles ... not easily described' were no doubt welcomed with necessary tact. Even more delicate was the thanks extended to 'the many gifts of great beauty and value presented by ladies' at the first General Meeting in 1832.[19] Perhaps they had the gift of Mrs Hawkins of Holywell, Hampshire – six cases of seaweed – and the donor of *Lady Morgan's Book of the Boudoir* (two volumes) in mind. In short, the Museum was 'swamped with ... stuffed animals and geological specimens' and all sorts of curiosities,[20] most notable of which were the crystal-stuffed skull of an extinct species of Himalayan elephant; a snake 'recently dead' donated by the Surrey Zoological Gardens; a pair of the late explorer Captain Dundas Cochrane's boots worn on his wedding to a young Kamchatkan girl (rather worn, as he had walked there from Dieppe in 1820–22); and a mummy from Thebes, which was unrolled in a public lecture in 1849.[21] A great number of ladies had certainly taken the opportunity to clear out a great many lumber rooms.

Unsolicited gifts would be a recurring problem for the Museum. In June 1853, for example, the Museum skilfully declined the natural history collection of a Mr Joseph Parker of Saville Row,[22] only to be faced in September with a battleship anchor thoughtfully dumped by Captain Ommaney, without notice, on the pavement outside the Museum. Only hearts of flint could refuse such well-meaning generosity and, after Ommaney (having dragged the thing from Limerick) refused all hints (however forcefully delivered) about taking it away, the anchor was duly found a home.[23] Nor could Master Hanby's pet centipede be declined, on similarly sentimental grounds.[24] By 1858, however, the patience of the secretaries had run out and the decision was taken, at the prompting of the new secretary, Captain Boughey Burgess, at a Special General Meeting, to sell off the natural history collections and accept only service-related artefacts thereafter. 'With regards to Natural History, in which the most extensive action of the pruning knife is required', the zoology department was to go almost in its entirety.[25] The sale of those items that could find a buyer realised £218 6s 8d. In 1869, the librarian, Mr Low, took this as a precedent to prune the collections further, reducing the coin collection to his own benefit – for which he got five years' penal servitude.

Notwithstanding this, the Museum quickly became a firm favourite and something of a tourist attraction – entry was free on Christmas Day, Easter and the anniversaries of Trafalgar and Waterloo – appearing in such popular guidebooks as *Mogg's New Picture of London and Guide to its Sights*, 1844. Two decades later, *Crutchley's London in 1865: A Handbook for Strangers* waxed lyrical about the Library, the nine rooms and three galleries of the Military Department, the three large rooms of the Naval Department and the Russian gun captured in the Crimea proudly displayed outside the entrance (no doubt serving to prevent further deliveries of battleship anchors). The Institute also built up an impressive collection of naval manuscripts dating back to 1693, including an account of the mutiny on the HMS *Bounty;* the secret orders of the USS *Chesapeake* taken after the HMS *Shannon* had captured her and demolished American pretensions to naval power during the War of 1812; and letters from Lord Nelson, Collingwood and St Vincent.[26] Inside, the eager visitor was able to take in such wonders as:[27]

> American, Oriental, and European weapons; military models, accoutrements; Chinese and Asiatic armour; the sword worn by Cromwell at Drogheda, and, the sword worn by Wolfe at Quebec; the sash which lowered the body of Sir John Moore into his grave at Corunna; the skeleton of Marengo, the horse which carried Napoleon at Waterloo; Colonel Hamilton's model of Sebastopol. The *Naval Department,* in three rooms, contains a large collection of naval models, European, Asiatic, and American; the Franklin relics, discovered in Captain Sir Leopold McClintock's expedition; the rudder of H.M.

Ship *Edgar*, sunk at Spithead; Drake's walking-stick; and Captain Cook's chronometer: these are a few of the more note-worthy treasures enshrined in the Museum. Recently has been added the model of the battle of Trafalgar, placed upon a table made from old planks taken from H.M. Ship *Victory*.

Some of the exhibits were of remarkable provenance – the coconut tree under which Captain Cook was killed, complete with the stone that finished him; a biscuit frozen for twelve years in the Arctic ice; yew bows retrieved from the *Mary Rose;* a piece of the conquistador Pizarro's standard (authenticated), donated by Mrs Heywood; and Nelson's hat. Among the curiosities were the jaws of a large shark which was caught by the crew of the HMS *Abergavenny*, engaged in hot pursuit of the slaver *Nancy* in the Caribbean. The captain of the slaver had thrown his real papers overboard to avoid arrest, only to find that the shark had swallowed them whole. The papers were 'Jonah-like recovered' from the shark and the slaver duly condemned.[28] Not so fortunate was the last meal of another shark's jaw exhibited – 'the mutilated remains of a little boy'.[29]

The prize exhibit was undoubtedly Siborne's model of the Battle of Waterloo. Commissioned by the Institute in 1830 to produce a centrepiece for the Museum, Lieutenant Siborne spent eight years researching the battle and then presented it to the public in the Egyptian Hall, Piccadilly, where 100,000 paying customers turned up to see its 75,000 model soldiers spread over 400 square feet of terrain. One customer was less than impressed however – the Duke of Wellington himself dismissed it as 'ridiculous and useless' and insisted that large numbers of Prussian soldiers be removed from it on the grounds that they were not there at the 'crisis of the battle' represented in the model (a point that Siborne vigorously defended).[30] This prevented the Institute from buying the model until 1850, when a subscription of £200 was raised to acquire it as the centrepiece for a model room attached to the new lecture theatre.[31] From then on the Museum treasured it, and at a shilling-a-go entrance fee, and the public flocked to see it – over 16,000 in 1869 and over 20,000 in 1873.[32] It remains a popular attraction at the National Army Museum in Chelsea, where it can be seen today.

Quiet Years

Dealing with hordes of tourists and fending off unwanted bequests were not the only hazards faced by the staff of the Institute in these years.[33] In 1836, when Downes became too ill to continue in his role as secretary an assistant, Lewis Tonna, was appointed to help with the day-to-day running of the Institute on an annual salary of £130, raised to £200 in 1838. This seemed to irk Lieutenant Acherley RN, who began a campaign to get this salary reduced to £130 – when put to the vote, Acherley lost by 63–2. Curiously enough, in June 1855, it was felt necessary to expel the similarly named Lieutenant Ackerley of the navy from membership of the Institute after he had formed the habit of expressing his opinions on the quality of scholarship of authors represented in the Library collection by commenting directly on the pages of the volumes themselves (though we have all been there). Lieutenant Ackerley felt strongly enough about this assault on his freedom of expression that he appealed against the Institute through the courts. The courts having ruled in favour of the Institute, Ackerley turned up at the annual general meeting in 1856 to make a forceful restatement of his case, and, being convinced that he was in possession of a professional reputation proof against all but the most serious faux pas, proceeded to berate the council (with the Duke of Cambridge in the chair). Not having gained satisfaction through this manoeuvre, he then returned to the Institute a month later, which necessitated his forcible removal from the premises. Intellectual arguments and appeals to reason having failed, Ackerley took his stick to Tonna, which resulted in a further court appearance – fined five pounds and bound over – and thus achieved a place in history denied to lesser scholars.[34] It is not recorded to which prison hulk or guano island governorship Ackerley was latterly appointed, but Tonna died a year later in 1857.[35]

However, even this unpleasant experience pales into insignificance when compared to the gas leak of 29 October 1855. The Institute being evacuated after a strong smell of gas was detected in the cellars and the gas company informed, the engineer called to investigate the problem went down into the cellars and, it being dark, lit a match to better see the problem. The resulting conflagration ripped up thirty-two yards of pavement and sparked off a series of secondary explosions in the area, but left the Museum intact. The meeting to discuss how to respond to the damage to the gas supply took place on 5 November – Guy Fawkes Night. There was also an ongoing problem with the nearby sewage works, which caused subsidence damage in 1851 and became so serious that in 1856 the building had to be shored up. The resultant leaks into the building necessitated a noticeable amount of cleaning up and led to complaints about the smell in the lecture theatre.

The finances of the Institute also required some management in the early years, mainly because the membership fee had been set at such a low level that collecting the subscriptions from globe-trotting officers was problematic. In 1832, the Institute almost went under when its bankers, Sir George Duckett & Co, suspended trading and froze the £1,279 that was virtually the only asset the Institute possessed. Ten years later, the Institute had still only recovered half of what it was owed. This problem was compounded when the accountant appointed in 1837 managed to lose £511/10 over the next five years and the council was faced with the unpleasant task of calling on Mr O'Brien to repay the money – a demand 'immediately complied with'.[36] The next accountant was drawn from a class of men thought to possess an endless store of financial acumen and attention to detail – a Royal Navy purser. Collecting the subscriptions continued to be a problem, however, and in 1852, 691 officers had their membership withdrawn for persistent non-payment, followed by another ninety-nine the next year, when the state of finances dictated a pay cut for the staff. An appeal for more members was made in 1854 by means of a circular to all serving officers to remind them that 'the subscription is small, the object is great', raising enough money to put the staff wages up again. However, 'the glorious contests in the Crimea and the great mortality in the Army at Varna and elsewhere … removed many valuable members',[37] to the point that the Institute was running at a loss, crippled mainly by taxes and rates.

In intellectual terms, the Institute also struggled in its early years. This was due to its roving focus beyond merely military and naval subjects and a lecture programme that reflected this background in natural history and geography. The first lecture, given on 13 March 1834 by Captain A Machonochie of the navy, secretary of the Geographical Society, was on the subject of 'The Actual State and Prospects of African Discovery' and the bi-weekly addresses that followed often illuminated the physical sciences rather than the military ones. Library subscriptions were taken out to French military and naval journals in 1835, but these were only in addition to the geographical and scientific ones already taken. The decision to establish a 'meteorological museum' in 1836 betrayed both the wideranging interests and the lack of focus of the membership. In 1837, a proposal was put forward to employ a lecturer specifically to instruct officers in general scientific principles and to take a more professional approach to the cataloguing of the collections, but this was not taken up. Instead, lecturers were paid to give series of talks on a particular subject in an attempt to impose intellectual coherence on the lecture programme. Papers read at the evening meetings were also offered to the *United Services Journal* for publication and from 1841 Henry M Browne, 'an intelligent youth', was employed as a full-time librarian. However, despite its varied achievements, for the first twenty-five years of its existence the Institute, variously known as the 'Naval and Military Library and Museum', the 'United Services Museum' and the 'United Services Institute', remained something of a curiosity.

There were several reasons why the Institute played only a subsidiary role in these years. The first was that, as already alluded to, its members were spread across the globe and often absent for years at a time and so a certain lack of continuity in membership, thrust and policy was inevitable. There was also the increasing incapacity of the Duke of Wellington to consider. His tenure as commander-in-chief from 1842–52 was far from his finest hour and engendered a great deal of frustration among reform-minded officers who increasingly regarded him as a block on necessary change. This reality meant that the Institute had to tread carefully if it was not to come into conflict with its patron, and therefore could not push its reformist inclinations as hard as it might have wished. Perhaps the main reason, however, was that the military debates of these years were aired most forcefully in the military press. Henry Colbourn's monthly *United Service Journal* was complemented in 1833 by the appearance of another title in his stable, the weekly *Naval and Military Gazette*, both of which were reform-minded. The more conservative view was represented by the *United Service Gazette*, which also appeared in 1833 and which debated vigorously – and sometimes libellously – with Colbourn's publications. The circulation of these publications was very strong – around 120,000–190,000 copies per year – and as copies were purchased by messes and other interested institutions, the readership was probably much higher. Wellington refused to read any of the publications, and let it be known that he frowned on those organisations that subscribed to them, which gave another check to the Institute's progress.[38]

A further problem existed in that although the Institute was convinced of its mission to push forward the idea that the practically educated officer would be the well-trained officer of the future, and of its role as a lobby speaking for the army and navy on procurement issues to Parliament and the Admiralty Board,[39] the international environment of the 1830s and 1840s was so benign that there was little urgent need to focus attention on military and naval matters.

France was firmly contained in a 'Liberal Entente' with Britain; the East India Company was proving more than a match for its rivals in India and would defeat its last, the Sikh army, at Sobraon, 'the Indian Waterloo', in 1846 (despite the setbacks in Afghanistan) and if the Russians were meddling in the Ottoman Empire, then Lord Palmerston's bluster and bluff diplomacy defended Constantinople. Even the civil unrest at home represented by the Chartist movement hardly presented a threat to the state.[40] And even though the rosy glow of *Pax Britannica* could not obscure the reality that the Empire and its trade had to be defended by the expenditure of blood and treasure on a regular basis, the fact that British troops and sailors had, in living memory, occupied Paris, burnt Washington, conquered India and established an unprecedented command of the seas indicated Britain's ability to hold its own in the world and even to be regarded by Russia as positively predatory.[41] All of this had been achieved without very much in the way of a conscious defence policy, imperial or otherwise, in this period, beyond a vague confidence in the Nelson touch backed up by Martello Towers and legendary British pluck. For the British government, it was the *threat* of British power wielded by diplomats that was the guarantor of British security rather than the maintenance of properly resourced and efficient standing armies.

Russians, Rebellion and Risorgimento

The failings of such a policy were exposed by the geopolitical turbulence of the 1850s, when a series of shocks first revealed the deficiencies of the unreformed British Army, and then tore up the rulebook of Congress Europe as the nationalist sentiment of 1848 became a tool of state. The first was the Crimean War, 1854–56, when public complacency over the state of the armed forces was shattered by the reports of William Howard Russell of *The Times* (his wife would donate several of his possessions to the Institute after his death). Fought to keep the Russians away from Constantinople, where they would be able to interfere with Britain's communications with India in the eastern Mediterranean, the war demonstrated serious shortcomings in British capabilities.

Neither the army nor navy was prepared for the war, and thirty years of neglect was paid for in blood and costly blunders. There were no reserves, weapons were outdated, and no adequate transport, medical or commissariat services existed. There was no clear system of command and the commander-in-chief, the Waterloo veteran Lord Raglan, had the habit of referring to the enemy as 'the French' rather than 'the Russians'. The system whereby officers purchased their commissions, combined with the social position required to rise to high command, had encouraged very wealthy aristocratic officers to rise far in advance of their capabilities: Lord Cardigan, commander of the Light Brigade is a famous example of a brainless martinet, but his brother-in-law and commander, Lord Lucan, whom he detested and refused to obey, was just as bad. General Scarlett, commander of the Heavy Brigade, did not know the words of command necessary to control his troops and only made up for his incompetence by an amateurish enthusiasm for a fight. Furthermore, it was officially decided that the Indian Army would not be employed in the war – its efficiency and experience were not considered great enough to outweigh its lack of social standing. The resultant long siege in a Russian winter left the troops to suffer in appalling conditions, while Lord Lucan lived on his private yacht anchored offshore. The fact that the British Army was not defeated in the battles at the Alma, Balaclava and Inkerman was, despite their equipment, due to the excellence of the soldiers, the quality of the regimental officers – Colonel Colin Campbell of the Thin Red Line is an example – and the Russians' even greater incompetence. Raglan died in disgrace in the Crimea, while the stress of explaining what had gone wrong to Queen Victoria caused the commander-in-chief, Henry Hardinge, to collapse with a stroke. The plan to burn the Russian naval base at Kronstadt and then St Petersburg, for which a purpose-built fleet was created – the Great Armament of 1856 – was frustrated because the Russians surrendered before it could be used; and to cap it all, it had been the French army that had finally broken the Russians at Sevastopol and scooped the laurels. Clearly, things had to change.

Within a year, that message was driven home when a combination of Benthamism, Evangelicalism, sheer snobbery and crass mismanagement violated a wide cross-section of Indian sensibilities and produced the Indian Mutiny of 1857. Put simply, a certain strain of British administrator believed that they had the duty and competence to sweep away Indian tradition and produce a more 'efficient' anglicised version based on Christianity and free trade. Running roughshod over the objections of those orientalist administrators – who believed that the way to rule India was to respect its particularities and tread softly – men like Lord Dalhousie (Governor General 1848–56) and Lord Macaulay (who led legal and educational reforms during the 1840s) and some truly dreadful Memsahibs who objected forcefully to British menfolk having anything to do with Indian women, interfered with and irritated Indian custom like never before. India was at heart a conservative society and although there were substantial groups who attached themselves to the British Raj in pursuit of the opportunities offered, there were many who felt threatened by the rapid and often fundamental shifts in their mental furniture. The immediate cause of the Mutiny was the issue of a new cartridge, which had to be bitten open. A rumour spread among both Hindu and Muslim Sepoys that the cartridges were greased with a mixture of beef and pork fat (offensive to each faith, respectively) and although there was no truth in the rumour, in May 1857 eighty-five troopers of the 3rd Light Cavalry refused the cartridge, were imprisoned and then revolted. From there the Mutiny spread to Delhi, Cawnpore, Lucknow, Agra and Jhansi, but despite later claims that this was the 'First Indian War of Independence', it had no clear leadership, no clear programme and no clear organisation. Its aim, if one can be ascribed, was simply to resist the changes brought about by the British in favour of established rules and custom.

What followed was fourteen months of bitter fighting in which the mutineers massacred any Europeans they could find: man, woman and child, military or civilian. The most notorious atrocity was committed at Cawnpore where all but four of a party of seventeen officers, 446 men, forty-six women and fifty-five children were shot in a trap after receiving a guarantee of safe passage. Those women and children who survived the ambush were later dismembered by butchers and thrown down a well. For many on both sides the conflict took on the character of a race war and after Cawnpore was re-taken and the details of the massacre revealed, the British Army went almost berserk. If the Sepoys felt their taboos to have been violated then the British, with their attitude that women somehow represented a higher, purer plane of existence, certainly felt that their own had been trampled upon. Captured Sepoys were made to lick up blood and then forced to eat beef and pork before being executed, while the new Governor General Charles Canning was branded 'Clemency' Canning after he attempted to restrain the most eager avenging angels. The final decisive act of the Mutiny came with the recapture of Delhi, the arrest of the last Moghul Emperor Bahadur Shah – who had reluctantly accepted the leadership of the revolt – and the shooting of the Moghul Princes by William Hodson in the Tomb of Humayun. The Mutiny had failed to drive the British from India, but it had forcefully emphasised to them that their rule of the subcontinent could not be taken for granted.

The third jolt of the later 1850s came with the French invasion of Italy in 1859. Dressed up as a war to liberate Italy from Austrian occupation, this unprovoked aggression had been cooked up in a plot known as the Compact of Plombières, which committed the French to aiding the Kingdom of Piedmont by ejecting the Austrians from northern Italy, in return for Nice and Savoy. In the event, both sides went back on the deal – one made in such secrecy that the French emperor and the Piedmontese prime minister turned up to the meeting wearing false beards – but what really rang alarm bells was that the French were now being led by a Bonaparte, Napoleon III, in possession of an army and an ambition to tear up the map of Europe. The battles of Solferino and Magenta were bloody enough to turn the stomach of Napoleon III into seeking an armistice and to inspire the foundation of the Red Cross and the Geneva Conventions. Within a year, a further Piedmontese expedition led by the swashbuckling soldier Giuseppe Garibaldi was dispatched to Sicily in distinctly murky circumstances – historians are still divided as to whether this was a freebooting expedition or a piece of state-sponsored opportunism. Startlingly, Garibaldi and his Redshirts overthrew the existing rulers, crossed the Straits of Messina, then marched up the boot of Italy and handed over the whole lot to King Victor Emmanuel of Piedmont. Europe now had a whole new country to deal with.

The effect of these three crises was to galvanise the British military and naval establishment into a more systematic approach to their business. At the forefront of this development were the Woolwich-trained officers of the Royal Artillery and Royal Engineers. The technical education that these men received instilled in them a 'scientific' approach to warfare that emphasised detailed mathematical analysis of military problems, and dispelled a lingering regard for emotive Byronesque adventurism that might have remained after the Crimean War.[42] Many of these officers, such as Garnet Wolseley, who fought in the Crimea, came back acutely aware of the need for this more professional approach. As George S Patton would later (allegedly) remark, patriotism was no longer about dying for one's country, but making your enemy die for his. For them, successful warfare was about logistics tables and physical sciences, and the *Journal of the Royal Engineers Institution* and the *Minutes of the Royal Artillery Institute* churned out masses of technical data which paid tribute to their mastery of their subject. These two institutes did not, however, confine themselves to technicalities, but also published wide-ranging articles on the experiences of their officers and on broader tactical developments. Like the Institute, they especially encouraged junior officers to contribute.

In parallel with wider shifts in military culture, the Institute's reaction to the Crimean War was similarly galvanised. The decision was taken to improve links with other military institutions, such as the School of Military Engineering at Chatham and Sandhurst, and to forge stronger links within the government. An approach to the Treasury in 1857 resulted in a £400 per annum grant to help offset the £205 of rent, £95 of tax and £130 of rates.[43] However, though this was a valuable boost to finances, the real aim was to have the government nominate a member of the Institute council in return for this financial support. That member would preferably be drawn from the Inspector-General of Fortifications (an influential body) or the educational branch.[44] In the event, Colonel Lefroy, already a member of the Institute, became the first government-nominated council member. This appeal was made in the context of an active debate about the education of officers in Parliament in which it was recognised that, along with improving the provision given by the School of Military Engineering at Chatham, Woolwich, Sandhurst and the Musketry school at Hythe: [45]

[The] United Service Institution was of the greatest importance to young officers, who had an opportunity of attending lectures there and acquiring scientific knowledge. It would be a great advantage to that institution to have some allowance made for the rent and taxes.

Pains were taken to place the Institute at the centre of the debates animating the public and military. In 1857, the Museum was thoroughly reorganised to make it accessible to 'even the merest saunterer' and the requirement to get permission of a member before visiting the Institute was ended.[46] That same year, the Institute emphasised its desire for a more focused contribution by taking the momentous step of publishing 'an instructive professional periodical'[47] to 'guide through rational debate ... the future course of the army'.[48] The *Journal of the United Services Institution* contained a mix of historical, scientific, but increasingly practical articles with an emphasis on military skills. The first volume included articles on new rifles, gunnery techniques, geometry, military engineering, the routes to India and military history. Demand quickly outran the initial print run of 3,500 copies.[49]

Not satisfied, the council also decided that the Institute needed a much higher profile if it was to wield more influence. It had already successfully approached the Duke of Cambridge with a proposal in 1853 that he succeed to the position previously held by the now-deceased Duke of Wellington and had persuaded Queen Victoria to visit the Institute on 21 June 1858. As a result, in March 1859, a Special General Meeting was called to apply for a Royal Charter. In this respect the Institute was pushing at an open door – Prince Albert had already (perhaps pointedly) donated a model of the fortifications of Sevastopol to the Institute – and the Charter was granted the following year (the costs covered by the proceeds from the sale of the natural history collections). The Royal United Services Institution was now commanded by the Crown to further 'the promotion and advancement of Naval and Military Science and Literature'. In today's Institute, this exhortation is framed above the door to the Council Room (having resisted to this day the RAF's efforts to get themselves included). The Institute was given a firmer purpose and stature; it no longer simply aspired to greater relevance, and was no longer characterised by its collection of curiosities. For this it had to thank in large measure Secretary Boughey Burgess, late of the 20th Bombay Native Infantry, appointed in 1858, who would continue to lead the Institute until 1892.

II. DEMANDING SECURITY IN A GREAT POWER AGE

1860–90

If the late 1850s had been a worrying time for the British military, the next decades were to offer no respite. There was a growing feeling within military and naval circles that the security of the home islands could no longer be taken for granted; that naval supremacy might be undermined; that its small army gave Britain few offensive options; that commerce raiding might starve it into submission and cause its industries to grind to a halt; and that the empire in the East was not as secure as it once imagined it to be. It was in the formulation of new approaches to these fears that RUSI was to make a major contribution and play a leading part in pressurising an often reluctant government to take defence matters seriously after a series of increasingly bitter debates during 1870–86. More controversially, it would be an advocate of the larger commitment that Britain would make to the security of the empire in the last quarter of the nineteenth century.

The unification of Germany demonstrated most forcefully that a new strategy was demanded. In 1864, Lord Palmerston's bluff was called by the new chancellor of a second-rank power, Prussia, when he tried to warn it off an invasion of Denmark. Otto von Bismarck had calculated correctly that the British means to intervene on the European continent were strictly limited, and forced Britain to watch helplessly as the newly reformed Prussian army quickly overran the Danes. Lord Salisbury went so far as to accuse Palmerston of cowardice for not intervening regardless,[1] but the reality was that

the British Army was only approximately 150,000 strong, divided in
equal thirds between the British Isles, India and the garrisons in the
rest of the empire, and supplemented by a post-mutiny Indian Army
of approximately 120,000 Sepoys. This was nowhere near enough
for Britain to take aggressive action on mainland Europe and the
inability of the British government to provide an army of sufficient
size had already forced it previously to concede leadership of the
Crimean War to the French. This reality also drove a great number
of schemes to raise reserves that could supplement the regular forces
in time of need, none of which worked particularly well, and which
were favoured mainly on the grounds that they would be cheap. The
Russian army, by comparison, conscripted 100,000 men each year to
serve for fifteen years,[2] while the Prussians fielded 1.7 million men at
the outset of the Franco-Prussian War.[3] The lack of a large continental-
style army meant that Britain held little sway over the construction of
a new European balance increasingly mapped from Berlin. The speed
of Prussia's wars of unification against Denmark and Austria in the
1860s also appeared to undermine Britain's traditional Napoleonic
approach to fighting a European enemy; amphibious warfare would
not decisively harm France, Russia or Germany, and it was hard to
envisage what Britain's small army could do if thrown in against
(or with) any of the large conscript armies. Blockade was a weapon
that could only work over time and even then the outcome of an
economic sanction was uncertain. Without a European ally ready to
accept British gold to finance its armies in the field, the prospects of
victory were nil.

Meanwhile, during the 1860s, the American Civil War advertised
to all who cared to look that the military potential of the United States
could at any time be mobilised to mop up Canada – in 1869, President
Grant called for a Canadian referendum on independence.[4] Nor had
the Russians been idle; if they had turned away from Europe after
1856, it was only to continue their advance into Central Asia, with the
army reformed to remove at least some of its Crimean shortcomings.

A major debate was subsequently sparked as to whether the Russians intended to get over the passes into India. Britain's commercial lead was also diminishing as Europe and America industrialised, while the revolution in military armaments and organisation brought about by the development of breech-loading rifles, better artillery and faster mobilisation schemes driven by the rapid expansion of the railways added to the tandem insecurities of a simultaneous revolution in naval design, as sail and wood were replaced by steam, iron and steel, which could undermine British naval hegemony.

From the outset the Institute was intent on promoting the discussion of these alarming developments. When France invaded Italy in 1859, a topographical department was formed by Colonel Alcock which managed to persuade the War Office to lend the Institute some large maps on which the members and the public could follow the course of the war – nearly 29,000 of them visited the Museum that year.[5] The Museum and Library were also given an extensive reorganisation after the Crimean War – 2,000 preserved birds that had been packed away in one of the cellars for over two decades were finally disposed of – and donations of modern European books, maps, journals and artefacts were actively solicited. Indeed, the Museum became less a place devoted to things past and much more one for consideration of the future. By 1871 there was an impressive display of modern weapons, an expanding collection of ship models (recommended in 1872 by Nathaniel Barnaby, chief constructor of the navy from 1870 and a founder of the Institute of Naval Architects) and a Library of 15,000 books. In 1873, the Kriegsspiel – the forebear of today's map-based wargames – was introduced for members to play, and in 1874 the decision was taken to start a Gold Medal essay competition, the winner to be announced at the annual general meeting. The first topic was on the formation of a reserve for the army.

It was in the publication of the new *Journal* that the Institute made its most notable contribution. Up until this point, the fact that Major Shadwell Clerke was both vice-president of the Institute (1829–41) and editor of the *United Service Journal* meant that an independent publication was probably thought unnecessary at that time. However, although a vigorous military press already existed, it was inclined to be *too* vigorous on occasion. John Philippart, editor of the *Naval and Military Gazette*, had been inclined towards rather more open campaigning journalism than was desirable while his rival at the *United Service Gazette*, A W Watts, was apt to be vituperative about reform and Philippart in equal measure. Even when Watts was replaced by J H Stocqueler in 1844, the *United Service Gazette* remained guilty of publishing too many personal attacks on those it felt stood in the way of reform, including Wellington himself.[6] The Institute's decision to publish its own journal was doubly brave in that several other attempts to produce rival military newspapers, such as the *British Army Despatch*, had met with bankruptcy and collapse. It was through the *Journal* that the Institute hoped to bring a more sober and professional tone to the very necessary debates without succumbing to the narrower focus of the professional, but particularly technical, *Professional Papers of the Royal Engineers*, after 1837, and the *Proceedings of the Royal Artillery Institute*, first published in 1839. After the death of the Duke of Wellington in 1852, the Institute was also able to more openly position itself behind prevailing arguments for reform.

The contents of the first *Journal* gave a good indication of how the Institute meant to proceed. From the outset, high-quality contributions were sought from senior sources but junior officers were also to be encouraged to write; the span of authorship by rank went from lieutenant to major general. Civilians were not to be excluded either as the presence of two fellows of the Royal Geographical Society on the contents list testified. The Institute agreed with the view of the Royal Military Academy, Sandhurst, that military history was a vital part of an officer's education and included articles on Hannibal by Lieutenant Colonel MacDougall, senior lecturer there, and by the Chaplain General, R Glieg, who disputed Clausewitz's argument that only up-to-date military experience was relevant by contributing 'The Armies of Ancient Greece'. Scientific and technical developments relevant to defence issues would also be a constant feature of the *Journal* from the outset, represented in Volume 1 by articles on medicine and metallurgy. Developments in practical soldiering came in the form of field fortification and military surveying, while the firmly held view of the Intelligence Branch of the War Office that officers ought to know something about their likely opponents before they met them in the field was represented in an article on French military education, and another entitled 'The Military Systems of France and Prussia in 1870'. Informed speculation on future developments was also encouraged by the inclusion of 'The Rifle, its probable influence on Modern Warfare' and 'Forms of Ships with relation to Naval Gunnery'. Broader strategic issues were also to become a regular feature, signalled by a discussion of the significance of the Euphrates route to India. Although the form and appearance of the *Journal* would undergo some changes over the lifetime of the Institute, the essentials remained; high-quality contributions from informed commentators on issues of present and future importance.

The Hedgerows of England

The first duty of the government was to prevent the invasion of the home islands: the restlessness of Napoleonic France (and the fact that it possessed, in *La Gloire*, the world's most modern steam ironclad) during the 1850s gave rise to a resurgence of fears that it might be possible for France or a French-led alliance to mount an invasion of Britain. With the invasion threat of 1805 just within living memory, there were many who regarded the possibility of mounting an invasion or a strong raid as something more than theoretical, often on the grounds that new technologies were eroding old certainties. Their opponents dismissed such fears as mere panic and pointed to Britain's preponderant naval strength, but this would remain an enduring issue throughout the nineteenth century and was one that the Institute could not ignore. Indeed at several points before the First World War, the entry of the Institute into the debate on Britain's vulnerability to invasion was to have startling and longstanding results.

After the Crimean War, there existed a widespread and well-justified fear that French appetites for military adventure had only been whetted and the Italian campaign of 1859 caused the Institute to look askance at 'that impregnable stronghold' of Cherbourg in an 1859 article entitled 'National Defence, or New Strategies in Warfare'. The clear implication was that the newly upgraded French naval base at Cherbourg was a pistol pointed across the Channel and that the dockyards at Portsmouth and Plymouth were vulnerable to a raid. Palmerston agreed and in 1860 began a programme of fortification, still visible today off Devonport and in the Solent, which was covered by the *Journal* extensively in 1860 and again in 1862–63. There was also a steady redeployment of the fleet towards a concentration in the Channel during the 1860s in order to rule out any possibility of a French 'bolt from the blue'. Naval design was also influenced by this possibility: the coastal defence ship HMS *Captain* was completed in 1870, designed to operate in shallow, inshore waters against a French raid, or perhaps for raiding Cherbourg itself. A model of this most controversial of ship designs was donated to the Museum and inspected with 'deep interest', shortly before the *Captain* was lost with all but eighteen hands in the Bay of Biscay in September 1870. (Its low freeboard and high masts had caused it to capsize, a danger repeatedly pointed out by the Admiralty professionals, but ignored by the government who dismissed their objections as Luddism. Hugh Childers, First Lord of the Admiralty, backed his judgement against the admirals by placing his son aboard it and duly paid the price of his hubris.) The Institute was the chosen forum in 1872 for the admirals to have their revenge by publishing a series of articles with pointed titles; 'The Causes of the Insufficient Stability of Her

Majesty's Late Turret Ship "Captain" and other Ironclads'; 'The Naval Hammock; its Buoyancy and Use in Saving Life at Sea in Cases of Collision etc'; 'The Necessity for a Permanent Commission on State Scientific Questions'.

A further development lay in the emergence after 1859 of the Volunteer movement, which, by 1870, had generated a part-time army of 200,000 men, officered by local dignitaries and manned, very often, by their employees and motivated by a patriotic determination to defend the country from invasion – the *Journal* offered 'A Sketch of the Militia, past and Present' to its readers in 1866. After 1867, when Britain acquired its first mass electorate, defence policy had to be publicly backed if it was to be paid for in taxes and the existence of this popular movement indicated that there was an appetite for more government attention to defence. Perhaps the first attempt to appeal to the enlarged electorate's sensibilities over defence came with the publication of *The Battle of Dorking,* a fictional pamphlet initially written anonymously for *Blackwoods Magazine* in May 1871, in which an unprepared Britain falls to a German (rather than French) bolt from the blue.[7] Although far-fetched, it indicated both alarm at the new level of potential threat and the suspicion that the defence professionals felt towards a Liberal government under Gladstone that was reluctant to spend on defence.[8]

The story caused a storm of excitement when it was published.[9] RUSI was not directly responsible for this publication, but the author, George Tomkyns Chesney, was the brother of Charles Chesney, Professor of Military History at Sandhurst and a *Journal* contributor. The Institute had also previously published articles on the defences of London in 1860, 'The National Defences of Great Britain, Especially with Reference to the Future Requirement of Floating Forts' in 1869, and in 1870 came out with 'Observations on the Defence of England' and 'On the Protection of London Against an Invading Force Landing on the East Coast'. That George Tomkyns Chesney's story was a professionally inspired work was shown by the choice of Dorking as the site of the decisive battle; an invasion force landing on the south coast and heading for London would indeed march for the gap in the South Downs at Dorking. The story was published against the background of a Liberal government elected on a programme of 'peace, retrenchment and reform' in 1868 which meant, in effect, defence cuts. However, after the Prussian army knocked out France in a lightning campaign in 1870, events seemed to call for an increase, rather than a decrease in defence spending. Gladstone certainly condemned the pamphlet as driven by a desire only for 'the spending of more and more of your money'[10] and took the intervention so seriously that he began to look for ways to rid himself of such troublesome Whitehall neighbours as RUSI. His solicitor general, Vernon Harcourt, was even more dismissive, declaiming to *The Times*, that he was 'more afraid of being run over by a Hanson cab than being slaughtered by a German' but felt it necessary to make a personal appearance at RUSI in May 1872 to deliver a lecture entitled 'Our Naval and Military Establishments Regarded with Reference to the Dangers of Invasion'. This was something of a coup, which established RUSI not just as *a* forum for debate, but *the* forum for defence debates. The Institute then underlined its success by inviting Chesney to make his case in person in the same month.

Neither Gladstone nor Vernon Harcourt could make the issue go away and fears of a sudden invasion would fester right up until 1914 and beyond. Indeed, the Institute made sure of it. Whether there was any truth in the possibilities envisaged by the Battle of Dorking remains a moot point, but Charles Adams of the Staff College probably came closest to the truth when, during the debate that followed Chesney's presentation, he argued that although the navy remained the first line of defence, a strong raid was still a possibility and land defences needed to be constructed. This convinced the editor of *The Times*, John Delane, who came out against the Cabinet. Major General Collinson kept the issue alive with 'Another Warning

Voice from 1805' in 1876 and in 1877 by arguing, in 'On the present facilities for the invasion of England and for the defence thereof', that if the fleet did go to confront Russia at Constantinople, then invasion was indeed a possibility. RUSI returned to the issue again in 1886 by inviting Major H Elsdale to publish 'The Defence of London and of England' in the May *Journal*, a statement adopted by the War Office and which became the blueprint for the construction of defences around London. It bears more than a very strong resemblance to the *War Office Handbook for the London Defence Positions 1903*. Indeed, as late as April 1917, First Lord Admiral Jellicoe was anxiously advocating an advance into Flanders to take Ostend and Zeebrugge in order to prevent Germany mounting a cross-Channel attack.[11]

There can be no doubt that the construction of a popular, informed, hypothetical scenario designed to galvanise the government into taking defence seriously, while at the same time raising the status and profile of the Institute, had been a spectacular success. Was RUSI behind 'The Battle of Dorking'? If a smoking gun was ever found, the fingerprints of the Institute would surely be all over it. Irrespective of whether it was directly behind it or not however, the Institute certainly drew the relevant conclusion as to the effectiveness of the tactic and would deploy similar ones on several occasions in the future.

Eviction

The bitterness of the defence debates of the period was also deepened by the fact that Gladstone had control of the Treasury for much of the time and that he was able to instil in it a belief that defence expenditure was wasteful and unproductive. After 1861, when Gladstone established the principle that all other departments of government should submit their spending plans for Treasury scrutiny before Parliamentary approval, the Treasury's views carried real weight. Building battleships that ran the risk of being obsolete within a few years went against all the instincts of the accountant;

even worse was the thought of paying a soldier to stand in a sentry box rather than contribute his labour to the economy. In 1860, defence expenditure stood at £24.9 million (approximately £2.58 billion today); incredibly, by the time that Gladstone was mid-way through his first premiership and Bismarck was marching on Paris, it was down to £21.5 million.[12] This not only hamstrung the military and naval reforms of Edward Cardwell and Hugh Childers, his defence ministers, but also ensured that any fighting in Africa or Asia would probably have to be done by the Indian Army – which did not figure on the Treasury's books. Nor did such financial stringency produce very efficient results. The German Army – which cost £19.3 million – was able to mobilise twenty times as many troops as the British Army, which cost £14.6 million. Britain needed an army that was twice as big as it possessed if it were to fulfil its commitments and guarantee its own security, but the Treasury was unwilling to spend more than approximately 1.5 per cent of Britain's worth on achieving it.[13]

Despite his claim to be guided in his actions by religious and moral principles, Gladstone was also possessed of a vindictive streak and a weakness for paying off old scores. The Institute drew his ire for a plethora of reasons (also discussed in more detail later in this chapter): it had done much to oppose his cost-cutting; it had been so bound up with the Dorking agitation; it had an increasingly popular lecture programme (in April 1871, it was decided to pay as much as £50 to visiting lecturers) as a result of more widespread advertising in the popular newspapers *Broad Arrow*, the *Pall Mall Gazette* and *The Globe*. All this marked it out for more attention, as well as a revamped *Journal* from 1871.[14] In addition, another favourite target of his, the Duke of Cambridge, was closely associated with the Institute, and if anything was guaranteed to raise Gladstone's hackles, the visit of the Crown Prince of Prussia to the Institute would. Even worse was the hiring of the lecture theatre by a Captain Walter to press for a resolution to be presented to the House of Commons 'to make the road to the civil service through the army and navy'.[15] These were dangerous developments: RUSI had an Achilles Heel in the looming problem of its insecure lease on its accommodation, it never having been clearly and legally defined. There had been questions in Parliament in 1864 about part of the Institute which had acquired the name of 'Fife House'[16] and by 1870 it became increasingly likely that Whitehall Yard would be up for redevelopment. The Institute was well aware of this and the secretary set up meetings with Cardwell and Childers, who were generally favourable to the Institute, in August 1871 to discuss the matter.

Although there is probably no way to prove a direct link, it seems more than coincidental then, that after forty years happy residence, and after the 'Dorking summer', the Institute was given an unwelcome Christmas present in the form of a Notice to Quit within three months of 23 December 1871 by the Lords Commissioners of the Treasury – after all, using financial means to undermine his opponents was a tactic often used by Gladstone. The secretary responded by calling an emergency Special General Meeting to mobilise opinion against this development and cannot have been more gratified by the response from the Institute's supporters; the Duke of Manchester, the Afghan veteran Field Marshall Sir George Pollock, Admiral of the Fleet and Trafalgar veteran Sir G Sartorius, four generals, five admirals, five lieutenant generals, seven major generals, including Napier, the queen's aide-de-camp, Colonel Adair, and numerous others all turned out. The Duke of Cambridge laid out the problem squarely: the Institute had an insecure lease on the buildings, had spent £10,000 on improving them over the years and, with only £7,000 in the coffers, simply could not afford to move or build within the Whitehall area. That the Institute should stay in the Whitehall area was seen as essential; to this day, it is an axiom that if one wishes to exert influence on the government, one must be in close physical proximity to it. Cambridge was determined that the Institute should not be 'turned into the street' or booted into the long grass in South Kensington and proposed that the traditional Whitehall tactic of appealing to your enemies' enemy for support be adopted. This had to be done quietly and with tact – an approach opposed by a Captain Craufurd, who made what *The Times* reported as 'remarks of an aggressive character in regard to the conduct of the Government', but accepted by the members who had a better understanding of the tactics needed by Whitehall warriors. Cardwell and Childers had no love for Treasury cheeseparing, and they would be approached. The meeting ended with a proposal that all members should double their subscriptions for the year – one not taken seriously. The Institute then flexed its muscles by persuading the Duke of Richmond to advertise their plight in the reply to the Queen's Speech in February 1872. This was no mean feat. He cleverly turned the government's desire for better educated officers into the case for retaining the Institute where it was:[17]

> We were told that the officers of the Army were badly educated. What, then, has the Government done with regard to any educational institutions connected with the Army? There is in this metropolis one connected with both branches of the Service—the United Service Institution, an institution of the very highest value, admirably managed, and, I believe, supported and maintained by the officers of the Army themselves. Well, what has been the conduct of the Government which told us that the officers must be better taught? The only thing we know of is that they have given the United Service Institution notice to quit the premises they now occupy, and that a great Institution, which has been got together and maintained with so much zeal, with so much trouble and expense, must quit the building it now occupies, and go to South Kensington, or somewhere else.

The Notice to Quit had been trumped by a promise to raise a hornet's nest of parliamentary trouble. In the event, Chancellor Lowe – too good a journalist to be unaware of what might potentially be in store – was approached directly and, being at that time aware that Gladstone's confidence in him was failing and that both Cardwell and Childers were circling, withdrew the eviction notice. The uncertainty over the lease remained a problem, but with Disraeli's government entering office in 1874, they could at least rest a little easier. In 1877 the War Office minister, Gathorne Hardy, chaired the Institute's annual meeting, which reported that a deputation to the First Lord of the Admiralty, W H Smith, had resulted in an assurance that its claim for a permanent site would receive due consideration – not quite a promise, but still, nowhere near a rejection.[18]

Weapons and Tactics

The tactical lessons of new developments in weapons after the Crimean War were of particular interest to the Institute. The first *Journal* contained an analysis of different breech-loading rifles then being issued to European armies, a development in weapons technology that would increase rates of fire from two or three shots per minute to as many as twenty – the logistical implications of this were investigated in 'Breech-Loaders, with Reference to Calibre, Supply and Cost of Ammunition' in 1867 and three articles on the subject dominated Issue 55 (1869). In 1860, Captain Tyler predicted that the increasing range, accuracy and rate of fire of rifles would make trench warfare the only practical way to conduct battles in the future. His lecture 'Rifle and Spade or the Future of Field Operations', and his 1861 article 'Rifle and Rampart' predicted the end of Napoleonic 'thin red line' tactics, an argument which if not fully borne out during the American Civil War gathered momentum during the next forty years until the South African War of 1899–1902 when smokeless powder and magazine rifles finally did create the 'empty battlefield' that he envisaged. Ten years later, R J Gatling himself was invited to lecture on 'Machine Guns'; the same issue also contained, appropriately, an article on 'Shelter Trenches, or Temporary Cover for Troops in Position' (1870). The real significance of this argument was that doctrine and planning for future war now had to take account of new technologies as never before and indicated that the Institute was developing a new approach to war planning, which was based on predicting the future and arguing for the provision of forces suitable for that prediction. No more, hoped RUSI, would Britain have to be merely *reactive* in the face of a threat, but would ensure security through preparation in advance.

Coming so soon after the new impetus of the Institute, the American Civil War naturally prompted a great deal of debate on a wide range of developments. The 1862 *Journal* included a 'Military Sketch of the Present War in America' while in 1864 Charles Chesney offered up a contemporary analysis of 'The Recent Campaigns in Virginia and Maryland' and then 'Sherman's Campaign in Georgia' in 1865. The role of cavalry in the war provoked a particularly interesting debate.[19] Both Union and Confederate mounted forces, while carrying on their traditional roles of screening and reconnaissance, had quickly eschewed the use of sabre and lance, the *arme blanche*, in favour of pistols and carbines and a return to operating like dragoons – moving on horse but fighting dismounted. This development set off a debate inside British cavalry regiments about the proper employment of mounted troops that was not resolved until the internal combustion engine settled it for good. The *Journal* also ensured that the reaction of other armies to these developments were considered; in 1861 it published 'Musketry Instruction For The Cavalry Carbine And Pistol, Recently Issued To The French Cavalry; With Suggestions For The Training Of Cavalry, And Its Important Function In Future Battles'. The raising of both the Union and Confederate armies was also widely studied – the regular army of the pre-war Union played little part in the war as a whole – with the respective merits of volunteers and long or short-service engagement regulars being of particular interest,[20] especially given the aforementioned contemporary upsurge in volunteering at home. This debate would also rumble on through the Cardwell reforms of the 1870s and right up until the raising of the Kitchener Armies in 1914. When Union forces began interfering with British shipping trading with the Confederacy and, in particular, carrying envoys in the *Trent,* the Institute was able to get a legal opinion on the issue from no less than the future solicitor general, Vernon Harcourt, who lectured in 1865. The welfare of the individual soldier was also widely discussed during the 1860s with welcome interventions on the 1864 Geneva Conventions (1866), 'Cooking for Troops' (1869), 'Military Hygiene' (1870) and, no doubt less welcome to those forced to endure it, 'The Value of a Gymnastic Training to the Soldier' (1862). Generations of blue-legged school children forced to endure PE on wintry mornings would also curse the Institute for giving the great Victorian sanitary reformer, Edwin Chadwick, a platform to demand compulsory gymnastic exercises for schools in a lecture which saw a fit population as the basis of an efficient army (1870). Nor were naval tactics ignored: 'Attack and Defence of Fleets' by Captain P H Colomb, who would become a respected naval historian in his own right, was also published in the first *Journal.*

The Rusted Trident?

The fact that in 1859 France had briefly led the world in naval design and technology with the appearance of *La Gloire* – the first ocean-going ironclad – was particularly unsettling to British defence thinkers on a number of levels. Firstly, there was the issue of cost: the HMS *Victory*, built in the 1760s, was still arguably fit to stand in the line of battle as late as 1850, but the launch of HMS *Warrior* in 1860 made every other ship in the world, including *La Gloire*, instantly obsolete (and *Warrior* herself was obsolete within eighteen months). As the pace at which revolutionary developments in warship design quickened, the spectre of obsolescence was raised for the Royal Navy unless it engaged in what was effectively a ruinously expensive pre-emptive naval race without end. On a second level was the fact that different technologies, particularly those concerned with gunnery and armour, advanced at different speeds and until such increasingly complex technical compromises could be resolved, outcomes would be ever more unpredictable as the plethora of ship types and classes proliferated – the Russians even experimented with circular ships. The complexities covered by the *Journal* included discussions on the limitations of iron as ship-building material (it rusted in seawater and quickly fouled with seaweed) in 1861 and 1862, and in 1867 a wide-ranging discussion of the relative merits of broadside versus turret-mounted guns. The Heath Robinsonesque issue of circular ships was also visited by the *Journal* in 1869.

As it was on land, so it was at sea, that tactics were increasingly dependent on changing technologies and in 1866 the signalling expert Commander P H Colomb strengthened his thirty-year relationship with the Institute by publishing 'Modern Naval Tactics' in the *Journal*, and then followed it up with the truly alarming 'Lessons from Lissa' in 1868. Colomb argued that this battle fought between the Austro-Hungarian and Italian fleets during the Third War of Italian Independence in 1866, off the Adriatic island of what is now Vis, Croatia, was 'the most important naval occurrence since Trafalgar'.[21] Gunfire had done virtually no harm to either ironclad fleet and unless guns could be made five times more powerful than at present, the Royal Navy could not sink a similarly constituted enemy fleet; the only ship to be sunk was the *Re d'Italia*, accidentally rammed by the *Ferdinand Max*. Colomb's aim was to persuade the navy that ramming was now the most effective weapon in a modern navy's arsenal, but to be truly effective, a ramming attack had to be delivered at a ninety degree angle to the enemy or it would be no more lethal than bumps at Henley – and no captain of a ship would allow this to happen. Much more worrying was the real point made by Colomb: it might now be theoretically possible for an enemy fleet to convoy an invasion force across the Channel by simply screening out the Royal Navy. Colomb had pointed out inadvertently that Britannia's rule of the waves was technologically nowhere near as secure as she imagined.

On a third and most important level, Britain had gambled on naval supremacy to protect the trade that was its lifeblood. The repeal of the Corn Laws in 1846 and the sweeping away of what tariffs remained in Gladstone's 1860 budget meant that Britain had opted for an economic policy that made it dependent on imported food and raw materials to feed its population and its industry. As an economic policy, this was an enormous success and British industry and commerce accounted for perhaps 25 per cent of the world's GDP during the mid-nineteenth century – a fact loudly proclaimed by the Great Exhibition of 1851.[22] The defence implications were, however, worrying. The Royal Navy had to maintain command of the sea now, otherwise the home islands would not simply face invasion – indeed invasion might not be necessary at all – but starvation into humiliating submission.

The threat to the shipping lanes came not from the great ironclad battleships but from small, lightly armed, converted merchant vessels acting as commerce raiders. These vessels, although no match for any regular man-of-war, were perfectly adequate for the interception of merchant shipping by reason of their much longer range. A merchant vessel might, under a combination of sail and steam, travel to Australia and back refuelling only once and such a vessel, filled up with coal and ammunition rather than cargo, and resupplied by rendezvous, could keep at sea almost indefinitely, moving at a speed of 8–10 knots, barring accidents. In contrast, an ironclad battleship burned up so much coal that it needed constant re-supply[23] and could barely keep up with cruisers able to steam at '*full speed* for almost as many *days* as our war cruisers can *hours*'.[24] Bolting a couple of guns onto a merchant steamer instantly turned it into a viable weapon of war when employed against unarmed steamers of a similar class,[25] and an absolutely lethal one when employed against the 25 per cent of the British merchant fleet that was still under sail in 1879.[26]

Just how lethal these commerce raiders could be had also been demonstrated in the American Civil War during the celebrated cruises of the Confederate Navy vessels *Alabama, Florida* and *Shenandoah*, which had wreaked havoc on Union shipping in places as distant as the Arctic, Australia, Brazil and the Sunda Straits.[27] This idea was quickly incorporated into Russian naval strategy, which adopted commerce raiding in the Atlantic and Indian Oceans as just one aspect of its strategy for a war with Britain. A further dimension lay in plans to attack the ports of the British Empire,[28] which were very inadequately defended. This was a standing disgrace. The director of ordnance had reported in 1867 that even such key bases as Malta lacked adequate defences and sufficient garrisons while those in Australia were 'in a very bad state of repair'.[29] The problem had still not been properly addressed when Britain almost went to war with Russia in 1878,[30] and the possibility of a Russian cruiser squadron leaving a string of burning ports from 'Cape Town ... to Trincomalie, Singapore and Hong Kong; in fact almost any British port abroad'[31] behind it was a very real one.[32]

The Russians were well aware of the vulnerability of these ports and had definite plans between 1876 and 1886 to take advantage of the situation should war breakout.[33] Similarly, if the French battle fleet was likely to be trounced by the Royal Navy in an ironclad Trafalgar, commerce raiding was another matter. France's bases at Toulon and Brest were difficult to attack or blockade, while there was a myriad of smaller ports capable of launching cruisers and privateers.[34] In the Indian Ocean, French forces could be sustained from Mauritius,[35] Madagascar (after 1883) and a number of other small islands. Further east, it was expected that the French *messageries* fleet would supply cruisers drawing supplies from Tonkin (after 1883) to attack shipping in the China seas and Australia,[36] which would also have to be hunted down.[37] On the west coast of Africa, the French development of a naval base at Dakar in 1878 gave it 'a position from which she could at any time harass British trade and the Lines of communication with India'.[38] The vulnerability of this trade was emphasised by its value – £900 million per annum with

£144 million worth of freight and shipping afloat at any one time.[39] The capture of even a small proportion of these lucrative cargoes and ships was a temptation to the enemy that could not be ignored. The considered opinion of the US Navy was that the Royal Navy could no more protect its colonies or commerce 'from an enemy than from a stroke of lightning or the shock of an earthquake'.[40]

Once again the Institute was at the cutting edge of the issue. The first foreigner to address the Institute was Captain Hamilton, a Confederate Naval officer.[41] The winner of the Naval Prize Essay for 1876 argued that cruisers have 'a value equivalent to that of the ironclad fleet'.[42] Sir John Coode, employed almost continually from 1856–92 on improving port facilities around the empire so that they could serve as 'harbours of refuge' for British commerce,[43] contributed 'On Military (or Strategic) and Refuge Harbours' to the *Journal* in 1876. Even when the building of the German High Seas Fleet after 1898 revived the possibility of a decisive fleet engagement, the essay prize for that year was awarded for another article on commerce raiding,[44] while between 1888–1905 there were a further eighteen articles published on cruiser warfare and the possibility of naval raids on commercial harbours. Until harbour defence schemes were upgraded to the point where they could inflict enough damage on raiders to deter them, this was a very real concern and Coode was only one of a number of defence thinkers involved in the construction of port defences. So great were these worries that by 1890 there had been such an improvement in harbour defences throughout the empire that the chances of a raid had diminished to almost nothing. This was largely because the raiding ships would now have to be so heavily armoured that they would lose their advantages of speed over the pursuing battleships – a real example of how the Institute promoted informed debate that was turned into practical action.[45]

Access to the necessary coal supplies would also be a problem for heavier ships after greater efforts were made from 1860 to 1890 to protect them. This was another issue that was regularly discussed.

T Symes Prideaux made recommendations in 'On Economy of Fuel in Ships of War', while in 1884 Lieutenant R S Lowrey explored the problems of cross-decking coal in 'On Coaling ships or squadrons on the open sea'. Before the advent of widespread telegraph communication, the great advantage of commerce raiders was their ability to disappear over the horizon and this too was recognised and discussed by RUSI in 1882 with Captain J C R Colomb's 'Naval Intelligence and the Protection of Commerce in War'. There was a steady increase in the number of cables laid by Britain from 1860 onwards and much of this was powered by the need for accurate intelligence in the event of war. The legal aspects of commerce raiding and especially privateering were also addressed by Lieutenant John Ross of Bladensberg in his 'Maritime Rights' of 1876. In the same year, the rising MP Thomas Brassey, who had previously written for the *Journal* on raising naval reserves in 1873, argued that the merchant marine itself should be armed for the protection of commerce.[46] Indeed the planning that went into the defence of commerce and colonial ports should stand as a case study for the correct anticipation and analysis of a threat, and the application of measured responses that negated that threat before it could turn real.

There was also the question of imperial defence to consider. Before 1860, there was little public or parliamentary interest in the empire beyond its capacity for adventurous entertainment and a colonial debate could empty the Commons chamber faster than a dinner bell. Most informed opinion assumed that it would disintegrate as the settlement colonies gained home rule and the main issue was to so manage that separation that it did not turn into another disastrous American War of Independence. Indeed, during the early years of the *Journal*, only limited space was given to imperial issues, although the Maori War was covered in 1860, the Abyssinian Expedition in 1868 and, curiously, in 1867, the 'Economy of the Chinese Army'.

The obvious answer to imperial defence – simplifying defence commitments by the straightforward abandonment of territorial empire – was not (nor could it be) contemplated without unimaginable upheavals. Kinship links meant that the British metropolis would always have to provide troops for colonials threatened with massacre in far flung places. The Raj was a major employer both in India and in Britain. France might well have taken advantage of a withdrawal to re-establish its mercantilist empire in the vacated regions and shut out British trade. The prophecies of peppery colonels that there would not be a 'Rupee or a Virgin between the Khyber and Ceylon' might well have come true in a post-Raj scramble by indigenous powers. The loss of India might have jeopardised trading interests further east in Singapore and Hong Kong. All this was accepted by even the most determined anti-imperialists. The corollary was that the empire and the trade routes connecting its constituent parts, especially the routes to India as its most valuable part, would have to be defended for the foreseeable future. In the decades before the Crimean War this was hardly onerous as maritime supremacy and financial power allowed Britain to arrange its forces around the globe at will. The long Cape route was the most secure for the transport of troops, goods and mails but the route of choice, the Suez Canal, was not secure at all. Built by French engineers with French capital and opened in 1869 with a view to further expanding French influence in an Egypt already used to it, the first ship to pass through the canal was the French imperial yacht *Aigle*.[47] Palmerston had used all his influence in the financial markets, in Egypt and in Constantinople, to throw obstacles in De Lesseps's (the mastermind of the canal scheme) way but by 1866 it was clear that the canal would be completed and the British government would have to deal with it.

Although the *Journal* allowed chimerical schemes for a Euphrates route to be aired in articles such as 'The Military Advantages of A Daily Mail-Route to India Through Turkey and The Persian Gulf' in 1869 (and again in 1873), but like all previous attempts there was no prospect of a viable alternative to the Cape or Suez routes appearing. Four years later, as the Prussian Army closed in on Paris, the Russians revoked the 'Black Sea' clauses of the Treaty of Paris 1856, which had forbidden it keeping naval forces there. This in effect gave the tsar the largest naval training area in the world and, if he could gain control of the Straits of Constantinople, a secure base from which his navy might threaten the route to India by attacking shipping in the eastern Mediterranean or by seizing the canal itself. Certainly, from 1870 onwards, it was the threat from Russia both on land and at sea that was seen as the most dangerous.

A re-run of the Crimean War was always more likely than a war with France largely because after 1870 the French were mainly concerned with finding an ally to help them take back Alsace and Lorraine, lost in 1870. However, if war had broken out between Britain and Russia at any time between 1870 and 1900, geopolitical realities ensured that there were few strategic options open to Britain. The Holy Grail for the Admiralty was an attack on the Russian naval base at Kronstadt which would open up St Petersburg for a raid, but this was unlikely to succeed, as the Admiralty reluctantly admitted:[48]

> Owing to the configuration of the channel, the strong defences which protect it and the limited range of the guns of our existing armour-clads, an attempt to bombard Cronstadt must be expected to result in serious injury to the attacking force, and an attack on the forts alone will be of little avail.

The most likely theatre of war would be therefore in the Balkans, where the best option for defeating a Russian advance on Constantinople was support from Turkey. When the possibility of a Russian war emerged in 1876, the insecurities of the military and naval lobbies led them to support, and indeed instigate, a series of wars in Malaya, Afghanistan, South Africa and Egypt which aimed to secure the routes to India and consolidate imperial defence even when doing so contributed to further overstretch. The Institute was, of course, right at the centre of the hurricane of war and imperial expansion that was about to take place.

The Emergence of a Defence Establishment

During its early years, the Institute had wielded a reduced influence not only because of the generally benign international environment, but also because its members were scattered around garrisons at home and abroad and were thus unable to co-ordinate any real intensity of debate. With the rapidly shrinking world of the nineteenth century, this began to change and more rapid communication allowed a greater concentration of influence close to the heart of government.

The Institute was increasingly home to men possessed of a belief that the current state of defence of the home islands and the empire provided, by and large, a standing invitation for a rival power to exploit; that defencelessness made the empire especially ripe for the plucking and that something ought to be done about remedying this. They felt that the existing justification of inadequate garrisons in the colonies – that an attack on them would be deterred by the threat of war with Britain – was no longer believable. They felt, further, that the common view of empire as a burden was incorrect and saw instead a potential which could preserve Britain's Great Power status. Being, by and large, capable men of experience, distinction and decision, they also felt a duty to ensure that the politicians did not waste the opportunities or shirk the responsibilities of empire. They believed that a war for survival with one or other of the Great Powers was inevitable and that urgent, even precipitate action, was needed to prepare for it. They also believed that this war, *when* rather than *if*, it came would be quick and decisive and that victory would go to the state that was best prepared in advance for it.

For these men, the model of future war would be the wars of German Unification: planned, decisive, intense. The idea that Britain could win any struggle by fighting a long war, in which its financial strength would inexorably bankrupt an enemy – the principle of the 'third campaign', whereby Britain could suffer defeats in two successive years but would always win because it could finance a further year of warfare while an enemy would dissolve in financial chaos – had, for them been negated by the Prussian experience. The existing example of the long American Civil War was disregarded on the grounds that *neither* side had been prepared for war and thus were incapable of launching the quick knock-out blow. Furthermore few, if any, of them questioned the underlying premises that the best policy was *si vis pacem, para bellum*, a mantra constantly repeated in the *Journal*.[49] They also questioned the ability of an increasingly democratic government created by the 1867 Reform Act to conduct an effective defence policy in a crisis.

The more professionally trained officers of the Royal Artillery and Royal Engineers were at the forefront of many of these debates and were intimately connected with RUSI. After the experience of the siege of Sevastopol, they were actively engaged in building the Palmerston Forts and were quickly deployed to do the same for colonial harbours too. Men like Lieutenant Colonel Crossman RE worked for the Inspector-General of Fortifications in Britain and Canada, was Director of Public Works at the War Office 1873–75 and established himself as the foremost expert on submarine defences. Lieutenant Colonel William Drummond Jervois RE, who had written for the *Journal* on coastal defences in 1869, took Captain J C Ardagh RE on his ground-breaking tour of colonial ports. Ardagh would become an aide to the Duke of Cambridge from 1888 and in 1896 was promoted to be the Director of Military Intelligence.[50] John Lintorn Araby Simmons RE headed both the Royal Military Academy Woolwich and the School of Military Engineering before gaining promotion to Inspector-General of Fortifications in 1875.[51] He would become one of the Institute's most influential members. In 1868, when the War Office appointed Lieutenant Colonel Cooke RE of the Topographical Section – shortly to become the War Office Intelligence Branch – to the Institute council, the Woolwich graduates also found ready employment there; Jervois had surveyed Kent and Surrey for the Topographical Branch.[52] The interconnectedness of the Royal Engineers and the Intelligence Branch is quite starkly illustrated by the fact that the Committee of the Royal Engineers Institute, which met in the War Office on 5 September 1878, contained Simmons, Home and Ardagh, all of whom were both Royal Engineers and Intelligence Branch.[53] In 1889, there was also a proposal on the table to amalgamate the Royal Engineers Institute with RUSI at the Institute's annual general meeting; Wolseley was in the chair, with Simmons present.[54] There was a corresponding connection with the Institute of Naval Architects, a body deeply concerned with the technical aspects of naval policy that attempted to bridge the problems of design and the demands of naval policy. Thomas Brassey, Nathaniel Barnaby and leading Admirals Milne and Cooper Key were all members. The Institute of Naval Architects also held its meetings at RUSI and contributions from its own journal were sometimes reprinted in the *RUSI Journal*.[55]

There was also a close relationship between the Intelligence Branch of the War Office and RUSI. Lieutenant Colonel Cooke's appointment to the council began an intimate connection which saw the views of RUSI conducted right into the heart of government policy-making. Lieutenant John Ross of Bladensburg, contributor on maritime law and commerce raiding, was both Coldstream Guards and Intelligence Branch. Major C Brackenbury, brother of Wolsey Ring member Henry, authored for the *Journal* 'The Intelligence Duties of the Staff Abroad and at Home', arguing that it was the duty of the Intelligence Branch to anticipate future threats and prepare plans for war in advance, and only a secondary duty to provide useful information for the army.[56] This link was mirrored in India where the Durand Prize Essay for 1874 was won by the 'Essay on the Formation of an Intelligence Department for India'.[57] That the particular thinking of RUSI made itself felt through the Intelligence Branch and on into government policy is perhaps most remarkably demonstrated with the first systematic attempt to learn from the Prussian officer-training technique, the *Kriegsspiel*. This handbook posed three separate scenarios for officers to study: a colonial war in Basutoland, a defence of the Straits of Constantinople and an invasion of Egypt. The choice is significant in that it showed an expectation that the wars that Britain would be most likely to fight were *imperial* wars to protect colonial possessions or secure the route to India; the author of this book was Captain Evelyn Baring RA – who would go on to be Lord Cromer, consul-general of Egypt.[58] There can be little doubt that the Institute and the Intelligence Branch developed a high degree of symbiosis; the Institute theorised and tested ideas, while the Intelligence Branch turned them into actual planning. The connection worked the other way too with the War Office and Intelligence Branch often passing on papers to the *Journal* that it wanted to publish but could not fund.

The increasing conviction that India was at threat from Russia meant that eastern interests were also represented in RUSI. The Scinde Irregular Horse, part of the Bombay Army, sticks out in this respect. This is largely because of Sir Bartle Frere's intimate connection with its commander, his great friend John Jacob. Originally an artillery officer, Jacob was seconded to the Scinde Irregular Horse in 1839 and by 1841, was in command of it. He was a dark, brooding man of terrific temper, who stuttered so much in company that he could barely make himself understood without speaking in verse form. Frere admired his energy for civil engineering, his active methods for ensuring a settled frontier and his brilliance as a cavalry leader, and by all accounts the regard was mutual.[59] After Jacob died in 1858, Frere continued to employ and promote his officers; Colonel William Merewether was particularly favoured becoming military secretary of the Bombay government in 1860; Sir Lewis Pelly led the negotiations with the emir of Afghanistan that led to war in 1878; Sir Henry Green chaired meetings at RUSI in 1874 and joined Crossman on the council in 1875. As Frere was promoted so his officers prospered too.

As governor of Bombay, Frere had developed a close working relationship with General Robert Napier, commander-in-chief in Bombay (and another engineer), so upon the outbreak of the Abyssinian crisis in 1867, it was Merewether who was chosen to perform the reconnaissance for the expedition.[60] Frederick John Goldsmid, intelligence officer, orientalist and RUSI member was another Jacob and Frere protégé and orientalism proved to be another link in this eastern connection. Charles Macgregor worked closely with Napier in Abyssinia before becoming an expert on Central Asia and confirmed Russophobe; he was instrumental in setting up the *Indian Army Review* in 1864,[61] and the United Service Institute of India (USI), RUSI's sister institution, in the Town Hall at Simla in 1870. Sir Henry Rawlinson worked with the Constantinople-based diplomat, and another confirmed Russophobe, Sir Henry Layard on Middle Eastern archaeology, and was named alongside Frere and Layard as the originators of anti-Russian propaganda by Gladstone during the Midlothian election campaign of 1880. Frere and Rawlinson were connected through the Royal Geographic[62] and Royal Asiatic Societies, while the *Asiatic Quarterly Review* was edited by Arminus Vambery, a campaigner for a forward policy in Central Asia since 1864, and contained articles by Fred Goldsmid.[63] It was determinedly imperialist and anti-Russian in tone. Vambery would also lecture on 'The Past and Future of the Turcomans' at the Institute in April 1880, with Rawlinson in the chair.

The eastern connection worked in other ways too. Napier, Merewether and many other RUSI members had been involved in the Abyssinian campaign of 1868, which had been sprung upon them by a home government insufficiently informed as to the difficulties of the operation – a hostage rescue in uncharted territory.[64] They had then performed a magnificent feat of logistics to successfully complete the mission and had then withdrawn with all aims accomplished.[65] However, in completing the mission they left behind a terrible state of internecine warfare, which required them to evacuate the capital of Magdala lest its inhabitants be massacred by their rivals. The retirement from Magdala left many officers scarred:[66]

> The cries of distress were most sad to hear … when we passed along the road two days after, many a dead body of an old man or woman or weakly child, showed the spot where some unfortunate had sat down to never rise again.

For many soldiers, therefore, there was a growing belief that perhaps the enforcement of a *Pax Britannica* was better than leaving the poor peasants of the world to their fate, even if it did mean the acceptance of greater responsibilities. A further consequence lay in the working out of the logistics of the campaign; Napier had had to improvise an enormous amount of animal transport, fodder and supplies to get the troops moving and a whole series of articles regarding supply and transport arrangements followed in the *USI Journal*[67] giving such useful advice on how to calm down animals driven mad by the stench of a ship's hold (ten or twelve buckets of cold sea water over the head), how to cure horse paraplegia (an electric shock to the anus was only the worst of any number of quack remedies) and how to prevent stallions masturbating (a collar of metal spikes around the girth).[68] Among the many challenges explored was how to load a telegraph pole onto a camel. The lesson drawn from all this was that improvisation was no longer a practicable solution – war needed to be planned and prepared well in advance.

There were also administrative responses to the perceived increased threat; after an article written in the *USI Journal* by Captain Colquhoun RA, Frederick Roberts sent Captain Edwin Collen RA to London in 1877–78 to study the workings of the War Office Intelligence Branch with a view to setting up a purely military intelligence service, as opposed to the political, geographical and diplomatic services with which India was well provided.[69] Collen was already known to RUSI through his writings on 'Military Transport and Supply in India' published in the *Journal* in 1873. Co-operation with the military establishment in London was also increased with the India Office providing regular intelligence on Central Asia[70] while the Colonial Office forwarded the correspondence on colonial defence.[71] Increasingly though, and perhaps more importantly, those officers who had fought in the mutiny were marked with a belief in pre-emptive action to stamp on military threats before they could gain headway, whether the politicians liked it or not. There was also the hardship and sacrifice to consider, which they felt gave them the moral right to a say in the formulation of policy.

The problems associated with the defence of India were also transmitted through the Institute and on into policy. It was Rawlinson, supported by Harry Green's book, *The Defence of the North West Frontier of India*,[72] Fred Goldsmid's book *Central Asia and its Question*,[73] both published in 1873, and Sir Bartle Frere who unleashed a tirade against the Liberal government's policy of 'Masterly Inactivity' which eventually resulted in the appointment of Lord Lytton in 1876 to carry out a 'forward' policy to create a 'scientific' or militarily coherent frontier.[74] Green and Goldsmid were both Institute council members in 1874–75; Frere was barred from the Institute because he was an Indian civil officer, rather than a military one – this restriction on membership would not be revoked until after the First World War – but he was now head of the Indian Council Political and Secret Committee, a body of worthy opinion formed to advise the Secretary of State for India in London. The 1873 Intelligence Branch summary dealing with the Russian advance quoted directly from Green's *The Defence of the North West Frontier of India* and its proposed solution was based extensively on Frere's proposals.[75] It was Frere who wrote the defence plan for India that Lytton and another member of the Wolsely Ring and *Journal* contributor, Sir George Colley, would develop into the scientific frontier and although the Institute never completely dominated the Indian Council – whose function was to advise the secretary of state for India, and was composed mainly of old India hands resident in London – its membership was well represented by Rawlinson, Wolseley and Merewether.[76]

Furthermore, the Institute was also beginning to attract the attentions of colonial governors with an appetite for expansion. Sir George Grey, ex-governor of South Africa and one of the first to press for confederation as a means of dealing with colonial problems, came out of retirement to call New Zealanders 'to a great destiny, with the whole future of the South Pacific dependent upon them'.[77] He had joined RUSI in 1864. Sir Hercules Robinson, the future governor of South Africa who would collude with Cecil Rhodes, joined in the same year. Sir George Young, founder of the Royal Colonial Institute in 1868, became a member in 1882. The Royal Colonial Institute was dedicated to imperial expansion; Young's father had been instrumental in the settlement of New Zealand. The focal point of this upsurge in concern at the present state of military, naval and colonial defence was without doubt the Royal United Services Institution and it was in this period that the Institute had a profound effect in drawing together all the strands of naval, military and imperial insecurities to call for a unified approach to the problems of defence. This took place initially with the expansion of its membership; with the publication of the *Journal* came an influx of new members from the Indian Army, the militia, the volunteers and the colonial forces as well as the regulars. By 1859, membership had reached 3,343 but perhaps more remarkable was the over 28,000 people who either visited the Museum or attended the weekly lectures.[78] In 1873 there were 4,116 members, almost 20,000 visitors and 21,000 copies of the *Journal* circulated each year.[79] After some grumbling from senior naval officers that their subordinates could not easily get to London, junior institutions were set up in garrisons and seaports; to avoid having to pay two separate subscriptions their members were allowed admission to RUSI on presentation of their membership cards.[80]

In 1878, RUSI had 4,485 members, 17,881 visitors and possessed a library of 18,700 books.[81] One of the leading lights of RUSI in these years was undoubtedly Captain J C R Colomb of the Royal Marine Artillery, brother of P H Colomb RN, who had authored 'Lessons from Lissa'. In fact for nearly two decades it was hard to pick up a copy of the *RUSI Journal* without finding Colomb or one of his followers in it. As an Irish landlord, Colomb enjoyed enough of a private income to retire from the Royal Military Academy in 1869 and devote his life to the cause of imperial defence until 1905. His first article, 'The Distribution of our War Forces', written in 1870, argued strongly that if Britain was to be secure then the first priority was to devise some integrated system of imperial defencem and his subsequent works in the *Journal*, 'General Principles of Naval Organisation' in 1872, 'The Naval and Military Resources of the Colonies' in 1880 and 'Naval Intelligence and the Protection of Commerce in War' in 1882 continually highlighted the vulnerability of Britain's commerce and colonial ports in the event of war.[82] His other main idea was that if the navy was to be considered the 'shield' of the nation, then the army should be considered its 'spear' for amphibious operations. His book *The Defence of Great and Greater Britain,* published in 1880, inspired the Imperial Federation movement. His writings not only encouraged a deluge of similar articles,[83] but also attracted the attention of Lord Carnarvon, the Colonial Office minister in Disraeli's 1874–80 ministry.

Attracting a key Cabinet minister to the cause of defence was a major advance for the influence of RUSI. Cabinet ministers had possessed automatic membership of the Institute since the 1860s and many of them had some sympathy with its aims – as long as it did not get them into trouble with the Treasury – but Carnarvon had always had an active interest in defence matters and now provided a mouthpiece in the cabinet for all those who argued that a more positive approach to the empire should be adopted. His particular confidant and troubleshooter was Lieutenant Colonel Crossman,

RUSI council member from 1875, and his first action on entering office in the new Conservative and pro-imperial government of Benjamin Disraeli was to order a complete review of the defence arrangements of each colony.[84] Understanding the importance of fuel supplies to the protection of trade, he sent Hercules Robinson to annex Fiji in order to provide for a coaling station between Australia and Canada in 1874.[85] What was worrying, however, was that many in the defence establishment read Carnarvon's appointment as a green light for a more active approach to imperial defence issues and that zeal for the cause might merit a certain amount of disobedience. This was apparent from the outset when Colonel Andrew 'Spicey' Clarke RE, an intellectual with interests in colonial emigration to Australasia, imperial and naval defence and possibly the first person to officially recommend buying the Suez canal, was appointed as governor of the Straits Settlements in 1873.[86]

The Perak War

On arrival at his post, Clarke decided on his own initiative to persuade the merchants of Singapore that their commercially driven desires for an end to the petty strife and piracy prevalent among the Malay states to the north ought to be subsumed within 'a really great and imperial question'.[87] That question was concerned largely with the security of the Australasian colonies and the security of trade. Without 'a single British soldier'[88] in Australia, the Colonial Office had already been moving in favour of taking measures to strengthen the British position in the Pacific but Clarke, understanding that the best place to defend the Pacific was at Singapore, decided to go ahead without waiting for specific orders and negotiated the Engagement of Pankore – a treaty that claimed British paramountcy over the whole Malay peninsula. This was too much for Carnarvon, who recalled him. The choice of replacement was striking for the similarities between the two men. Colonel William Drummond Jervois RE had been assistant-inspector general of fortifications since 1856, secretary to the Defence Committee in 1857, secretary to the Royal Commission to enquire into the defence of the UK in 1859 and, after travelling constantly between 1862–75, author of a report into the defenceless condition of coaling stations and naval bases in the colonies, which set out the first War Office departmental acceptance of a rational concept of imperial defence.[89] He was also a RUSI member.

Jervois had Carnarvon's permission to accept the Engagement of Pankore, but he certainly did not have his permission to begin a war when the Sultan of Perak had one of the budding imperialists posted as resident to his court murdered. Carnarvon was understandably furious when he found out and told Jervois that he 'entirely disapproved'[90] of his actions. Jervois thought Carnarvon and the Colonial Office to be 'timid and vacillating' and that 'this is the time for ... acting, once and for all'[91] to achieve complete annexation of the peninsula. Faced with a war that seemed to be spiralling out of control – Jervois had asked for two infantry regiments and a million cartridges – Carnarvon finally decided to give in to Jervois and despatch the forces that he demanded. After all, the 'great and imperial question' was one of defence and what Clarke and Jervois had done would strengthen the defence of the Australasian colonies. And Carnarvon did not sack Jervois, but appointed him to the governorship of Australia specifically tasked with drawing up schemes for defence there. A willingness to disobey the politicians, in the expectation that expansionist schemes would be retrospectively condoned, was to be a disturbing feature of the defence establishment during these years.

The Balkan Crisis, Afghanistan and the Anglo-Zulu War

It is a common trait in the historiography of the period 1876–80 to treat the Balkan Crisis, the Afghan War of 1878–80 and the Anglo-Zulu War of 1879 as separate issues, yet in the minds of those soldiers, administrators and politicians involved there was a very strong connection between these events: the prospect of a war with Russia, which would rapidly turn into a global war as the Ottoman

Empire collapsed. The defence establishment was almost universally united on this point and made its views known through the Institute, on into policy and into actions sometimes in advance of policy.

The Balkans

The decline of the Ottoman Empire during the nineteenth century and its gradual withdrawal from the Balkans created a power vacuum that Russia, with its ambitions to gain the prize of Constantinople, turned into the repeated crises that became known as the 'Eastern Question'. In 1875 a series of revolts there exploded into a full-scale Bulgarian rebellion, which neither Turkish brutality, Gladstone's outrage or European diplomacy could avert, and the tsar decided to intervene more directly by sending his armies in. This created a major dilemma for British policy-makers: should Russia be supported as the 'moral' response to Turkish misrule or should the tsar be opposed in his ambitions to capture Constantinople and destroy the Ottoman Empire? If Russia did take Constantinople then it would have control of the imperial jugular in the eastern Mediterranean. Morality might condemn the Ottomans, but realpolitik demanded they be supported.

As the Russian armies advanced through the Balkans in 1877, the Institute began to publish a series of articles designed both to inform the decision-makers about the issues involved, but also to undermine Gladstone's attempt to galvanise public opinion against British intervention to stop the Russians from taking Constantinople, that he had begun with his 'Bulgarian Horrors' campaign.

In 1876 a special lecture on 'The Turkish Forces and the Military Aspects of the Eastern Question' and a paper on 'Recent Reforms in the Russian Army' given at the Institute opened up the fundamental question concerning the Russian interventions (which began with the despatch of officers and 'volunteers' to help the rebels in 1875) as to the likely victor of the looming conflict. Eager to get the latest on infantry tactics, the Ritter Von Arnim led an evening meeting on 1 May 1876 in which security on the march, skirmishing and outpost duty was covered. Given the present size of the army, the title of Von Arnim's lecture – 'Trial of a Method for Effectively Training a Company in Skirmishing and Outpost Duty, in a Limited Time, and Under Unfavourable Circumstances' – was particularly apt. In December 1876, Richard Wilebraham lectured on the Russo-Turkish War of 1828–29, and in January 1877 the 'Military Geography of European Turkey' was investigated. Fred Goldsmid underlined the importance of Islam to the British Empire in 'Islam: From Constantinople to Calcutta' in February; after the Ottoman Empire, Britain was the world's largest Islamic power and this implied that if it wished to retain the empire then support for the Caliphate in Constantinople was vital. W S Lindsay reminded the Institute of the complexities of blockade and privateering in 'Belligerent Rights – The Declaration of Paris 1856' three weeks later and the shipping magnate Donald Currie lectured on the need for upgraded port and telegraph facilities for imperial commerce in time of war on 2 March 1877, with Garnet Wolseley, then deeply involved with the planning for both a Turkish war and, as a member of the India Council, Indian defence, in the chair. Colonel Fletcher's special lecture on 'A Volunteer Force, British and Colonial, in the Event of War' in 1877 gave further indication that the resources of the whole empire would be needed to fight the expected war.

During 1877, however, the number of contributors to the *Journal* fell off, largely because officers were involved in the preparation for war, but the Institute was able to get the leading journalist Archibald Forbes to lecture on the war in Bulgaria as Russian forces bogged down outside Plevna while C B Norman covered the war in Armenia. Emphasising again that any war would be fought on the north-west frontier of India as well as the Balkans, A H Wavell, father of the future Field Marshal Archibald Wavell, contributed 'A Russian View of the Indian Army'. After Plevna fell and the Russians imposed the Treaty of Stan Stefano on Turkey in early 1878 – a treaty that would give it possession of Constantinople in the near future – the crisis deepened as Disraeli demanded the revision of the treaty at a European Congress or war would follow. The Institute duly published an account of the fighting at Plevna, speculated 'On the Employment of the Reserve Forces in Case of an Expeditionary Force Being Sent Abroad', before virtually drying up on the subject in the middle of 1878 as officers waited for the results of the Congress of Berlin. Despite Disraeli's brilliant diplomatic triumph over the Russians there, tensions did not relax immediately: although the tsar was required to send his armies home and give up virtually all his gains (and, to add insult to his injuries, Britain gained Cyprus without firing a shot), they remained outside Constantinople until May 1879.

Wolseley was paying attention to the discussions taking place at the Institute. In the event of war he envisaged sending 50,000 British troops to Turkey in 1877 and enough British special service officers to lead 150,000 Turkish, Egyptian, Albanian and Moroccan soldiers.[92] If Constantinople did fall then Gallipoli could be seized,[93] however impractical it would be to hold it in the longer term. A *coup de main* might be feasible, but given the need for replacements, the rotation of units and inevitable reinforcements, the army would need a permanent expansion of 40,000 new men. Construction of the necessary fortifications would cost another £2.8 million and even then the chances of holding the area forever were assessed as slim. Crucially, Gallipoli had no port facilities. It would, concluded General Simmons, Inspector General of Fortifications and a leading light at the Institute, 'be like resuming possession of Calais'.[94] What gave heightened anxiety to this issue was the fact that Russia did actually possess the capacity to take Constantinople and was confident that it could hold it against a British counter-offensive.[95] The unsettling fact was that the British shark could not beat the Russian wolf in the Balkans without allies and by studying the issues properly, the Institute provided a major service in tempering the growing anti-Russian 'Jingoism' that threatened to drown Gladstone's anti-Turkish agitation. The army would fight, of course, but they warned the politicians against unrealistic expectations.

Indeed, Simmons's long experience of both the Balkans and defence debates in and out of the Institute allowed him to play a substantial advisory role in the formulation of British foreign policy during the Balkan Crisis. During the Crimean War, he had surveyed the Turkish defences on the Danube and Bosphorus and had then operated with the Turkish army in their defeat of the Russians on the Danube before being instrumental in persuading the Turks that their army would be better employed at Sevastopol rather than advancing further. When Sevastopol fell, he then led a Turkish force in the Caucasus before serving on the Boundary Commission there with Charles Gordon, with whom he became firm friends.[96] When in 1876 he was asked to investigate the likely course of a war in the Balkans,[97] he despatched a team from the Intelligence Branch led by Colonel Home, and supported by Ardagh and six other officers of the Royal Engineers, to 'prepare a line of defence for a British force' and to 'send home as soon as possible a report of the present state of the defences of the Dardanelles and Bosphorus against attack by sea'.[98] In addition to this, Captains Baring and Clarke RA were to study the probable future course of a Russo-Turkish war, building on Baring's earlier work in the *Kriegsspiel*.[99] Home's reports then provided the basis for Simmons's Memorandum of 2 December 1876, which argued that the Turks would need 135,000 men to hold the line of the Little Balkans to Varna and that Britain would need to pay and command an additional 100,000 Turkish troops plus provide a field force from India, while another 10,000 British troops would be needed to hold Gallipoli.[100] This obviously caused some startled and adverse reactions in the Cabinet because two days later he submitted a further memorandum designed to argue that Britain should declare war on Russia the moment the Russians marched because 'If once the Turks are routed, England will lose the most efficient ally … it would be simple madness to allow the Turks to be crushed'.[101] He then made clear exactly what the consequences of not fighting would be:[102]

> The struggle will be one for life and death. A British force of 50,000 men will be quite inadequate to ensure success; that is, if by success it is understood that Great Britain is to do more than sustain a siege in front of Constantinople. By carrying on such a war she would descend from her position as a first-class power, and lose her prestige in the East.

> There never was a time when it was more necessary to sit down and consult whether with the force at the disposal of England she is able to meet the power that is against her.

As yet the Cabinet was not convinced and when Lord Salisbury went to the Constantinople Conference in late 1876, Colonel Home failed to convince him of the necessity of supporting Constantinople, to the point that he told Home and Ardagh to start looking for somewhere suitable to take in compensation if Constantinople fell to the Russians.[103] The fact that Salisbury wanted Home to go to Egypt and that he seemed to be spending a lot of time surveying Gallipoli rang alarm bells in Simmons's mind and he quickly moved to argue that seizing Gallipoli was not a substitute for support of Turkey; it could not be another Gibraltar. The size of the force needed would mean conscription; and Russian gains in the Caucasus would allow it to march down the Tigris and Euphrates to the Persian Gulf and 'give Russia a preponderating influence as an Asiatic power'.[104] Simmons's fears were increasingly shared by Gathorne Hardy, secretary of state for war, and prompted him to ask him to prepare a series of reports for the use of the Cabinet.[105] As the war began in April 1877, Simmons was invited to brief the Cabinet directly on 1 May 1877 and predicted that the Turks would be defeated, Constantinople would fall within seventy-five days, the Turkish fleet would fall into Russian hands which 'would at once make it one of the leading maritime powers in the Mediterranean'[106] and reiterated his argument that to seize Gallipoli would be a disaster; it could not be supplied and it would be inevitable that the army would get sucked into the hinterland. Furthermore, argued Simmons, if war did break out:[107]

> I cannot conceive that any matter can be more urgently necessary than attention to our coaling stations, which are absolutely defenceless, but upon which the protection of our commerce entirely depends. In the event of a break up of Turkey, a coaling station should be secured ... at the eastern end of the Mediterranean.

After the Treaty of San Stefano in April 1878, with Simmons present, the War Office Council unanimously approved the emergency arming of colonial ports and coaling stations.[108] Furthermore, among Simmons's papers is a 'Very Confidential Memorandum' dated 8 July 1878 arguing for the establishment of a British coaling station at the eastern end of the Mediterranean. On the side, Simmons scrawled:[109]

> Given to me by Colonel Home when going with Ld Beaconsfield to attend Congress at Berlin in 1878. It was upon this paper that the convention then secret had been agreed upon with Turkey for ceding Cyprus to Great Britain.

This might have been the end of it, but the Russians had long been used to playing on British fears of a thrust across the north-west frontier of India and just as the Congress began they sent a diplomatic mission to Afghanistan – perhaps as a bluff or perhaps as a prelude to conquest. Lord Lytton, viceroy of India, interpreted the move as the latter and, defying strong representations from London not to, issued an ultimatum to the emir of Afghanistan on 14 August 1878 after he had refused to receive a British mission, which began the Second Afghan war.

The Second Afghan War

Looking from the other end of the line of imperial communications, India herself had long been protected by its geographical isolation, but by the 1870s this was no longer the case as Russia mopped up one after another of the decayed Islamic states of Central Asia: those of the Caucasus in 1859, Tashkent 1865, Samarkhand and Bokhara 1868 and Khokand 1875.[110] The lecture offered up by R A Shafto to the Institute on 'The Communications, Commercial and Military, Between the Steppes of Central Asia and Hindustan' in May 1867 put an unusual cast on the later assertion that 'trade follows the flag', but as each step brought Russian troops closer to India – and just as the British at home were reassessing their security needs in the light of changed circumstance – so the British in India felt they had to look at new ways of defending the northwest frontier and securing the lifelines to home.

The longstanding debate over whether there was a Russian threat to India – what rapidly became known as the 'Central Asian Question' – was encouraged in the *Journal* with lectures and articles published in 1873 and 1874 at the same time as old India hands like Sir Bartle Frere and Sir Henry Rawlinson also began to worry in public. Sir Charles McGregor too picked up his pen to begin thirty years of campaigning for a 'scientific' frontier on the Hindu Kush.[111] The Russian advance through Central Asia had been viewed with a certain amount of complacency in Calcutta, especially under Viceroy Lawrence, who believed that the correct strategy was to await a Russian army, if indeed it ever came, on the Indus where, in an exhausted state at the end of tenuous supply lines plagued by Afghans, it could batter itself to pieces against the fortress at Attock. This strategy of 'masterly inactivity' was, however, under increasing challenge, especially after the publication of Sir Henry Rawlinson's *England and Russia in Central Asia* in 1873, and Sir Bartle Frere's *Letter to Sir John Kaye* in 1874, both of which demanded a more active policy in response to the Russian advance.[112]

Frere and Rawlinson had deliberately started an agitation against masterly inactivity and their call was subsequently taken up by RUSI. Fred Goldsmid, Institute stalwart and long-time associate of Frere's, offered 'On Certain Roads between Turkestan and India, Independent of the Oxus, or of Any Oxus Boundary in 1874', while other contributions included 'The Russian Campaign against Khiva in 1873'. In 1875 he returned with 'On Journeys between Herat and Khiva' to supplement Valentine Baker's 1874 'On the Military Geography of Central Asia' – despite Valentine Baker's disgrace after an unfortunate incident in a railway carriage, the Institute continued to recognise his expertise.[113] In the early 1870s, the lack of adequate maps meant that geographical knowledge was power on the northwest frontier and the case that Frere, Rawlinson and RUSI made ensured that in 1876 Lord Lytton abandoned masterly inactivity. Having no previous experience of Indian affairs, Lytton took as his starting point Rawlinson's *England and Russia in the East*, and told Sir Bartle Frere that they had 'an almost exact coincidence' of views.[114] Lytton employed another Frere protégé and Scinde Horse officer, Colonel Lewis Pelly, to conduct the negotiations which would bring Afghanistan within the British orbit as part of a general 'forward policy', but which ultimately failed. Again this led to bitter divisions within the cabinet on how to respond to Russian forward moves in Asia; Salisbury was firmly against a British invasion of Afghanistan, but Lord Lytton believed that he had enough support both within the government and from public opinion to discount it. His decision to enforce British influence over the Afghans by issuing an ultimatum was only just the right side of outright disobedience.

As the centre of likely conflict shifted from the Balkans to Central Asia in the middle of 1878, so the *Journal* reflected the changing centre of gravity. Military geography was again a subject of particular interest with 'The Kurdistan Mountain Ranges, Considered in Reference to a Russian Advance on the Tigris Valley' and Fred Goldsmid's 'On Communications with British India Under Possible

Contingencies', as were the resources of the semi-independent India, which were explored by G B Malleson in 'The Native States of India in Subsidiary Alliance with the British Government'.

Hostilities began in November 1878 when Sam Browne VC occupied the Khyber.[115] On 2 December, Roberts defeated the Afghans at the Peiwar Kotal[116] and on 8 January 1879, Stewart entered Kandahar. The Russian mission withdrew and the Treaty of Gandamack, 26 May 1879, brought a successful end to Lytton's campaign to bring Afghanistan under British influence.[117] The Institute followed the issue closely in two lectures in December 1878 chaired by Sir Henry Rawlinson and another in March 1879, but then forgot about the issue as events in South Africa took centre stage. When the British mission in Kabul was unexpectedly massacred by an Afghan mob in September 1879 and war flared up once more, the *Journal* offered a view of logistics in Afghanistan with 'A Transport Service for Asiatic Warfare, with a Brief Account of the Transport Operations from Sukkur to Quetta in 1879', 'Between Russia and India', 'A Streak of the Afghan War – Lieutenant-General Sir Donald Stewart's March from Kandahar to Ghazni, with Actions of Ahmed Khel and Urzu' and 'The March from the Indus to the Helmund and Back, 1878, 1879'. A hundred and thirty years later, the last of these places would be a familiar name in British households once more. In July 1880, British forces were defeated at Maiwand after being abandoned by their Afghan allies, a defeat which prompted Robert's epic march from Kabul to Kandahar and the administering of another crushing defeat on Afghan forces, incidents which were covered in 'The March from Kabul to Kandahar in August, and the Battle of the 1st September, 1880'.

The survival of the myth of Afghan invincibility is something of an historical oddity; in their dealings with the British they scored two notable successes – the Khyber Pass in 1842 and Maiwand in 1880 – yet were roundly thrashed in all three Anglo-Afghan wars. For the Victorians who dealt with Afghans and the tribes of the northwest frontier, respect was due to them as worthy opponents – the red balls on a snooker table are said to represent the wounds incurred in various skirmishes by the tough frontier fighter and inventor of the game, Colonel Sir Neville Chamberlain – but it was also true, however, that the Afghans held no terrors for men like Fred Roberts.

Zululand

A further by-product of the Balkan Crisis was another piece of disobedience that led to war. In March 1877, Sir Bartle Frere had been sent out to South Africa to implement a policy of confederation that was driven by Carnarvon's desire to see the empire put into a state of defence. Again, the historiography on this period has tended to view South African affairs in isolation from the concurrent crises in the Balkans and Afghanistan yet Frere was a major influence on Indian defence policy. He had also written in favour of robust support for the Ottoman Empire in 'The Eastern Question'[118] for the *Quarterly Review* in October 1876, and had been extensively briefed by the Colonial Office on the likelihood of war with Russia, a feature of which would be a naval attack on colonial ports such as Cape Town by privateers or cruisers. He had barely arrived in Cape Town in March 1877 before he heard the news of the outbreak of the Russo-Turkish War and the unauthorised annexation of the Boer Transvaal Republic by Theophilus Shepstone and his aide, the novelist Rider Haggard. From that point on he was overwhelmed by a series of frontier crises which included a major Xhosa revolt, the possibility of a major Boer revolt in the Transvaal and, in the summer of 1878, border violations by the Zulus which Frere mistakenly interpreted as the precursor to invasion.

With the Russian army outside Constantinople and an Afghan war about to begin, Frere decided that he had to break the back of the Zulu army (estimated at anything from 25,000–40,000 strong) before the Balkan passes opened again and the Russians could finish their march on Constantinople in the spring of 1879.

Ignoring (admittedly contradictory) orders from London not to invade Zululand,[119] like Clarke and Jervois in Malaya and Lytton in India, in January 1879 Frere sent the troops in confident that Martini-Henry breech-loaders would hose down the ardour of the Zulu *impis*.[120] Thus began the most famous of Britain's colonial wars, even though it would not enter the popular imagination fully until the making of the 1963 film *Zulu*, starring Stanley Baker, Michael Caine and, appearing as Cetshwayo, Chief of the Zulus, Mangosuthu Buthelezi – who would go on to head the Inkatha Freedom Party in the closing days of Apartheid.

The war proved to be an epic struggle and although there could be no doubt that it would end in a British victory, the Zulus were able to inflict a major defeat on the British forces at Isandlwana before being themselves defeated later in the day at the iconic defence of Rorke's Drift. The Institute was, of course, well represented during these events. The General Officer Commanding when Frere went to the Cape was General Cunyghame, a member since 1864, and his successor, Lord Chelmsford, who had been Napier's logistics chief in the Abyssinian campaign, had joined RUSI in 1861 and had written on infantry tactics for the *USI Journal* in 1873 before appointment to the RUSI council in 1874.[121] Colonel Glynn of the 24th Regiment had encouraged his officers to join RUSI and Lieutenants Mostyn, Melville and Cavaye, all of whom would die at Isandlwana, were all members. Lieutenant Carrington, credited with inventing the British approach to mounted infantry in South Africa, was also an officer of the 24th and RUSI member; he escaped the fate of his brother officers because he was on detached service. Charles Nugent RE was employed by Frere to draw up the coastal defences for Cape Town and would contribute three articles on harbour and imperial defence to the *Journal* in 1883–84. When Frere was disgraced for his disobedience, his successor was none other than RUSI contributor and Lytton's *éminence grise*, George Pomeroy Colley. And when Private Hitch VC's wounds, received at Rorke's Drift, resulted in an honourable discharge, RUSI gave him a job.

The lessons drawn by the *Journal* from the engagements at Isandlwana and Rorke's Drift were aired in 1881 with 'Carrier Corps and Coolies on Active Service in China, India, and Africa, 1860–1879', a reflection in part of the fact that Chelmsford had lost most of his transport at Isandlwana and had thus been forced to withdraw and begin the invasion of Zululand again. The fact that the loss of 1,500 men at Isandlwana during the morning had not deterred Lieutenants Chard and Bromhead, with just over a hundred men at Rorke's Drift, from making a stand behind an improvised wall of mealie bags and biscuit boxes prompted the timely contribution 'Notes on Hasty Defences as Practised in South Africa'. Rumours that the British line had crumbled at Isandlwana because the lids on the ammunition boxes were screwed down so tight that they could not be opened prompted 'The Supply of Ammunition to Infantry on the Field of Battle'. This theory has since been disproved – there was enough ammunition at Isandlwana, just not enough riflemen to take on 25,000 warriors – but asking an officer in a Welsh infantry regiment if he has remembered his screwdriver will still provoke a droll response today.

The Other Side of the Debate

Not everyone thought RUSI was on the right track. Indeed, an altogether different view emerged in parallel to the growing disquiet within the defence establishment about the state of the home and imperial defence, and produced a corresponding determination among parliamentary radicals and Gladstonian Liberals to challenge the growth of what they saw as a dangerous imperialism that looked uncomfortably like preatorianism. In the period before 1868, radical assaults on imperialism had made little impression, and tended to be more concerned with correcting abuses and encouraging self-government, rather than pursuing an overtly anti-imperial agenda.[122]

Both the aristocracy and the squirearchy were prepared to leave foreign policy to Palmerston more or less; pragmatic responses and patriotic sentiment were all that was expected. However, the death of Palmerston in 1865 seemed to open up new opportunities for the radicals,[123] especially as his successor to the leadership of the Liberal Party, the formidable William Ewart Gladstone, was apparently inclined to entertain many of their ideas. However, it was the Radical John Bright MP who battered away most regularly at what he saw as the iniquities of the defence establishment and nailed into the mainstream an acceptance of the 'moral' school of foreign policy.[124]

Bright's basic view was that 'the moral law was not written for men alone ... [but] as well for nations',[125] and that only by following such 'eternal principles'[126] could greatness and happiness be achieved. Failure to do so would bring down God's wrath upon the nation and only expiation of past wrongs would ward off disaster: British rule in India was only justifiable if its westernisation worked to expunge 'the original sin of conquest'.[127] Taxation for defence purposes was 'draining the veins of the body to supply ulcers';[128] war was a device of those 'jackals of the desert'[129] the international landed interest, and its prosecution no more than a 'gigantic system of outdoor relief for the aristocracy';[130] the standing army and navy was, in his view, doubly in excess of what was required for effective defence[131] and the empire a 'showy equipage' based on no logic, but pride.[132]

Bright was tapping into a vein within a Britain rediscovering its religious feeling. Non-conformism was a powerful and growing force at local, municipal and national level and many of its worthies were outraged at the apparent amorality required for the conduct of foreign policy.[133] An increasingly literate, but essentially uneducated, public opinion existed to which simplistic moral notions in foreign policy were an attractive alternative to an equally simplistic bombastic Jingoism, and its force was making itself felt on the national political scene. This was a groundswell of vague feeling that material progress might be matched by moral progress, that the beneficial British example of thrift, trade and godliness might be extended beyond its shores and that the industrial revolution might translate eventually into a New Jerusalem of the brotherhood of man, if only Britain gave a lead. What made Bright's alternative vision important was its partial adoption by Gladstone when, on succeeding to the leadership of the Liberal Party in 1867, he fused it with his ideas of international law, anti-imperialism, the separation of the colonies and of conciliation rather than coercion.[134] Out of it came the first attempt at 'moral force' diplomacy and what would later be recognised as 'ethical' foreign policy.[135]

There was, however, something of Gladstone's beliefs that was rooted in some more sober elements of liberalism. Charles Dilke's *Greater Britain* had argued that the colonies were a succubus and that it was ludicrous to make 'Dorsetshire agricultural labourers pay the cost of … Maori wars';[136] that the extension of empire simply made it more vulnerable to attack; that for the colonies, attachment to Britain simply exposed them to an attack in time of war, while at the same time, they were too weak to provide meaningful help to the metropolis. Nor was retention of them necessary for the purposes of trade; 'America is a truer colony of Britain than is Canada'.[137] Paradoxically, argued Dilke, loosening the bonds of empire would strengthen the bonds of kinship and culture between the English-speaking peoples. In a similar vein Gladstone's Chancellor of the Exchequer R A Lowe, extended the argument to India; no matter how highly popular feeling regarded India as a source of strength to Britain, he argued, the opposite was in fact true. Indian finances, he argued, were so poorly managed that Britain was perennially bailing them out, while the need to base 70,000 troops there put the safety of the home islands at risk. India also complicated the dangers of a coherent foreign policy; 'What might have been the result had the Indian rebellion taken place one year earlier and the Crimean war lasted one year later?'[138] Discounting the idea of an imperial federation on the grounds that the differences between the colonies

would outweigh any value that an intensified connection to the
metropolis would bring (would 'Australia submit to the legislation
of Jamaica?'[139]), he also pointed, like Dilke, to the problem that
while Britain had an obligation to defend the colonies, they could
do little in return to defend Britain. Lord Blatchford, ex-permanent
secretary at the Colonial Office, also poured scorn on any idea of
imperial federation on the grounds that devising a practical system of
administration for it would be impossible.[140]

From these roots, Gladstone came to the conclusion that the
settlement colonies must eventually go their own way and that there
must be no repeat of the American War of Independence. More
controversially, he believed that India was a poisonous legacy to be
managed but not exalted in, and was in no way an addition to British
power.[141] In many ways, Gladstone believed, the empire drained
Britain of the energies that it could devote to putting its own house
in order. Most of all, however, he was determined that under no
circumstances would there be a repetition of the conquest of India.
For him, empire was an elephant trap and entertaining arguments for
its expansion on the basis of supposed defence imperatives was the
quickest way to jump into it.

This was no doubt true: 'It is an axiom that one cannot hold a
port without sooner or later becoming involved in the politics of
the hinterland'[142] and Gladstone correctly dismissed any argument
that Britain could gain the security it desired for the Suez Canal by
limiting its occupation to the canal itself and perhaps the delta.[143]
Occupation of the Suez, he argued, would inevitably suck Britain
down the Nile until its dominions linked up with those in Southern
Africa.[144] The experience of colonisation in Southern Africa seemed
to bear this out too: inexorable expansion had seemed to override
any and all attempts to curb it. Security, he argued, was best sought
in the Concert of Europe and if all else failed then naval supremacy
could more surely guarantee Britain's safety than by occupying more
territory, however strategically vital it was deemed to be. The problem

was that Gladstone undermined the force of his arguments in the eyes of his opponents by his resolute opposition to large expenditures on armaments[145] – as Palmerston's chancellor 1859–65, he had used his position to 'chip away'[146] at such expenditure in the hope that by removing the *pecuniam* the *sinus bellum* would disappear.[147] Furthermore his dislike of soldiers and his unwillingness to study war meant that his grasp of strategic and military theory was somewhat tenuous. His contentions that the loss of the Bosphorus to Russia would have no effect on the security of the route to India and that control of the Suez Canal by another power had no effect on strategic security provoked several strong responses.[148]

What was at issue here was a fundamental disagreement between the strategic thinkers at RUSI and Gladstone. He believed that an active approach to imperial defence, which involved the occupation of strategic points, was not just an elephant trap, but unnecessary and repulsive.[149] He discounted both French and Russian threats on the grounds that they were unlikely to complicate their own international positions through expansionism or, in the case of Russia, run the risk of bankruptcy and the internal upheavals that would follow. These were fair points, but open to objection on the grounds that following such a policy conceded the initiative to France and Russia. Furthermore, it took no account of the sensibilities of the colonies themselves. It discounted the possibility of German colonialism or that other Great Powers might build ocean-going navies constructed with new technologies in the future. For the defence community entrenched in the Goose Pie just up the road from No. 10, possession meant guaranteed security and the responsibilities contingent on possession, manageable – and even beneficial for the populations concerned, because with occupation would come good government.[150] Gladstone was also inclined to believe that there was more than an element of panic in the defence establishment and that their 'womanish and unworthy fears'[151] would 'sacrifice ... the future to the present'.[152] This too was a fair point, but for the defence community their insistence on preparation for war grew out of a fundamental belief that they did not have the strength to win a quick war and that therefore they had to show 'a bold front' to dispel any notion that Britain was 'the Sick Man, not of Europe, but the World' and thus avoid the need for fighting at all.[153]

Gladstone's approach to foreign and imperial policy was simply one of a number of battlegrounds, such as franchise reform and the Royal Titles Bill, on which to fight what he saw as an emerging praetorianism, a Jingo tendency based substantially in and around RUSI, in alliance with a despised Tory Party. In this respect, it may be argued that his foreign policy was not primarily concerned with foreign and colonial issues at all, but with an internal struggle for the soul of Britain against the bogeyman combination of imperialism, militarism, nationalism and Toryism, which abroad, he believed, had produced the empire of Napoleon III and Bismarck's truncated parliamentary element in an overwhelmingly military and royalist constitution. Lord Northbrook, ex-Viceroy of India, had earlier protested at the rising power of the military voice in India[154] while the *Spectator* suspected that Disraeli was trying to advance an 'alliance of the monarchy with the mob'[155] thus undermining both the middle classes and traditional conservatism. Lowe argued that the essence of 'Imperialism' was 'the apotheosis of violence'[156] and required a large army 'unless we are prepared to be as ridiculous as we have been presumptuous',[157] which in turn meant conscription. For him, it was the potential of power that was important in convincing a potential enemy to desist from threats, rather than actual boots on the ground. Importing 'imperial' practices would also be deleterious to liberty, as being symptomatic of 'arbitrary power'.[158] Gladstone held up a mirror to RUSI which presented imperialism as being a dreadful vision of the future, not just abroad, but at home too, and as a result was prepared to accept reverses abroad in order to undermine these domestic opponents. Just as he had tried to frustrate Palmerston through budget cuts, so too did he attempt to hamstring what he regarded as the praetorian imperialists frequenting RUSI by restricting the opportunities of empire and the arms that went with it.

From Debate to Crisis

The real crisis in the battle between the defence establishment and Gladstone came during his second ministry of 1880–85. This was because his anti-imperialism made no sense so long as Britain ruled India; and unfortunately for him, Gladstone lacked both the political strength and the political courage to pull out of India and accept all the upheaval that would go with it. Lord Hartington, second only to Gladstone in the Liberal Party, and an increasing number of Whigs, Liberals and even Radicals therefore accepted the logic that if the empire was not to be abandoned, then it had to be defended. And if it had to be defended, then it needed to be expanded.

Majuba

Gladstone's barnstorming Midlothian Campaign of 1880 swept him into power on a wave that was partly driven by the humiliating defeat at Isandlwana and the massacre of the Kabul Mission. His forthright condemnation of Frere and Rawlinson for whipping up what he considered to be false fears of Russian aggression signalled a very strong determination to roll back the tide of imperialism. Fortified by his personal triumph, he forced the defence-minded official leader of the Liberals, Lord Hartington, to hand him the premiership and immediately began moves to reverse the forward moves that had taken place as far as he was able. Foremost among these was his attempt to reverse the settlement that had been imposed on the defeated Zulus and restore Cetshwayo to power – a misguided policy which quickly produced a miserable civil war – and a determination to withdraw from Afghanistan as soon as possible. Both these policies were accepted with varying degrees of frustration by the defence establishment, but it was Majuba that really stung.

The Transvaal had been annexed in 1877 on a flimsy pretext and too much optimism. When Gladstone went back on his election promise to restore the Transvaal to independence in May 1880, it was obvious that the Boers would rise up against the British. Hostilities commenced over the seizure of old Piet Cronjie's wagon for non-payment of taxes and the 94th Connaught Rangers were ambushed on the morning of 20 December 1880 at Bronkhorstspruit as they trudged up to Pretoria eating peaches.[159] General Colley reacted immediately and sent his troops to seize the pass at Laing's Nek on the border between Natal and the Transvaal, only to find it held against him by Boer forces which repulsed him. Trying to outflank the position, he seized Majuba Hill which overlooks the pass, on the morning of 27 February, but was driven off it in a humiliating rout in which he was killed.

Their blood up, the army cried out for revenge, but Gladstone refused to give it and demanded a negotiated settlement, which would grant the Transvaal its independence in all but name. The First Anglo-Boer War ended in the greatest humiliation for the British Army since Yorktown. For negotiating the treaty Colley's deputy, Colonel Evelyn Wood VC, was virtually ostracised by the officer corps, who considered that he should have resigned rather than have anything to do with it. The *Journal* printed nothing.

The Bombardment of Alexandria and the Invasion of Egypt

Within a year, however, Gladstone was forced to revise his opposition to forward policies following the meltdown of order in Egypt. The wild spending of the Khedive had resulted in a debt that if repudiated would precipitate a banking crisis and economic collapse in Britain and Europe; attempts to restructure the debt by cutting Egyptian government spending brought to power the nationalist leader Arabi Pasha, who was determined that ordinary Egyptians should not be held responsible for the profligacy of their former rulers. After a series of anti-European riots and threats to dynamite the Suez Canal,

Gladstone was pushed ever more reluctantly by Lord Hartington and his more hawkish-minded cabinet colleagues into sending the fleet to Alexandria to warn off Arabi Pashi. Indeed, the exasperation of Lord Hartington at Gladstone's reluctance almost resulted in a fist fight during the Cabinet meeting of 20 June 1882[160] while Lord Northbrook, an established opponent of forward policies in India was persuaded into Hartington's camp by his nephew, Captain Evelyn Baring RA, amidst a raft of defections by the service and colonial office ministers.[161] When the fleet did arrive, Arabi Pasha began the construction of earthworks to retaliate in kind if the Royal Navy opened fire, which guaranteed that the fleet *would* open fire – it was widely understood that gunfire from forts was much more effective than naval bombardment of forts.

This was a debate that had rumbled on since Napoleonic times and despite the reluctance of many naval officers to accept the facts, the weight of evidence lay heavily on the side of the forts. It was an issue well covered by the *Journal* in 1882 as the fleet made ready to sail for Alexandria; 'The Attack of Armour-Clad Vessels by Artillery', 'On the Forts of to-Day' and 'The Effects of the Bombardment of the Forts of Alexandria, July 11th, 1882' all appeared in the 1882 *Journals*. In 1858, it had been pointed out that the reduction of Cherbourg would require 100 ships of the line and 100,000 men.[162] Given that electrically fired mines, contact mines, spar torpedoes (a charge on a long pole wielded by *very* brave men) and locomotive torpedoes were increasingly an integral part of fortress defence, Chaband Arnault's 'On the Employment of Torpedo-Boats Against Ships' in the 1879 *Journal* presented much food for thought. Nathaniel Barnaby was also moving in this direction when he argued in his 'Battle Ships—A Forecast' in an 1883 *Journal* article that the power of a battleship to attack or even blockade sea forts was gradually approaching extinction. When the fleet did open fire on 11 July 1882, the results were alarming. Despite the spectacular explosion caused by hitting the Egyptian magazine, the arguments of the 'forts' protagonists won the day; the guns had only been silenced because the Egyptian gunners ran away; had the battle recommenced, the navy would definitely have had the worst of it, as both the War Office and the Admiralty admitted after detailed reports had been commissioned.[163]

The naval bombardment resulted in further riots and disorder and on 20 July, Hartington won the cabinet battle that despatched the army to Egypt and blew Gladstone out of control of his own foreign policy. Garnet Wolseley's subsequent campaign went like clockwork – aided by the fact that Major Tulloch, a RUSI contributor, had reported on the state of Egypt to the War Office in 1881,[164] and that Captain Baring had written this very scenario for the *Kriegsspiel* in 1872, which had subsequently been played at the Institute.[165] When Wolseley made his feint at Alexandria, followed by a shift to Ismailia, the mid-point of the Suez Canal, and a march up along the sweet water canal to Cairo, he knew exactly where he was going – the fortified camp at Tel el-Kebir identified by Lieutenant Collen, RUSI and Intelligence Branch member, who had identified it as the decisive ground in 1878.[166] Wolseley pitchforked Arabi out in thirty-five minutes after a night march and a dawn attack on 13 September 1882,[167] and threw a flying column into Cairo to prevent it going up in riot and looting. The imperial lifeline that the Suez Canal represented was now firmly in British hands and would remain so until the debacle of 1956.

After the occupation of Egypt, foreign, imperial and defence policy was progressively removed from Gladstone's control by Lord Hartington and a series of forward moves initiated:[168] Somaliland in 1884, Bechuanaland, Malaya and Pondoland in 1885, Zululand in 1887, and a clear threat of war with Russia if it moved any closer to Afghanistan during the Penjdeh crisis of 1885. Gladstone resisted, digging his heels in and using every tactic he could to dissuade or delay, but he was swimming against the tide as Liberal Imperialism attracted an increasing number to Hartington's banner. Even Radical

Joe Chamberlain, who had led the parliamentary attack against Frere over the Zulu war, morphed into 'Jingo' Joe. The last gasp of Gladstone's resistance was the abandonment of Gordon at Khartoum in 1884–85, which turned his nickname from GOM (Grand Old Man) to MOG (Murderer of Gordon). Thus the paradox; the Liberals elected on a platform of anti-imperialism actually went further than the pro-imperial Tories in expanding the empire as a result of defence imperatives suggested by RUSI.

Nor was this the whole of it. Colomb responded to his disappointment at not gaining a place on the Carnarvon Commission on Imperial Defence (see Chapter III) by publishing *The Defence of Great and Greater Britain* in 1880,[169] and when Gladstone attempted to bury the Carnarvon Commission reports,[170] he co-operated with Carnarvon and Hartington (through his private secretary, Reggie Brett, the future Lord Esher)[171] on an article entitled 'Imperial Defence' which appeared in *The Times* in November 1884.[172] The Institute had also given the floor to Colonel C H Nugent RE, lately secretary of the Commission, to push forward his ideas on imperial defence in April and May 1884, while Major General Wemyss, a veteran of the 'Notice to Quit' crisis and avid letter writer, pushed the idea of an imperial defence federation to *The Times* in November 1884.[173] Carnarvon was going further by correcting the proofs of W T Stead's 'The Truth about the Navy' articles,[174] again based on Colomb's work. Colomb returned the compliment by leaking the existence of the Carnarvon Commission reports, whose existence was by now an open secret, to *The Times*. The effect was to drive Gladstone into another retreat and force him finally to accept that foreign, colonial, imperial and defence policy would be controlled by a new grouping within his party, the Liberal Imperialists, led by Lord Hartington who agreed substantially with Carnarvon, RUSI and Colomb.

In March 1885, a new interdepartmental Colonial Defence Committee was set up by Hartington which made the concept of a defence policy based on an active, planned system of imperial defence the political orthodoxy (elaborated further in the next chapter).[175] The influence of Carnarvon and Colomb on Hartington's subsequent involvement in the Royal Commission on the Civil and Professional Administration of the Naval and Military Departments (1888–90) can also be seen in that Hartington concentrated largely on bridging the gap between the military and naval perspectives to rectify what many thought was an overemphasis on the navy in their work.[176] There is no irony that Hartington, 8th Duke of Devonshire, still stands on Whitehall between the RUSI and Old War Office buildings today (and you can find Frere round the corner on the Embankment).

Colomb (elected to Parliament in 1886) and RUSI had, however, already gone one step further. For them, an imperial defence policy made no sense without active co-operation from the colonies themselves, and if this was to be achieved then some form of equitable division of costs and responsibilities was necessary. To achieve this there would need to be some forum where British and colonial officials could meet to plan revenue raising, expenditure and strategy; an imperial parliament, no less, overseeing an 'imperial federation for defence'.[177] Nor was Colomb going out on a limb here; he began his article on the subject with a quote from W E Forster, one-time Gladstonian Radical cabinet minister and educational reformer and now first president of the Imperial Federation League (another Colomb-inspired organisation) set up in August 1884. Forster had been persuaded into the ranks of the Liberal Imperialists by his adopted son H O Arnold-Forster, who had agitated against Gladstonian naval unpreparedness since 1883.[178] The cry was immediately taken up in parliament when Howard Vincent MP asked Gladstone if he would call an Imperial Federation conference 'for the imperial purposes of the defence of the Empire, the extension of the interchange of commerce, and the regulation of Foreign affairs',[179] taking advantage of the fact that several former governors and statesmen of the colonies were in London for a Colonial Exhibition.

Gladstone replied that he was 'not struck with the great felicity of the idea'.[180] Sir Henry Barkly, Frere's defence-minded predecessor as governor of South Africa and Carnarvon Commission member, took the chair at RUSI in July 1886 when Thomas Brassey MP, another ex-member of the Carnarvon Commission, called for a colonial naval conference.[181] Two weeks earlier, Carnarvon himself had chaired a discussion in which he had declared that 'Defence, in reality, is the prime factor in all federations'.[182] When, the following year, the first Colonial Conference took place, the Tory Prime Minister Lord Salisbury stated that it was to consider the empire not as 'a Zollverein', but a 'Kriegsverein'.[183]

Was RUSI responsible for the expansion of the empire in the last quarter of the nineteenth century? It is a tantalising prospect. Undoubtedly, it played a major part in creating the climate of opinion necessary for the politicians to react to the worries of the defence establishment and 'Jingo radicalism'[184] was rapidly picked up by the popular press.[185] A very strong case can be made for the argument that defence and security was the principle motor for imperial expansion in this period; after all, the expeditions to Mexico, Peking and Abyssinia during the 1860s were not accompanied by any large-scale annexations, whereas after 1874, territory, once occupied, was expected to remain under the British flag.

It is also the case that many of the areas annexed were economically worthless at the time of annexation: Bechuanaland, Pondoland, Zululand, Somaliland and Afghanistan were unproductive; Egypt was bankrupt; Malaya without infrastructure and gold was not discovered in the Transvaal until 1886 – after most of the forward moves in southern Africa had taken place.

There is also no doubt that the Institute was the principal platform for defence debates. Sir Charles Dilke made the point that it 'can claim credit for having been almost the only scene … of that sort of politico-military criticism … that this country has exhibited'.[186] There is no doubt at all that it took a proactive approach to defence issues, was

connected into the heart of government and the press, and that its
views were taken very seriously indeed. However, not all the credit (or
blame) can be laid at RUSI's door. It had no actual executive power.
It was unable to influence the outcome of the 1880 election when
Gladstone returned to scourge 'the Fiend of Jingoism'[187] and even
Hartington was unable to prevent the withdrawal from Afghanistan
or the even more humiliating retrocession of the Transvaal in 1881.
Imperial Federation never came to much in the end, and it was
Dilke's ties of sentiment that bound the empire together rather than
an imperial parliament.

What RUSI did do, however, was to frame the argument in stark
terms: if the empire is to be retained, then it must be defended; if it is
not to be defendedm it must be abandoned; if the politicians have not
the courage to accept the political and human costs of abandonment,
then the soldiers have a duty to the peoples of the empire to ensure
their security regardless. This stark logic was, in the event, persuasive
enough to ensure that plenty of politicians could be found to agree
with it and although there were plenty of others who found in it a
dangerous threat of praetorianism, they could never come up with a
workable alternative beyond some vague notions of a 'moral' foreign
policy.[188]

In effect, RUSI, by promoting *informed* debate among *informed*
actors, was able to make its influence felt within government
ministries and on into parliament and the cabinet and, by framing
the debate, ensured that security was indeed debated.

The sustained pressure from the Institute and the rest of the
defence establishment told even more when Gladstone was bundled
out of office in 1885–86. In 1888, the decision was taken to double
the defence budget over the next ten years after Sir Garnet Wolseley
stood up in the House of Lords and told the government that the
British Army was not fit for purpose.[189] In 1889, the Naval Defence
Act established the 'Two Power Standard' whereby Britain would
maintain a navy as large as the next two powers combined and the

decision was taken to build ten new battleships, forty-two cruisers and eighteen torpedo boats – the largest peacetime naval-building programme to date.[190] In the last decade of the nineteenth century defence was now to become a serious priority and there would be no more Gladstonian moralising to stand in its way. Much of this concern for the provision of adequate resources for defence and security came about as a direct result of the Institute's efforts. It was a major achievement in policy terms but also in institutional terms: during his first two decades as secretary, Captain Boughey Burgess had moved RUSI from the edges of the defence debate right to the very centre.

III. LA BELLE ÉPOQUE
1890–1914

The nations of Europe are all preparing for war; they have taken
to heart the proverb *si vis pacem, para bellum* and are preparing
in the most thorough way for war; it is our duty, therefore, not
to be behind them.

(Field Marshall Sir John Lintorn Simmons, 1897)[1]

It is easy to forget what bizarre propositions the philosophical
and scientific minds of the late nineteenth century inflicted on an
unsuspecting public. Spiritualism attracted both Gladstone and
Arthur Conan Doyle; Frederick Nietzsche's sister so bungled his
legacy that it was mixed up with that other pseudo-science, Social
Darwinism, to produce the first serious concept of a master race. Up
until the last decades of the century the terms 'race' and 'nationality'
were virtually interchangeable and had nothing to do with biology.
The Protocols of the Learned Elders of Zion provided the first and
most persistent conspiracy theory centred on international Jewry,
while Emile Durkheim wove old prejudices towards racial character
into the new science of sociology. In truth these were by-products of
an extraordinary fecundity of scientific and philosophical advance.
Given the absurdities of crystal healing, aromatherapy and *The Holy
Blood and the Holy Grail* that appeared a century later, we should be
wary of judging the later Victorians and the Edwardians too harshly
for the 'Military Millenarianism' that was to grip them.[2]

The ideas that made up such military millenarianism derived from a fervid extrapolation of some quite sensible ideas. During the 1850s, the military theorist Antoine Jomini had argued that armies ought to be maintained in peacetime as a precaution against a sudden blow, but that a balance should be maintained between the needs of defence and the distortion of a balanced society that too much military influence could incur. The Prussian military reformers Scharnhorst, Gneisenau and Blücher forwarded the idea that an army was the physical embodiment of the moral force of the nation, while Clausewitz concurred with the nationalistic lessons these Napoleonic-era warriors had learnt fighting the French in arguing that a trained citizenry was essential for a nation's defence. So far, so good; but it was Heinrich von Treitschke who posited the idea that the army was the perfect model for the state, while Helmuth von Moltke (the Elder), the embodiment of Bismarck's blood and iron, thought that the army should sit on an elevated plane, because without it no civic institutions could survive. He also saw war as a noble endeavour which would prevent the debasement of the human soul through excessive materialism. The sociologist Walter Bagehot pushed the European intellect a little further down the slippery slope by arguing that war was akin to Darwin's survival of the fittest and that 'the hard impact of military virtues beats meanness out of the world'. Alfred Thayer Mahan, who wrote three articles for RUSI in the 1890s, argued that the world was driven by 'the free play of natural forces' of which the most important were 'national efficiency … and armament'.

None of this meant that war was inevitable of course, but there were enough people in influential positions who accepted the basic tenets of militarism and Social Darwinism to make them potent influences. Indeed, Conrad von Hotzendorf, Chief of the Austro-Hungarian General Staff from 1906 onwards and a prime mover on the road to war in 1914, was a Social Darwinist; while Helmuth von Moltke (the Younger), Chief of the German General Staff in

1914, advocated preventative war as necessary for German survival.[3] What all this added up to was the idea that war was a natural and unavoidable part of human existence and that in it would be revealed all the highest virtues of men. Henry Newbolt caught this mood perfectly in his 1897 poem *Vitai Lampada*:

> The sand of the desert is sodden red, –
> Red with the wreck of the square that broke, –
> The Gatling's jammed and the Colonel dead,
> And the regiment blind with dust and smoke.
> The river of death has brimmed his banks,
> And England's far, and Honour a name,
> But the voice of a schoolboy rallies the ranks:
> 'Play up! play up! And play the game!'

Romantic defeat was not what Jomini, Scharnhorst, Gniesenau, Blücher or RUSI had had in mind at all – indeed, when reading Rudyard Kipling's paean to the virtues of the British officer and colonial administrator, *If*, it is hard to miss the infuriated whirr of Clausewitz spinning in his grave.[4]

Serious theorists like Mahan provided an unintended disservice in adding to the pervading air of militarism by using their historical studies to produce apparently immutable rules which could be used to predict the future. In short, continued great power status for Britain depended on a large battle fleet, colonial trade and, if she commanded the seas, she could ignore whatever went on by land. This meant, in effect, that she need not worry about France, Russia or Germany, unless they built navies – which was precisely what they did. It did not matter to those who fêted Mahan in Britain that neither the French or Russian navies were up to much, because it was the *potential* for challenge that was feared by the defence establishment. Their fears were far more justified, however, when it came to the German High Seas Fleet, which was efficient and designed specifically to cripple the Royal Navy. More worrying were the predictions of Halford Mackinder, the father of geopolitics and first holder of the readership in geography at Oxford established in 1887, who told Edwardian England that in the coming century it was doomed to decline. This was because the industrial potential soon to be realised in the US and Russia would make sea power irrelevant to future economies centred in the heartlands of continents where sea power could not reach. Railways able to transport armies and goods across the interior would become more important than ships; the implication of this was that the Russians *could* get over the North West Frontier into India, and the Americans could get over the Canadian frontier, whatever the strength of the Royal Navy. When the Russians started building railways into Central Asia and to the Far East, it looked like this doom would shortly be realised. The future for Britain was bleak unless Mahan was right after all. Following Mackinder, it seemed to make sense to be sending armies into areas as remote as Sokoto in 1903 and Tibet in 1911 in search of an imperial power base that would preserve Britain's Great Power status.

The Apogee of Low Imperialism

The expansion of empire that had taken place between 1874 and 1882 had been justifiable on the grounds of security, and as Lord Hartington progressively wrested control of foreign and imperial policy from Gladstone during the ministry of 1880–85, the job of taking physical possession of the imperial lifelines was quickly completed. In southern Africa, Gladstonian appeasement of the Boers was seen to have been disastrous as Kruger went on an offensive against the defeated Zulus and the fragile Tswana, egged on by Bismarck's annexation of Namibia in 1884, which was only halted by the despatch of the Bechuanaland Field Force and the annexation of Zululand in 1887. Had gold not been discovered in the Transvaal in 1886, a lasting settlement would have been possible that would have obviated the need for another South African war in 1899–1902 to ensure that the Cape remained in British hands – a prospect aired in the *Asiatic Quarterly Review* (available in the RUSI Library from its first publication in 1886) as early as 1888.[5] The result of this was that both the Suez and Cape routes to India were now firmly under British control and the subject of harbour defence programmes aiming to keep them that way. Similarly, the clear, unambiguous threat issued to Russia when its forces once again drew near to Afghanistan during the Penjdeh Incident of 1885 that any further step forward would mean war – the fleet actually did put to sea and the Indian Army was mobilised – enabled an agreement to be reached that confirmed Afghanistan's status as a buffer between the two empires.

The problem was, however, that the success of these forward moves had set all sorts of other hares running. To Social Darwinism and Geopolitics were added new hopes of finally abolishing slavery by marching into the interior of Africa, wild dreams of bringing business to Africa to help raise it out of its dreadful poverty and attendant miseries, of bringing the light of Christianity once and for all to the 'dark' continent – Stanley's first trans-Africa expedition returned to England in 1878 and by 1882 he had become King Leopold's Congo cat's paw. There were also the baser motives of unrestrained exploitation to consider along with the pegging out of claims on 'undeveloped estates', and the even more eccentric notion of a world colonised and run by a benevolent Anglo-Saxon supremacy. 'Take up the White man's burden', Kipling urged the Americans on during their conquest of the Philippines, while Cecil Rhodes dreamed first of a Cape-to-Cairo railway and then the British colonisation of China. What resulted were a series of imperial acquisitions which to many seemed like a good idea at the time, but which to others, like Lord Salisbury and Gladstone, appeared indicative of a 'fit of absence of mind'.

The first of these episodes of pointless imperialism was the attempt by General Gordon to tack on the occupation of the Sudan to the occupation of Egypt. Gordon, who had a reputation for alcoholic messianism, was meant to evacuate the Egyptian garrisons there, but disobeyed his orders and offered himself up as a martyr to drive Gladstone into sending an expedition to rescue him from Khartoum, an expedition which he hoped would be the prelude to occupation and the extinction of the slave trade. The distinctly murky circumstances in which he had been sent to Khartoum by Hartington and Wolseley, and the fact that it was an open secret that Gordon would disobey his orders, like Clarke, Jervois, Lytton and Frere before him, indicated that this was the defence establishment taking matters increasingly into its own hands.[6] In the event, Gladstone was strong enough to delay a relief expedition until it was too late (and Gordon got his martyrdom), but it cost him the last of his political capital as far as imperial policy was concerned. As far as security was concerned, the Sudan had no value whatsoever.

This also went for Cecil Rhodes's seizure of Zimbabwe and Zambia – today, Southern and Northern Rhodesia – which he believed were full of minerals that would finance further expeditions northwards towards Cairo. His disappointment at finding nothing there was palpable and the 'Pioneers' were forced into farming rather than mining after dispossessing the Matabele and Shona; his British South Africa Company set up to exploit the expected bonanza did not pay a dividend until after the First World War. Much the same could be said of the British East Africa Company, which at one stage forced the annexation of Uganda on an unwilling British government to stave off bankruptcy – the humanitarian impulses that had driven schemes to extend legitimate trade through railway expansion and thus undermine the slave trade were simply too expensive. The expansion of control in southern and northern Nigeria made even less sense; an unhealthy climate made European settlement impossible, and palm oil – the main economic interest – could be sourced elsewhere while the dangers of a reintroduction of slavery if Britain withdrew were no worse than elsewhere. During the 1860s, the British presence in the coastal protectorates of Nigeria consisted of little more than a solitary consul and even with the appearance of Sir George Goldie's West Africa Company, malaria and yellow fever meant that it lived up to its nickname as 'the white man's grave'. When Major Lugard did annex northern Nigeria, it was done simply to keep the French out – and simply because they were French, rather than for any good reason of economics or security. Had it not been for the 'open door' brought about by the implacable opposition of the US and the rivalry of both Russia and Germany, it is not beyond the realms of possibility that China would have been subjected to similar attempts of carving-up. As it was, both Australia and New Zealand developed sub-imperialisms of their own. Of the settlement colonies, only Canada seemed to maintain its sanity.

The Institute quite sensibly kept out of most of this nonsense as far as was possible, even when many of its members were willing to be seduced by the romance of exploration and adventure in far flung places. Between 1880 and 1884 the Institute published nothing on the 'Scramble for Africa', even when Germany was actively encouraging Boer expansionism in southern Africa and acquiring colonies there and in the Pacific. Not even the appointment of Fred Goldsmid to set up an effective administration of the Congo for King Leopold in 1883 could draw a comment. In 1885, Charles Nugent contributed 'Recent Colonial Acquisitions by Foreign Powers, and their Commercial and Strategical Aspects', and there were two articles drawing on events in Egypt and the Sudan, but the focus was very much on imperial rivalries in Asia and European warfare in these years. Indeed, it was not until 1892 that imperial actions in Africa were given an airing in the seven-page long 'The Lagos Expeditionary Force'. Even then, such a short contribution was broken down over two issues, the last two pages being squeezed into a *Journal* dominated by articles on how mobilisation for a European war would be managed. By comparison, 'The Army and Navy of Japan', published in 1893, ran to twenty-five pages, reflecting the importance of this newly emerging power. It was not until 1894 – when French forward moves in west Africa, two minor rebellions in the Gold Coast and the Nigeria protectorates, and a rebellion in Rhodesia ensured that some attention was directed towards these events – that the *Journal* got round to publishing on them; a total of four articles in 1894–96. It might also be significant that Gladstone was back in power 1892–94 and the Liberal imperialist Lord Rosebury was keen to undermine him; no-one in the defence establishment wanted Gladstone back, especially on a platform of home rule for Ireland – P H Colomb gave 'Notes on the Attempted Invasions of Ireland by the French in 1796–8' to the *Journal* in 1891.

For a flavour of how crass and ultimately pointless this sort of imperialism was, it is hard to beat 'A West African Expedition' by Lieutenant C E Vickery RFA in the *United Service Magazine* of April–September 1906, or 'Somaliland Expeditions 1902–1904' from *The Royal Engineers Journal* of 1 October 1904 – indeed, the British involvement in Somaliland from start to finish should stand as a vindication of the Gladstonian viewpoint. The most important event in Imperial Africa during the mid-1890s, Rhodes's failed coup in the Transvaal, the Jameson Raid, was not covered at all. What went for Africa was also true of the endemic warfare on the North West Frontier of India. Between 1878 and 1899, there had been thirty-seven sizeable expeditions (and countless smaller ones) on the frontiers of India; RUSI covered 'The Miranzai Expeditions, 1891', 'On Mountain Warfare: India' (1895) and Francis Younghusband's 'The Chitral Campaign' (1896).

Where RUSI did excel itself, however, was in spotting the talent of Charles E Callwell; his 'Lessons to be Learnt from the Campaigns in which British Forces have been Employed Since the Year 1865' won the Gold Medal Prize Essay in 1887 and his 'Foreign War Offices' appeared in the *Journal* in 1893. His 1896 work, *Small Wars*, remains a classic. On this occasion however, the *Journal* was scooped by the *Proceedings of the Royal Artillery Institute*, who published 'Notes on the Tactics of our Small Wars' in 1884.[7] His analysis of the Anglo-Zulu campaigns of 1879 stands up well even today.

Popular Imperialism

One of the most striking features of this era is that for a brief period, between the late nineteenth century and 1914, Britain fell in love with its armed forces, taking militarism and imperialism seriously, as though these were the measures of national success. The 'Great' in 'Great Britain' ceased to be a geographical description – an appendage of Brittany in France – but a puffed-up chest of national pride. That great *post facto* justification for the scramble for Africa, the 'civilising mission', began to gain intellectual currency as it became ever-clearer that monetary fortunes in Africa were rarer than Cecil Rhodes would have one believe. Popular culture began to celebrate militarism and imperialism on everything from cigarette cards to tea caddies and stamps. This became evident as the debate on defence and imperial concerns quickly spread beyond RUSI and other professional journals and into the diverse popular media.

Political journals such as the *Asiatic Quarterly*, the *Nineteenth Century*, *The Spectator* and the *Quarterly Review* provided regular forums for informed debate drawing contributions from leading politicians, colonial administrators and journalists.[8] Edward Dicey, editor of *The Observer* from 1870–89, debated directly with Gladstone through the pages of the *Nineteenth Century* about the strategic importance of the Suez Canal, while Chesney took on R A Lowe on the pros and cons of imperialism in the same journal.[9] *Broad Arrow*, *The Army and Navy Gazette: Journal of the Militia and Volunteer Forces* and Colbourn's *United Services Gazette* were aimed at increasingly literate officers and non-commissioned ranks, while *Brassey's Naval Annual* further popularised service matters. Daily and weekly newspapers such as *The Graphic* found endless opportunities for exciting copy. '"Soldiering Sells" might have been the motto of … *Blackwood's Magazine*',[10] while *The Times*'s letters page acted as a semi-official notice board for debates on both the politics and the technicalities of defence. Hamley and Chesney's publication of *The Operations of War* was welcomed with an article almost 6,000 words long,[11] while Chesney's 1871 lectures on Prussian tactics at Aldershot was also covered in some detail.[12] The publication of *The Battle of Dorking* raised tempers so much that by 1881 *The Times* was convinced that it was this publication that brought defence within the realm of practical politics for the first time.[13] George Sydenham Clarke wrote on naval issues during the 1890s under the pseudonym 'Navalis' before going on to serve on the Committee of Imperial Defence.[14] Indeed, planned press campaigns were used by the defence establishment on several occasions to attack what they felt was a neglect of defence issues.

Editorials were another way in which contributions were made. W T Stead made his name at the *Northern Echo*, supporting Gladstone's Bulgarian agitation; but he then swung around, as editor of the *Pall Mall Gazette*, to a more positive view of empire, campaigning for the despatch of Gordon to the Sudan, improved naval and colonial defence and supporting Alfred Milner. When Stead founded the *Review of Reviews* he did so with a loan from Cecil Rhodes and repaid the compliment by giving him public support.[15] He was also personally friendly with G E Buckle of *The Times,* H S Wilkinson, defence expert and leader writer of the *Morning Post,* and E B Iwan-Mueller of *The Telegraph* who went to Bechuanaland with Sir Charles Warren's Field Force.[16] Charles à Court Repington became a hugely influential military correspondent on *The Times* in 1903 after being drummed out of the army in a sex scandal, so much so that he was reprieved and given the *General Staff Quarterly* to edit in 1911. Furthermore, the tone of the press shifted during these years towards a much greater acceptance of the tenets of the defence establishment and even the liberal-leaning *Times, Telegraph, Spectator* and *Punch* all became increasingly critical of the more pacific and anti-imperialist policies of Gladstone.[17]

Trying to adequately weigh the actual influence that the press had is still problematic and remains a subject of debate today, but it is certainly the case that in this period it was regarded as a fairly accurate indicator of public opinion by many leading policy-makers[18] and that editors themselves believed that they had an important part to play in forming public opinion.[19] Palmerston fully understood the need to appeal to popular support before the creation of a mass electorate in 1867 made it an absolute necessity;[20] J A Hobson implicitly blamed the press for stirring up Jingoism before the Second Anglo-Boer War.[21] In 1875 Lord Kimberley made the observation that:[22]

> The London newspapers are persistently seeking to stir up the nation to a policy of large armaments, interference in continental affairs, & extension (any where, any how) of our Colonial possessions. This indicates ... that there is a growing desire for such a policy among their readers.

Similarly, in 1882, Lord Derby noted:[23]

> [A]s curious the unanimous feeling expressed by the newspapers & at public meetings ... in favour of extending our influence in S. Africa. It is impossible to doubt or mistake the strength of this sentiment: & it is exactly the opposite of that which prevailed 10 or 20 years ago, when colonies were generally regarded as encumbrances, & the burden of empire was thought greater than its benefit....When the *Daily News* and *Pall Mall Gazette* are with the *Standard* & *Morning Post*, the practical unanimity of opinion which may be inferred is irresistible by any minister.

The shift towards discussion of military problems, and popular militarism, was also reflected in popular literary tastes in the era of mass education. The tabloid journalist William Le Queux was a famous master of Dorkingism, but G A Henty must also be considered. As a war correspondent, Henty had been alarmed by the scale of Prussian power while covering the Franco-Prussian war; he had also been to Magdala with Napier in 1867, to Kumasi with Wolseley in 1874 and with Frere to India on the Royal Tour of 1877. He then became editor of the *United Service Gazette*, working closely with Wolseley, and the boy's magazine *Union Jack*, but it was his output as a novelist that helped to encourage the popularisation of empire and all things military. Writing over 120 books, mainly for children, many on imperial, military or 'sport and manliness' themes, he was acclaimed by readers and educationalists;[24] *Through the Sikh War* was less a story of derring-do than a manual on how to hold a hill fort in a siege.[25] He was followed by many others such as Herbert Strang (*One of Clive's Heroes; Kobo – A Story of the Russo-Japanese War; Boys of the Light Brigade*, all published before 1906) and F Cowley Whitehouse (*The Sniper*, of 1907 – which included a chapter with the quintessentially Edwardian title, 'The Exit of the Bounder'[26]). This was matched by an increasing interest in imperial and military matters in the art world. Lady Butler's paintings attracted enormous numbers of visitors; 20,000 for *The Roll Call* in 1874, and 50,000 for *Balaclava* in London alone, before a national tour.[27] Frederick Burnaby, the author of the bestselling *A Ride to Khiva*, 1876 and *On Horseback through Asia Minor*, 1877, was painted by Tissot in 1870.[28] This popular imperialism, it has been well argued, was not evidence of a confident country, but rather pointed to a great deal of national self-doubt[29] and it is to the credit of RUSI that the realities of Britain's vulnerabilities found their way into the national discourse rather than being obscured by Jingoistic posturing and the cries of dunghill roosters.

The voice of the defence establishment was also strongly represented in Parliament and a military or naval background was seen as a good qualification for a potential MP. Significant numbers of soldiers and sailors sat, or had family members, as MPs on both sides of the House. Lieutenant Colonel William Crossman RE sat as a Liberal Unionist 1885–92; Henry Havelock, son of the defender of the Residency at Lucknow – and defender of RUSI during the 'Notice to Quit' affair in Chapter II – sat as a Liberal 1874–81, a Liberal Unionist 1885–92, and acted as chairman of the parliamentary army and naval service committee; two RUSI stalwarts, J C R Colomb, also a Conservative, sat 1886–92 and 1895–1906, as did George Chesney 1892–95; and also Henry Hildyard, who translated articles from German for RUSI. This is by no means an exhaustive list of MPs with service connections, colonial experience or interests: as George Chesney put it, 'there is hardly a middle-class English family which has not a relative employed in some official capacity in India'.[30] Even parliamentarians who never visited the Institute were no strangers to RUSI, as both Commons and Lords were often regaled with questions that began with a reference to its lectures and *Journal*. Wolseley's views on the vulnerability of the Suez Canal expressed at the Institute were referred to in the debate on Egypt in June 1882;[31] the technical issues surrounding ship signalling and the operation of rifle breechblocks as discussed at RUSI were brought up in April 1883 and June 1886;[32] Henry Labouchere brought up the costs of the British as opposed to the German Army in 1884;[33] Brackenbury's comments on army organisation were quoted in July 1887 as a speech 'of considerable national importance'.[34] In May 1890, commerce raiding was brought up, while Sir Charles Dilke used papers prepared at RUSI for three interventions between 1895–98; 'one of the best documents ever prepared on a military or naval subject was the Naval Prize Essay which was read before the *Royal United Service Institution*'.[35] Nor was this an accident, as Colomb pointed out at the AGM in 1889:[36]

> No question arose in the Houses of Parliament respecting … national defence without evidence being given that the debaters relied upon the journals, papers and discussions of this institute … to guide the legislature.

The raised voice of the defence community in Parliament was noted especially by those who were not particularly in sympathy with it. John Bright complained in 1882 that it was 'painful to observe how much of the "Jingo" or war spirit can be shown by certain members of a Liberal cabinet',[37] while Gladstone recognised the 'latent Jingoism still cherished by a portion of the country' over Egypt in 1882.[38] Three years later he complained of a *rabies* for more land oversea',[39] blamed firmly upon 'the Fiend of Jingoism' represented by the Tory Party and used his powers of patronage to combat its rise in the public schools and universities.[40] Liberals felt surrounded: Kimberley noted that over the Afghan and Zulu wars 'our side are almost as "Jingo" as the Tories: indeed some of the most furious Jingoes "sit" with us'.[41] Lord Derby identified the existence of a 'war party' in 1882[42] and equally believed the Tories were becoming 'exclusively a military & clerical party'.[43] By the 1890s, Jingoism permeated much of British society and found expression within the cabinet in Joseph Chamberlain, Liberal Unionist and imperialist, who tried unsuccessfully but persistently to wrest control of foreign policy from Lord Salisbury and set it on a more overtly imperialist course. Salisbury thought much of the empire was worthless; Chamberlain was prepared to go to war over such places as Samoa. Salisbury urged caution over joining alliances; Chamberlain wanted an Anglo-Saxon alliance of Britain, Germany and America. RUSI, as we have seen, tended much more towards Salisbury's point of view as regards empire, and continued to emphasise that, if the latent strength of Britain was actually mobilised and trained, then there would be little to fear from anyone and little need to go on acquiring territory.

Occupying the Palace of Whitehall
In the dying moments of Gladstone's 1880–85 ministry, the government again issued eviction orders against the Institute, but could not make them effective before it was turned out.[44] However, the question of what to do with the Institute would not go away.

Its insecure tenure and the shock of the December 1871 Notice to Quit meant that RUSI would venture no more funds on the upkeep or extension of the building and as the redevelopment of Whitehall began to gather pace, the 'Goose Pie' began to 'get into a state of disrepair, and the appearance [brought] a certain amount of discredit to a valuable institution'.[45] A 'perfect disgrace to the locality' was a stronger way of putting it.[46] Deputations went to the Admiralty, War Office and the Treasury in 1888 and 1889 but without gaining much more than a promise to look into the matter. The problem was that the Institute was sitting on prime real estate and it could not justify its existence there simply by claiming to be a useful library, museum and lecture theatre, when space was needed for an enlarged, centralised War Office. At the same time the Institute could not afford to move its £43,000 worth of books and models to new premises – and nor did it want to give up the access to government that its location gave it. The case for the Institute being given a new home was made forcefully by *The Times*:[47]

> The extinction of the Institute at the present juncture through the failure of Government to recognise its value and come to its assistance would be … unfortunate in its moral effect and…disastrous in its practical results. … If it did not exist, it would be necessary to invent it. … when national defence is more than ever a matter of national concern.

It was no exaggeration that the existence of the Institute was at stake if they could not persuade the Treasury to foot the bill for a major new building. The government did offer a subsidy that would add up to £1,700 per annum if the Institute built new premises, but it was estimated that a new building would cost £20,000 to erect, well beyond the ability of the Institute to pay, especially as subscriptions were declining as members became reluctant to stump up for an organisation that looked like it might have to close.[48] As a result the Institute tried the tactic of offering two possible alternatives to the government. The first was no more than a smoke screen – that the government should simply pay for a new building for them – that was bound to be rejected. The second alternative contained a real sting in the tail, however. The Institute asked for alternative accommodation to be provided by the government and cited the precedent that when Somerset House was taken over for government use, the Royal Society, the Society of Antiquaries, the Linnean Society, the Chemical Society, the Royal Academy, the Geological Society and the Royal Astronomical Society had all been granted free accommodation elsewhere. Here was an argument pregnant with parliamentary possibilities and perhaps even a lengthy legal wrangle carried out in the public gaze. No government could possibly want the trouble or adverse publicity that a controlled outburst of Jingoism would produce, especially when the approach was supported by a large number of MPs and a wide section of the press.[49] There might even be trouble in the colonies after Australian RUSIs were founded in Sydney in 1888 and Melbourne in 1890.

In the event, the networking skills of RUSI paid off when someone pointed out that the Banqueting House of the old Whitehall Palace, more properly known as the Chapel Royal, had never really been used for religious purposes – indeed society weddings had taken place there – and was cavernous enough for any number of displays and collections. There was also a high level of official support; the First Lord of the Admiralty was Lord George Hamilton, and Edward Stanhope was at the War Office. Both men took:[50]

> [G]reat interest in the Institution, and for a long time we have been endeavouring to bring about an arrangement with the Treasury. Although I am unable to announce any decision, yet I hope to be able to do so at no distant date.

When the Duke of Cambridge sent a memorandum to Queen Victoria in October 1890 requesting the use of the Banqueting House for the Institute, he was pushing at an open door. In the last week of October the Chapel was closed by the Queen's Order in Council.[51] A favourable reply was forwarded on 2 December 1890 granting the use of the Banqueting House to the Institute. The deal was done and the Institute took over the building on 1 January 1891. All that had to be done now was to physically move the Library and collections, a task that Secretary Burgess decided was beyond him – both he and the librarian took the opportunity to retire in favour of Lieutenant Maltby as secretary and Lieutenant Colonel Bowdler as librarian and editor of the *Journal*. Moving the 26,000 books, including 400 books dated between 1494 and 1700, plus the discovery of 573 sets of parliamentary papers and diverse other articles proved too much for Bowdler too, who resigned in 1894, handing on the *Journal* to Captain F N Maude. Two years later the effort of cataloguing – by hand, for the umpteenth time – the entire collection caused a further changeover and the editorship went to Captain H J G Garbett RN (Rtd) with his assistant Major Holden. Major Dashwood of the 16th Lancers finished the catalogue just in time to receive a further donation of 300 volumes on cavalry. He left in 1897 to be replaced by Lieutenant Colonel Lonsdale-Hale, a regular contributor to the *Journal*. Increasingly, the direction of the Institute became the business of the President, General Erskine, assisted by Simmons and Lord Chelmsford. As the membership of the Institute expanded by 50 per cent after 1895, the donations to the museum continued to arrive and space once more became an issue. The patents collection was given away to the Birmingham Free Library in 1896 in order to make way for what was now the finest collection of model ships in the world. The chain of the garden gate at Hougoumont, acquired in 1894, was also saved for the nation.

The use of the newly renamed Banqueting House was conditional on no major alterations being made to the structure, and that the Reubens ceiling was taken care of.[52] This condition was no doubt prompted by Alfred Waterhouse, President of the Royal British

Institute of Architects who had been moved to write to *The Times* on this point in 1892. The organ would be moved out to the chapel in the Tower of London – RUSI council member Lord Chelmsford was also Constable of the Tower – while the pews and other accoutrements would be sent to other royal chapels.

The problem was that the Institute would also need some purpose-built rooms, and so made a pitch for a vacant plot of land on the south side of the Chapel Royal which might be big enough to build offices, reception rooms, a library and a lecture theatre on, if the existing, run-down stables were demolished. Riding a wave of optimism, the Institute proposed that the government build them suitable accommodation there – it would only cost a mere £22,000, after all. Mr Jackson from the Treasury replied that the government had already shown the Institute 'its high appreciation' by the grant of £600 per annum and the use of a 'noble and historic building in one of the most convenient situations in London', rent free. This was Whitehall code for 'do not push your luck', but this is exactly what the Institute did.[53] Holding their first meeting in the Banqueting House in March 1891, they invited Lord Stanhope to take the chair where they regaled him with thanks while Simmons pointed out that they had lost £10,000 on the previous building and really did need the stables next door. An expert on the innovative use of museum space and old supporter of the Institute also nodded in agreement – Vice Admiral Erasmus Ommaney RN, of battleship anchor fame. The Treasury remained firm, however, in its refusal to pay for a new building, but did offer a site on Jermyn Street.[54] When it became clear that the site would not be available for five years, the offer was rejected and the Treasury was approached again. This time, they did agree to let the site to the south of the Banqueting House to the Institute in 1893 for eighty years at a rental of £350 for the first year and £580 a year thereafter, as long as the Institute paid for the erection of the buildings themselves.[55] This was a major victory. At last, the Institute had a security of tenure that stretched until 1972 –

or so they imagined. All they had to do now was raise £20,000 for a new building, which they intended to achieve by public subscription and gambling on an increase in membership that the new building would bring.[56]

Unfortunately this was not to be. The public appeal raised almost nothing whilst, by 1892, less than a fifth of the sum required had been subscribed by members of the Institute and the armed services, drawing the glum comment in the 1892 Annual Report that 'there must be many ships and many military units in which officers give hardly any support to the Institution'.

Not to be deterred, a special fundraising committee was formed led by Admiral Sir G Willes, but which called upon the financial acumen of the lock and safe magnate (and volunteer officer), Sir George Chubb. The result was a 'Fancy Bazaar' set for the week of 6 June 1893, when the foundation stone of the new building would be laid by the Prince of Wales under a red and white striped marquee, accompanied by military bands, a variety of parades and a guard of honour furnished by the Coldstream Guards, the Duke of York's Military School and the Chelsea Pensioners.[57] Inside the Banqueting House a variety of stalls selling fashionable bric-a-brac – 'it could not be said that the goods they contained were rich or rare' commented *The Times* acidly[58] – would be manned by aristocratic ladies, including the Duchess of Edinburgh, Princess Victoria of Battenburg, Viscountess Wolseley, and Lady Brassey. Lady Methuen sold fruit and flowers from the Guards' stall while the Maharajah of Bhownuggur professed himself delighted with a clockwork bear beating a drum, for which he stumped up £5. Lady Jephson's daughter told fortunes, but it was not recorded whether Lord Methuen or Redvers Buller availed themselves of her services to foresee what would shortly happen to their reputations. There was also a musical café and performances of the mandolin to entertain the crowds, but none could really top the rather racy Miss Letty Lind, the burlesque performer presently starring in 'Morocco Bound' at the Shaftesbury Theatre, who would go on to reveal in public the dangers of performing with a broken petticoat string. In the end, however, not even Miss Lind's petticoat string could raise enough and the decision was taken to raid the Institute's capital reserves. These had been built up since the 1830s by investing the life membership subscriptions in gilts which were now worth £20,000. In the end, the building and moving costs came to £24,000, of which half was paid by selling off the capital.[59]

By 1895 the new building was ready, but not everyone was pleased by it. The Earl of Wemyss was distinctly underwhelmed by its appallingly modern architecture and asked in the House of Lords 'was there ever a more dreadful building seen in this world than the United Service Institution building adjoining the banqueting hall?'[60] The fact that the Banqueting House was being used by the Institute for the storage of 'old uniforms and arms' was not much to his taste either; he attacked the government for not using the opportunity to redevelop Whitehall in the original style of Inigo Jones's Banqueting House.[61] This was rather unfair, as the architects had used Portland stone to blend in with Jones's building and had also spent a considerable sum in cleaning up its crypt, which had been used to store coal, and opening up the lower floor windows. The only major alteration work that had been done to the original fabric was the insertion of two doors (with Chubb locks, naturally) to connect the Banqueting House to the Institute directly. It was officially opened in February 1896.

The newly revived Institute began to attract visitors to the Museum in increasing numbers – 27,500 paying visitors plus 6,000 members' guests and servicemen who went free – and membership numbers rose to 5,620 in 1899, even though the cost of life membership was raised to £15 (well over £1,200 in today's currency). In 1897, stands were erected around the Museum so that people could view Queen Victoria's Jubilee procession; ticket sales from this piece of enterprise raised £1,300, while after Kitchener conquered the Sudan in 1898 a special exhibition of his collections brought more visitors in. The variety of journals taken in 1897 showed that the intellectual life of the Institute was flourishing – from America came the US Cavalry and Artillery journals, the *US Naval Institute Journal* and the *Annual Report of the Smithsonian Institute*; Argentina's *Boletin del Centro Naval* sat along the shelf from the *Proceedings of the Canadian Institute of Civil Engineers*; eighteen French journals were taken, thirteen German and five Italian, along with Russian, Japanese, Swiss and Belgian periodicals. This was in addition to all the leading military and scientific British journals and a selection of newspapers.

In 1895, Colonel F C Trench Gascoigne of the Yorkshire Volunteers, veteran of the Gordon Relief expedition (and holder of the Royal Naval Volunteer Reserve Officer's Decoration – which allowed him to put VD after his name, and which the wits claimed was the most prevalent of naval decorations) tried to encourage more officers to write for the *Journal* by donating 60 guineas for an annual essay prize and then two years later donated £5,000 worth of Hull, Barnsley and West Riding Junction Railway and Dock ordinary stock. This put the financial reserves up to £12,000 and allowed the Institute to go back to investing the life membership subscriptions for the longer term. In 1898, the Chesney Gold Medal Award was also established for particular written contributions to the Institute. On the eve of the Boer War, the Institute was therefore in good shape, both intellectually and financially.

The Century Turns

Despite Lord Salisbury's exasperated gibe in 1892 that 'If they were allowed full scope they would insist on the importance of garrisoning the moon in order to protect us from Mars',[62] (and six years before H G Wells's *War of the Worlds* promulgated the notion that they should have) the defence establishment were able to point to the precarious diplomatic situation that Britain faced between 1895 and 1907 to give weight to their points.

Having sacked his Chancellor, Bismarck, Kaiser Wilhelm II engaged a series of policies that were a direct threat to vital British interests, driven by the underlying belief that war was not just an instrument of policy but a desirable end in itself. These policies were not limited to the decision to build a navy to rival Britain's; also irksome were his interference in the Balkans and the Middle East with the putative Berlin-Baghdad railway, his support for the Boers and his genocidal colonial policy in South West Africa (covered by the *Journal* in 1906). *Weltpolitik* came to look increasingly like a plan for world domination. On a visit to Jerusalem in October 1898 he made his entrance on a white charger; the wags at the time noted that even Jesus had had to make do with a simple donkey.[63] The *Journal* used the Kaiser's portrait as a frontispiece in December 1896, as if to point out who the most dangerous man in the world at that time was – no other statesman was so honoured between 1887 and 1906.

Tensions flared up further when the Fashoda incident brought Britain to the brink of war with France in 1898. A series of colonial disputes in Africa and the Pacific culminated in a French attempt to grab control of the Nile, after Kitchener had gone to the trouble of securing it for Britain during the invasion of the Sudan and the Battle of Omdurman. What made this more serious was that since 1894 France had held an entente with Russia (in Kipling's *Kim*, the enemy spies on the northwest frontier of India are Russian *and* French officers). This meant that when Lord Salisbury considered intervening in Armenia to end the brutal Ottoman suppression of a revolt there, both the army and the navy felt it necessary to point out that this would present the Franco-Russian entente with an opportunity to attack the British empire in such force as could not be resisted with the manpower at their disposal.[64]

More worrying was the new assertiveness of the US, as President Grover Cleveland passed a resolution in Congress in 1895 to appoint the Venezuelan Boundary Commission and enforce its findings 'by every means' against British objections. This new threat was reinforced by the appearance of the 'Great White Fleet' in European waters in 1889. This first real ocean-going American battle fleet, brainchild of

Alfred Thayer Mahan and others,[65] was a demonstration that the US was about to become a serious naval power, and not just a home port for potential commerce raiders. In 1896, the *Journal* also pointed out that the enormous industrial capacity of the US was increasingly evident in 'The Production of Modern War Material in the United States of America'. After the Spanish-American War of 1898 its six modern battleships rapidly became twenty-four,[66] while in 1902 the *Journal*'s 'Naval Notes' were contributed by Theodore Roosevelt himself.[67] This was a point not lost on the War Office planners who considered that conflict with the US would inevitably result in the loss of Canada: even though 'facts of this nature may be galling to our national pride … it is necessary to look them in the face'.[68] In March 1896, H H Wilson, editor of the *Navy League Gazette* summed the reality up well; 'It is clear that we have no certain ally in Europe or in the world'.[69] Splendid isolation was not all it was cracked up to be in the absence of adequate armed forces.

The Boer War

The fact that Britain had an army to send to South Africa in 1899 at all was due to the exertions of the defence establishment and its centre in RUSI. In 1879, the despatch of eight battalions to fight the Zulus had stretched capacity to the utmost, a lesson that was repeated again in Egypt in 1882, but not remedied until Salisbury's Conservatives came back into office after 1885. By 1898, despite the fact that defence expenditure had been doubled and now made up 40 per cent of the government's budget, the amount spent still only added up to 2.5 per cent of Britain's net worth, which still left Britain with an army about half the size that it needed to be if it was to fulfil its imperial and home defence functions.[70] This remained a bone of real contention for the defence establishment, especially as the tendency of the newspapers to whip up patriotic fervour on every possible occasion gave opportunities for politicians like Chamberlain, Lord Curzon and Winston Churchill to push for an active foreign policy based on gunboat diplomacy.

This was not at all what the soldiers and sailors had in mind. They wanted a system of imperial defence based on adequate forces and secure bases and felt that the politicians were issuing threats which could only end in humiliating climb-downs or bloody disaster once the disparity between ends and means became apparent. Given the serial crises of the 1890s as the world was carved up in search of imperial glory – whether 'Manifest Destiny' or 'a place in the sun' – it was only a matter of time before one of them would touch national pride, as understood by newspaper editors keen to get their circulation figures up, and end up in bloodshed. However skilfully politicians like Salisbury tried to steer clear of colonial conflicts, there were plenty of others who hoped to ride the millenarian tiger into Downing Street.

The Boer War of 1899–1902 was a case in point and was without doubt the creation of the ambitious radical imperialist Joseph Chamberlain and his High Commissioner in South Africa, Sir Alfred Milner. The roots of the war lay in the discovery of gold on the Witwatersrand in 1886 which had transformed the South African Republic from an economic basket case into the centre of gravity in the region. Its virulently anti-British president Paul Kruger had made repeated overtures to Germany in search of an alliance and since the failure of the Jameson Raid in 1896 – Cecil Rhodes's attempt at a coup – had imported large numbers of Mauser rifles to reinforce his ingrained intransigence. What was more threatening was that Johannesburg was drawing power and influence away from the British centre at Cape Town and there was a very real possibility that the long-sought confederation of South Africa might come about – but it would be Boer, not British-led. This was something unthinkable for both Milner and Chamberlain and they set in train a policy designed to provoke Kruger into war. Flooding troops into South Africa was all it took for Kruger to issue an ultimatum and then invade Cape Colony and Natal.

Kruger knew that he could not beat the British Empire, but with memories of the First Anglo-Boer War in 1881 fresh in his mind, he gambled on striking a series of humiliating blows which would result – he hoped – in an electoral revolt in Britain which would bring some Gladstonian appeaser to power. Times had changed, however, and despite the early British reverses of the war, the possibility of defeat did not exist. But the Institute still lost nearly 400 members from bullets or enteric before Kruger's hopes were extinguished.

The flood of books that came out of both the popular and military presses as a result of the Boer War was unprecedented and the Khaki Election of 1900 was probably the first election in which war fever played a decisive role – and probably the last one until Margaret Thatcher's post-Falklands victory in 1982. The *RUSI Journal* responded too with a real determination to explore lessons learned. Twenty-five articles on the subject were published between 1900 and 1903, which included contributions translated from German, Dutch, Afrikaans and Italian, and with a diverse range of authors, amongst whom were Winston Churchill, a Chief Petty Officer from P&O, two German General Staff Officers, an Austro-Hungarian legal expert and, not least, R M Holden, Secretary of the Institute from 1899. Even M Jean de Bloch, Russian councillor of state, was invited to lecture in 1901 – remarkable, because Russian volunteers were actively aiding Boer forces in Natal – on 'The Transvaal War: Its Lessons in Regard to Militarism and Army Re-organisation'. Jean de Bloch was also the author of *The War of the Future*, and his predictions of the results of a general European war were worth listening to, especially if one happened to be a Russian.

[A] great war would bring forth terrible catastrophes without solving the questions in dispute, owing to the exhaustion of economic resources; and probably internal revolution would force the conclusion of peace, with the social order of Europe in dissolution.

The Museum benefitted too; a chair looted from a Boer *dorp* and subsequently sat on quite frequently by Earl Roberts, and an India Rubber Stamp from the Orange Free State, were among the more prosaic treasures.

Smokeless Powder

In July 1863 Robert E Lee had ordered the 12,500 men under General Longstreet forward to deliver what he hoped would be the *coup de grace* against the Union forces holding Cemetery Ridge at Gettysburg. Advancing across three quarters of a mile of a gently rising glacis, they were met with a withering fire that prevented them from taking the ground directly in front of the Union line and drove them back with 50 per cent casualties. Standing on that ground today, one can only be struck by the insanity of launching a mass of men, shoulder to shoulder, across such an obvious killing ground; the target for the Union riflemen was about a mile wide and it would hardly be possible to miss it. However, what Lee was counting on was the fact that for much of the advance his Confederates would be shrouded in an obscuring smoke generated by thousands of rifles and hundreds of guns using black powder, and that the effective ranges of the Union rifles would be no more than 150–200 yards. Dixie's finest would then emerge with the rebel yell and quickly cross the last hundred yards to come to grips with an enemy who had mainly been firing blind for most of the advance. The charge almost worked, and the two sides did close at bayonet length in several places. That smoke was a defining factor of eighteenth- and nineteenth-century battlefields was shown again at the battle of Isandlwana, when the smoke generated by Martini Henry breechloaders allowed the Zulu warriors to close with the British line and slaughter it. Theoretically, the volume of fire deployed by the British infantry was enough to stop the 25,000 Zulus thrown against them – at one point, it almost did – but smoke, long grass and a partial eclipse provided enough dead ground to cover the Zulu charge.

However, as new technology brought increasing rates of fire and longer effective ranges, smoke began to lose its importance as a factor; at the Battle of Gravelotte in August 1870 the Prussian Army assaulting uphill against French bolt-action rifles and *mitrailleuse* fire suffered almost 20,000 casualties before being forced to withdraw, smoke or no smoke. The increasing rate of rifle fire was a contributory factor in Wolseley's decision to march on Tel-El-Kebir at night in order to suprise the Egyptian defenders and successfully assault before they could properly resist. It was increasingly clear that however much smoke would be generated by both sides, the volume of bullets fired against a massed target would still be substantial.

From 1888, rifle fire took on an even more lethal aspect with the introduction of smokeless powder. Invented in France in 1884, smokeless powder was more powerful, did not obscure the firer's view, allowed machine guns to function more efficiently through fouling less and made it possible for a marksman to hit a target as far off as 1,000 yards – perhaps 2,000 if the target were a group of mounted men. It also allowed the position of the firer to be easily camouflaged, especially if he were entrenched. These realities had connotations that went beyond increasing lethality and the increasing difficulty of closing with the enemy, in that the necessity of looser formations demanded a decentralisation of command that few armies were ready to countenance. At Waterloo, battalions standing shoulder to shoulder delivered volley fire on the word of the Colonel. At Isandlwana, companies dispersed at 5-7 yards between each rifleman had delivered a mixture of volley and individual aimed fire on the word of the company commander, a captain, but it was becoming increasingly evident that this would not suffice in the future.

On the eve of the Boer War, the conception of battle was, roughly: effective cavalry reconnaissance to discover the enemy dispositions; an advance to contact in a recognisably parade-ground formation; followed by dispersal as the firefight began. Supports would then be gradually fed into the firing line until, supported by artillery pushed well forward, the enemy's fire was sufficiently suppressed to allow for a bayonet charge to take the position. The cavalry would then undertake the pursuit of the broken enemy. The need for greater dispersal, however, meant that orders issued at company level would not be heard and the increased level of junior leadership and initiative required therefore meant that it would be platoons – and even squads – that would need to form the basic tactical units. In the age of mass, short-service conscript armies, it was a reasonable surmise that the training of officers, NCOs and men to utilise this initiative under fire and engage their courage without notice from their superior officers would not be possible. Experience seemed to indicate that individual riflemen under fire tended to go to ground in the killing zone resulting in a prolonged, murderous but indecisive firefight and there were fears that unless the 'spirit of the bayonet' could be instilled into the conscript, then an attack once stalled would never get going again. German officers who had seen this happen 1870 were apt to describe it as *Massen-Drückebergertum* or 'wholesale skulking'.[71] Few, if any, of these insights could be tested by military manoeuvres and peacetime exercises that could not adequately simulate the new tactical realities; large bodies of men were regularly allowed to cross ground that would be killing zones in a real war. This was the background to the shock administered to the British military system by the Boer War.

The Institute had, of course, identified many of these trends and had busily debated the issues involved. Colonel Home had posed the question in 1882 in succinct terms:[72]

> A certain space of from 1,500 to 2,000 yards swept by fire, the intensity of which increases as troops approach the position from which the fire is delivered has to be passed over. How shall it be crossed?

During the 1880s there were so many *Journal* contributions dealing with the introduction of machine guns, quickfiring guns (breechloading artillery) and smokeless powder that the 1891

Military Prize Essay was set on 'The Tactical Operations of the Future (Including Questions of Supply and Transport of Ammunition) as Affected by the Introduction of Magazine Rifles, Machine and Quick-Firing Guns, and Smokeless Powder'. Responses to the problems of effective reconnaissance included an article on 'Employment of Dogs for Military Purposes' in 1889; it was imagined that they could be used to find a concealed enemy; clearly the author had spent too much time fox hunting. More futuristic was the lecture on the use of photography for reconnaissance given in March 1892 and the growing interest in the use of aircraft for both scouting and the delivery of 'aerial torpedoes'. The vexed question of the proper function of cavalry – were they mounted infantry who, like the dragoons of old, rode to battle then fought on foot or were they to continue to deliver a massed charge – was revived yet again. This debate would be revisited often and without resolution as the cavalry desperately hung onto their swords and lances.

There was no agreement either on how to best respond to the implications of this new wave of technology and the British Army went to South Africa almost completely unprepared for the style of warfare that they were to face. At Stormberg, Magersfontein and Colenso, reconnaissance was unable to discover the Boer positions, parade ground formations were ambushed and pinned down before they could disperse, guns pushed forward had their crews picked off and officers were unable to get their men moving again. The effect of accurate rifle and artillery fire on exposed infantry was devastating in terms of both casualty rates and morale; a visitor to Spion Kop today cannot but be struck by the fact that a determined bayonet charge by the British troops would have carried the position quickly had they had enough respite for the officers to regain the initiative. The despatch of light horse or mounted rifle units from across the empire to take on the Boer Commandoes seemed to finally settle the cavalry argument in their favour, except that on one or two occasions, charges *had* been successful and thus allowed the *arme blanche* enthusiasts to claim that they still retained a useful role.

There were also observations made that the colonial and volunteer units tended to display greater initiative than regular soldiers as a result of having a better education and having been spared the inculcation of excessive dependence on officers that drill was supposed to impart. This had major implications for the debate on whether the future constitution of the army should be professional, conscript or volunteer.

The truth was that RUSI had kept up to date with military developments during the period before the Boer War; but, without a real testing ground, the issues had necessarily been stalled at the theoretical level. It is to the credit of the British Army that they did learn much from the experience; the Russian, German and Austro-Hungarian infantry were still prepared to advance in mass formations in 1914, and were shot flat for their pains.

National Efficiency
The British defence establishment looked facts square in the face after the indignities of the Boer War. The military shortcomings were all taken note of, but more worrying still was the state of the volunteers who did come forward to fight. Cramped up in industrial slums, overworked and underfed, the British working classes were often in too poor health to be considered for military training and the number of potential recruits thus rejected was truly alarming – in Manchester, 8,000 volunteers out of 11,000 failed the medical. It was true that for many years social reformers had been campaigning against urban poverty, but it was only now that a widespread feeling emerged that something had to be done about the health of the nation – for many, it was about the health of the *race* too.

Social Darwinist fears were raised as it became ever clearer that Tommy Atkins resembled much more of an under-sized weakling than something out of a Ford Madox Brown painting. Within the Liberal Party there was a strong feeling that money spent on battleships and guns would be wasted unless the health of the men expected to man them could be improved, and this meant that the state ought to actively intervene in society to alleviate these ills as it already did in the Kaiser's Germany, where various social insurance schemes were effective in combating the downward spiral of poverty, unemployment and poor health. From the defence establishment, led by Lord Roberts, came the view that 'National Efficiency' would now depend on compulsory military training for all males, which would serve not only to spread military skills more widely through the population but promote public health. The National Service League resulted and Roberts devoted much of his time between 1905 and 1914 to it, but the whole concept was anathema to the Liberal government and controversial within the army itself.

The *Journal* debated the idea on several occasions. In 1896 the Gold Medal Prize was given for an essay on 'The Relative Advantages and Disadvantages of Voluntary and Compulsory Service, both from a National and Military Point of View', which suggested that military training was good in itself. In 1902, 'The Advantages of Compulsory Service for Home Defence' appeared while the ominously titled 'Conscription or Compulsory Volunteering' was published in 1903. Adjutant General Ian Hamilton co-operated with Secretary of State for War R B Haldane to reject the idea in 'Compulsory Service' (1910), which led to an ugly public spat with Roberts. Baden-Powell, surprised that his *Aids to Scouting* (1899) was being used as a manual for spontaneous military training by the Boys Brigade and various Church youth organisations, thought that this was a better way forward and produced *Scouting for Boys* in fortnightly parts from January 1908. By March 1910, the spontaneous growth of the Scout movement persuaded him to retire from the army and devote all his time to boys' education based on 'character' and military skills.

The Committee of Imperial Defence

Gladstone's view on bodies set up to look into defence matters
was that if generals were allowed to plan for wars then wars would
happen, and that nothing like a General Staff would be tolerated on
his watch. Britain had no official machinery for planning for defence
issues at a time when major shifts in the security environment were
taking place. It was therefore Lord Carnarvon's greatest long-term
influence on imperial defence issues that he brought together the
army, navy and colonies into a unified planning forum under his own
aegis in 1878.

Previously, the army had operated through the Defence
Committee, a permanent deliberative body chaired by the Duke
of Cambridge at the War Office, while the navy planning resided
with the Board of Admiralty.[73] Both of these bodies had begun to
co-operate on a formal basis after the Admiralty requested army
help in garrisoning its overseas bases, but in general the government
tended to seek military advice on an ad hoc basis. In this way, the
declaration of war by Russia on Turkey found I G F Simmons
explaining the importance of colonial defence to the Cabinet in April
1877, while Secretary of State for War, Gathorne-Hardy, opened up
discussions with Carnarvon for an interdepartmental committee to
be formed.[74] This finally came to fruition in the establishment of
the Colonial Defence Committee (CDC) in early 1878,[75] which,
despite Carnarvon's resignation in January 1878, brought together
Simmons, Admiral Alexander Milne and Sir Henry Barkly (ex-
governor of Cape Colony), to represent the Colonial Office, into one
forum with a brief to properly examine the subject.[76] By September
1878, the CDC had come to the conclusion that the matter was of
such complexity that a more thorough investigation was required[77]
and Carnarvon's successor, Sir Michael Hicks-Beach, authorised the
creation of a permanent commission in February 1879, which by July
had become a Royal Commission presided over by Carnarvon and
manned by Hugh Childers, Sir Henry Holland, Milne, Simmons,

Barkly, Thomas Brassey and Robert Hamilton (Accountant-General of the Navy and Comptroller of Navy Pay).[78] This was not quite an Imperial General Staff, but it was at least an attempt to systematically investigate the problems and, by implication, set up some body to deal with them.

For a while, however, the Carnarvon Commission was kicked into the long grass by Gladstone when he came to power in 1880. John Bright considered it to be 'an insane scheme',[79] and both of Gladstone's colonial secretaries, Lord Kimberley and Lord Derby, wanted nothing to do with it. But the Commission's work was widely supported (even when it was supposed to be secret – its secretary was Colonel Nugent, a RUSI contributor, and its existence was leaked in the *Journal* in 1882)[80] and allowed to continue its work. In the event, Kimberley attempted to bury all three reports in the Colonial Office secret cupboards, but Lord Hartington had other ideas. He had read the first report in December 1881,[81] and was determined to do something about it by encouraging the Duke of Cambridge to revive his Defence Committee's interest in colonial issues[82] – there was a strong whiff of collusion with Carnarvon in his decision to try to bring together the army, navy and Colonial Office representatives to discuss imperial defence issues after Gladstone had refused to discuss it in Cabinet in March 1884.[83] In March 1885, Hartington announced that there would be a new interdepartmental Colonial Defence Committee, made up of four War Office nominees, one from the Admiralty and one from the Colonial Office, but Hartington could go no further due to the fall of the Liberal government in 1886.[84] Under Lord Salisbury, Hartington was encouraged to continue his work from inside the Foreign Office but no minutes were kept of the discussions held.

The Boer War changed all this, however, and the more thorough approach to planning long demanded meant that in 1902, Salisbury's successor, Arthur Balfour, founded the Committee of Imperial Defence with a Chief of the Imperial General Staff to look into the whole question of co-ordinating a more rational defence policy. For the first time, Britain now had a properly constituted war-planning organisation. Nor was this all: Hartington's ex-private secretary (and co-conspirator with Colomb, Stead, Jackie Fisher and Carnarvon over the 'Truth about the Navy' affair) Reginald Brett, Lord Esher subsequently set up a committee (with Fisher and George Sydenham Clarke RE as secretary) to look into the running of the War Office, reorganised it and established the Army Council and the General Staff. This lead also encouraged a greater spirit of co-operation within the empire and the emphasis began to shift away from imperial *defence* to the concept of Imperial Expeditionary Forces employed independently or as reinforcements to British forces deployed on offensive operations outside Europe. By 1912, the concept of a single Minister of Defence to replace the separate Secretaries of State for War and the First Lord of the Admiralty was being discussed at RUSI by Lord Esher himself with the Chief of the Imperial General Staff Sir John French in the chair.[85]

The End of Splendid Isolation

The lonely position of Britain during the Boer War was extremely threatening, and it was clear that the days of 'splendid isolation' had to come to an end. Sooner or later Britain would have to make a choice about whether to settle with its old rivals in the Franco-Russian Entente or accept a junior partnership in the German-led Triple Alliance (with Austria-Hungary and Italy). The first indication that things were about to change came with the signing of the Anglo-Japanese Alliance in January 1902 which was aimed at restraining Russian ambitions in the Far East by establishing Japan as a local counterweight. This was followed with the signing of the Anglo-French Entente in April 1904 and, after Russia had been defeated by Japan in 1904–5, the Anglo-Russian Entente of August 1907, which tidied up a whole series of disputes in Asia. The rapprochement with Russia was fundamentally the result of the Kaiser's attempts to upset an Anglo-French colonial carve up of North Africa, in which Britain gave France a free hand in Morocco in return for a free hand in Egypt. The First Moroccan Crisis of 1905–06 convinced the British that it was Germany, rather than Russia, which was now the more likely antagonist. Even more momentous was the opening up of military talks between Britain and France in 1906, which posited the despatch of the British Army to aid France in the event of a German attack. This had been a theoretical possibility since the 1888 Stanhope Memorandum had listed this as one of the functions of the army, but no one had really thought that an expeditionary force landing on French soil would actually be there to help – Wolseley thought its most likely task would be to raid the dockyards at Brest.[86] This really was the world turned upside down.

The hardening of Europe into two blocs – although in reality neither was as tightly bound as they looked – and the Kaiser's aggressive naval building programme fed the growing feeling that war really was inevitable. The tenor of popular opinion in Britain meant that even when a new Liberal government came into office in 1906 intent on widespread social reform, which included for the first time, a real attempt at the redistribution of income through social insurance schemes, it could not ignore demands for adequate defences. Even the People's Budget of 1909 carried provisions for eight new Dreadnought-class battleships.

The Battle of Hitch VC

The Institute had acquired several Victoria Crosses (VC) for its medal collection over the preceding forty years. Now recognised as the highest award for bravery that the British Army can award, before the First World War it was highly valued by soldiers more for the £10 per annum pension that came with it. One of the first VCs to be awarded, that of Surgeon F James Mouat VC, earned by saving the life of the Colonel of the 17th Lancers after the failed charge of the Light Brigade, belonged to the Institute.[87] He would later contribute

'A Visit to Some of the Battle Fields and Ambulances of the North of France' to the *Journal* in 1871.[88]

One VC that did not belong to the Institute, however, was that of Frederick Hitch, late of the 24th Regiment of Foot. Hitch was a twenty-year-old labourer from Edmonton (today a north London suburb) when he enlisted in the army in 1877. Posted out to South Africa for the Anglo-Zulu War, he was present at the Battle of Rorke's Drift in January 1879 where, despite having his shoulder blade shattered by a Zulu bullet (the surgeon took thirty-nine pieces of bone out without anaesthetic), he fought on using a borrowed pistol in his left hand and helped evacuate his wounded comrades from the burning hospital building (something he did not bother to mention in his own account). Gradually weakening, and politely turning down an offer to be put out of his misery, he then finally fainted from loss of blood. As the great Zulu war raconteur David Rattray said: 'They broke the mould when they made Hitch'.[89]

Hitch was sent back to England and invalided out of the army in August 1879. He was snapped up by the Corps of Commissionaires in October, but drifted in and out of employment with them for the next three decades. He tried his hand at being a railway porter and as a caretaker at the Imperial Institute – set up in 1887 to promote scientific research for the benefit of the empire – in South Kensington. In 1894 he became a publican but a year later had his licence rescinded. By 1901, he was working at RUSI when he fell from a ladder and was knocked unconscious. Rushed up the road to Charing Cross hospital, when he came to he asked about the medal which was on his tunic in the Institute cloakroom. Someone was sent to fetch it, but could only report that it had, in the meantime, been stolen. Hitch, understandably furious, blamed the Institute, but the Institute refused to take responsibility. Indeed, there was some suspicion that Hitch had engineered the fall to cover up the fact that he had sold his medal – he had seven children with another on the way at the time. This was an unlikely probability, however, because the pension attached to the award had been raised to £50 per annum in 1898 and the medal never did turn up. Hitch, somewhat disillusioned, returned to his old job at the Imperial Institute before becoming a cab driver and only received a replacement medal in 1908 after his son had petitioned the War Office. For this act of graciousness he was charged £3 7s 6d. Hitch died in 1913 after catching pneumonia while on strike in protest at Winston Churchill's decision, as Home Secretary, to refuse a rise in cab fares to cover the increased cost of petrol. In 1929, the widow of his eldest son put his VC up for sale; it was bought by his second son, then RSM in the 24th, and donated to his regiment.[90]

This was not the only misfortune visited on the staff in these years. One of the curators had been given the job on condition that his wife acted as housekeeper at the Institute. Unfortunately she developed a taste for the bottle over the years, and on one unfortunate evening sat too close to the fire after her accustomed tot (or tots). Her crinolines went up in flame and she died before her distraught husband could extinguish her. This was traumatic enough, but fearing that he would lose his job as a result of the death, he chose to hide the body until such time as he could hatch a plan to dispose of it. A charred body has a certain presence, however, and the unfortunate man was found out. He kept his place, however, after a severe ticking off. (The stove, now covered up to prevent soot spilling in, is still in its original configuration on the fourth floor of RUSI's main building).

The Battle of Dorking Revisited
J C R Colomb told RUSI that he had written the articles that culminated in 'The Defence of Great and Greater Britain' partly in frustration that The Battle of Dorking had, in his opinion, entirely distracted the necessary debate about defence away from the problem of commerce raiding to an unnecessary panic about invasion.[91] However, this was a difference of nuance; imperial and home defence were two sides of the same coin – there were those in the defence community who

were less sure that the Dorking scenario could be ignored entirely and were prepared to use alarmist tactics again. The Gold Medal Prize for 1898 was concerned with raising a Home Defence Force, while the raising of a system of local guides for home defence was discussed in 1903. In 1904, the *Journal* published 'Southern England as a Theatre of War'. Lord Roberts, increasingly concerned that his hopes for National Efficiency through compulsory military service would fall foul of the Liberal's social insurance schemes, decided that the Dorking tactic might well pay off dividends again. That a public campaign might generate more funding was not incompatible with firmly held convictions that Britain was vulnerable to attack; indeed what gave 'Dorkingism' its power and credibility was that it was indeed informed.

In 1886, Major Elsdale presented to RUSI a paper entitled 'The Defence of London and of England', which laid out a credible invasion scenario.[92] Elsdale, a runner-up for the Institute's Gold Medal Prize essay contest in 1877,[93] argued that the navy was too stretched to guarantee that a *coup de main* against London would not succeed; in the audience, General Collinson RE (a friend of Ardagh[94] and one of the judges of the competition in 1877) remarked that it would be a simple enough manner to land 150,000 men from steam ships before the navy could seriously intervene and then regain control of the sea to leave the invader beached. In 1885, the *Journal* had published 'The Dutch in the Medway, June 9-13, 1667' as an example of how a successful raid had been conducted during the seventeenth century; in 1911, Kipling used the same title to claim that Britain was in danger because of the perennial unwillingness of the government to spend on defence:[95]

Mere powder, guns, and bullets,
We scarce can get at all;
Their price was spent in merriment
And revel at Whitehall.

Concern at the possibility of a German invasion continued to mount, resulting in the publication in serial form of a new and bigger restatement of the *Battle of Dorking* theme. *The Invasion of 1910 with a Full Account of the Siege of London* was written by William Le Queux[96] – a third attempt; he had already written *The Poisoned Bullet* in 1893, which was reissued as *The Great War in England 1897* on the theme of a surprise French invasion – at the behest of Field Marshall Lord Roberts. Serialised in the popular press, the invasion this time featured a German landing at several points around the East Anglian coastline, with volunteer forces brushed aside at the battles of Chelmsford and Harlow, Audley End burned, London bombarded and occupied, and the final ignominy in the victorious General Von Kronhelm setting up his headquarters in the (then) newly built War Office in Whitehall. Although deliberately alarmist in tone, Le Queux obviously had access to informed opinion; the defences of London are breached at Chipping Ongar, the very spot that Elsdale had identified as the north easterly keystone of his defence lines. One of his informants was Colonel à Court Repington.[97] Furthermore, Le Queux finally sent Von Kronhelm packing by a popular revolt in London which results in terrible street fighting and the swamping of the German forces; the very tactic which Elsdale had advocated as a last resort.

Leading Liberals, busy in 1906 with plans for the establishment of a welfare state, thought much the same of Le Queux and Roberts as Gladstone had of Chesney. Indeed, Lord Tweedmouth went so far as to accuse Roberts of taking bribes from a 'little ring of wild, though self-convinced alarmists' during the 1907 official inquiry into the possibilities of invasion.[98] In resisting calls for increased armaments and fortifications they pointed out the two main flaws in the whole Chesney concept; firstly, that the navy had not been properly taken into consideration and secondly, that it would be impossible for an invasion armada to be established in such complete conditions of secrecy that Parliament and the Admiralty would not get wind of it and take pre-emptive action. These were very fair points. In *The Invasion*, Le Queux had Chatham closed by block ships scuttled in the Medway; the destroyer force on exercise in Irish waters; while the dreadnought contingent was so weakened by a surprise torpedo and mine attack on its anchorage at Rosyth, it was trounced by the German High Seas Fleet in the subsequent battle in the North Sea. Taken each in turn, the individual incidents were all more or less credible – indeed, they appeared likely after the Japanese navy defeated the Russians by similar measures in 1905 – but taken together, they represented such an avalanche of bad luck and poor judgement as to be completely incredible.

Nor was it necessary for Erskine Childers to solve *The Riddle of the Sands* to know that an invasion force could not be assembled in secret; even the most rudimentary diplomatic, consular or intelligence service would pick up on the enormous activity contingent on moving an army to the ports. Le Queux stretched his credibility beyond breaking point in having Antwerp occupied and the Belgian army disarmed, the telegraphs cut, the invasion flotilla assembled (where Erskine Childers said it would be), an entire army embarked and every scrap of British shipping in German ports interned without anyone in Britain noticing. The troop trains and mobilisation plans might well have proceeded with 'the punctuality of clockwork'[99] but the ticking would have thundered through the afternoon snooze of even the most blimpish of War Office staff officers. This was something that Roberts himself knew very well; in 1871 he had written a very detailed article for the United Services Institute (in India), in which he discussed the problems of shifting an Indian Army Corps of 24,000 men and worked out that it would require 155 ships and 8,500 pack animals. It was inconceivable that this could be done in secret.[100]

Certainly, Roberts and Le Queux had fallen into the trap of overstating their case in the hope of generating publicity and thus undermining the thrust of the argument by exposing it to ridicule;

but the fact remained that they had a valid point to make. The First World War would show that the German navy did possess the capability to raid the east coast. Had the Kaiserliche Marine shown perhaps a little more dash, possessed a few more ships, and had a little more luck in their attempts to lure Jellicoe's Grand Fleet over their mine and submarine traps, they might well have landed marines at Hartlepool or Scarborough to embarrass the government severely.

Even if a lasting occupation was dismissed as impractical by both Chesney and Le Queux, it was widely considered that a strong raid delivering a knock-out blow on an undefended London followed by a Carthaginian peace was, in fact, feasible. In 1888, Ardagh wrote a memorandum on the possibility of an attack on London that was taken seriously enough for the government to begin buying sites for forts in 1889 and 1890 – they became known as 'Stanhope's Storehouses'.[101] Furthermore, the 1903 'Handbook for the Defence of London Positions', issued by the War Office to divisional commanders, contained a line of fortification drawn up by Ardagh that bore a striking resemblance to Elsdale's *RUSI Journal* contribution.[102] When the Chief of the General Staff asked the British military attaché in Berlin, Lord Edward Gleichen, for his opinion of whether the Germans could embark 150,000 men in thirty-six hours, as Roberts had asserted, the answer was affirmative, even if it could not be done in secret.[103]

'Dorkingism' was a symptom of the continuing and underlying insecurity of a defence community unsettled by unprecedented technical and geopolitical change, which they felt might result in a catastrophic, unforeseen calamity destroying British naval supremacy and thus exposing Britain and its empire to calamitous assault. *The Defeat of the Navy in the Battle of Dorking*,[104] and *Rasplata* ('The Reckoning'; translated from the Russian, a fictionalised account of the defeat of the Russian Navy in 1905), which the *Journal* offered in serialised form between 1909 and 1911, differed little in their sentiment or intent from the 'Concentration of a Force to resist

Raids or Invasion: Training, Organisation and Rapid Deployment', which the Institute published in 1908. This itself based on a *Times* article called 'Invasion', which was reprinted in November 1907 in the *National Review*, and in which the possibility of a large-scale attack on Britain was accepted as 'gospel'.[105] There was even a brief flirtation with the idea of a pre-emptive strike against the German High Seas Fleet which, given the defences of Heligoland and Kiel, was quickly abandoned.

One of the symptoms of British insecurity in these years was the often ludicrous obsession that a German fifth column existed, ready to rise up the moment that a German army appeared off the coast. That there was an abundance of German waiters employed in hotels across the south coast was, in the wilder imaginations, proof positive that something dastardly was afoot. The fact that Britain had no secret intelligence services – the War Office Intelligence Branch and the Naval Intelligence Department were not intended to be clandestine organisations – allowed novelists, fantasists and tabloid journalists to indulge themselves to the full. Prominent among these was William Le Queux, who invented his own imaginary intelligence service to foil the plots of these imaginary enemies.[106] There were, however, a number of considerations that were worth investigating. The first was that the German army had used German nationals resident in France as guides during the invasion of 1870 and would probably seek to replicate this tactic in any future invasion. The second was that a well-placed intelligence agent was worth a great deal in the right circumstances; in 1897 the *Journal* carried an article on 'Schulmeister the Spy', a German in Bonaparte's service, who had provided the vital tip off for the capture of the Duc d'Enghien in 1804 and was then credited with providing such disinformation to the Austrians that they were forced to surrender to Napoleon at Ulm in 1805.

In 1905, during the debates over the possibilities of a German invasion, Colonel Ovens held out the possibility in the *Journal* that the Germans would indeed use resident nationals as guides in

'Fighting in Enclosed Country' and although this was rather flimsy stuff when it came to hard evidence, the outburst of Dorkingism in 1907 resulted in the possibility of German intelligence operating in Britain being taken seriously. Indeed, there were German naval intelligence rings operating in this period, but they did not consist of waiters or tourists with false moustaches reconnoitring invasion routes on bicycles. The result was the appointment of Captain Vernon Kell and Commander Mansfield Cummings as Britain's spymasters; MI5 and MI6 had at least some of their roots in RUSI.

The Reformers

Richard Burdon Haldane came to the War Office against the background of Earl Roberts's declaration of 1905 that, yet again, the army was not fit for purpose – it was, after all, still smaller than Switzerland's.[107] Haldane brought with him, however, a willingness to listen to his professional advisers and a genuine desire to build on what Esher, RUSI and others had done before him and contributed his ideas to the *Journal* in 1907 with 'The Military System of the Future in the British Empire'. His aim, in short, was to produce a sizeable British Expeditionary Force (BEF) for despatch to France and to finally create a system of reserves that might allow for rapid reinforcement and expansion in time of war, without spending so much money that the Liberal social reformers would rebel.

In 1907, his Army Order of 1 January put in motion plans for a BEF of one cavalry and six infantry divisions, with a seventh to be scraped together from odds and ends scattered around garrisons at home and overseas. The Territorial and Reserve Forces Act of 1907 swept up all the cherished eccentricities of militias, volunteers and yeomanry into the new Territorial Army of fourteen infantry divisions and fourteen mounted brigades which, by 1910, had a quarter of a million part-time soldiers enlisted at 88 per cent of full strength. Eleven articles in the *Journal* charted the progress of the Territorials from 1906–13, including one by Baden-Powell in 1908.

Mobilisation arrangements were also sped up through the co-opting of railway managers, and the University Officers Training Corps were established to increase recruitment and popularise the army among the educated. There is no doubt that Haldane achieved a lot, but there was a cost too and that was paid in equipment shortages – much of the volunteer artillery never saw a functioning gun for years at a time. In the event Kitchener decided not to expand the Territorials in 1914, but to build a whole new army altogether. The volunteers were, by and large, sent off to do garrison duty.

Admiral Sir John Fisher had long been deeply involved in naval politics and was one of W T Stead's informants for his 'Truth about the Navy' articles. His mantra of 'economy and efficiency' was one guaranteed to appeal to both sailors and politicians throughout his tenure as First Sea Lord 1904–10 and, despite a sometimes despotic, often abrasive and vindictive manner, it was his reforms that ensured the navy went to war in 1914 in very good order indeed.

From 1899 to 1904 he had worked on improving the conditions, morale and training of the crews of the navy on the time honoured principle that happy ships were efficient ships. This was followed by a sweeping reform of the Reserve Fleet, which involved scrapping a large number of older vessels and redeploying their crews to those that remained. These ships would be manned at 40 per cent of their wartime complement and made to exercise on a regular basis. There was also a major cull of over 150 obsolete warships scattered around foreign stations and a reform of those foreign stations themselves. The Cape Squadron would look after the whole of the Americas and the South Atlantic; the Eastern Fleet based in Singapore would control the Indian Ocean; while the Mediterranean Fleet was reduced in strength as co-operation with France reduced the level of potential threat there. In time of need the Atlantic Fleet, based on Gibraltar, could reinforce the Mediterranean Fleet or the new Home Fleet concentrated in the North Sea against Germany.

Fisher then sought to simplify the plethora of ship types developed

over the last half century into four main categories. The most famous
were the big-gun dreadnoughts, but the new battlecruiser class,
which was designed to run down commerce raiders while still being
fit to stand in the line of battle, was a real innovation. Similarly, his
championing of the fast, torpedo-armed destroyers and his insistence
on the development of the submarine for coastal defence were major
developments. Fisher was fortunate in that three successive First
Lords, Tweedmouth, McKenna and Churchill, all supported his
belief that a big navy was vital to British security, and that it was
the Liberal imperialists, rather than the Liberal social reformers, who
took over the defence ministries. He also had good fortune in the
new foreign secretary, Sir Edward Grey, who was convinced that a
war with Germany was inevitable and that the naval challenge had
to be met.

Naval cuts were never on the cards after the last serious attempt to
effect them by the Liberal government – in particular, reducing the
dreadnought order from eight to six, and then to four – was defeated
by the famous Navy League agitation of 1908. When Churchill
became First Lord of the Admiralty in 1911, he continued to follow
Fisher's lead, introducing the new *Queen Elizabeth*-class battleships
and took the fateful decision to convert the navy's energy supply
from Welsh coal to Persian oil. The Royal Naval Air Service was also
formed, and the submarine arm expanded and developed into an
oceangoing force. In 1912, a Naval War Staff was established, the
Kriegsspiel introduced and an Anglo-French Naval Agreement allowed
the Royal Navy to virtually withdraw from the Mediterranean and
concentrate in the North Sea. Perhaps most impressive was the speed
at which the Fleet could now be mobilised – just two days in the
summer of 1914.

Any thought of an invasion of the Home Islands now was gone.
This was not achieved without pain, and serious concerns were
raised by the Foreign and Colonial Offices and the Dominions
about the repercussions for imperial defence that these withdrawals

and redeployments entailed. For Fisher, and especially Churchill, these concerns were secondary and they consistently built up a navy designed to defeat Germany. Once this was done, they argued, everything else could be mopped up afterwards. What they did in the process was to progressively abandon any pretence of the maintenance of the Two-Power Standard, whereby Britain would maintain a navy equal to the next two competitors combined.[108] Perhaps the only real criticism that could be levelled at Fisher was that his contempt for the army – 'a bullet fired by the navy' – stood in the way of a proper co-ordination growing up between them and his reluctance to talk to his French allies.

There was also something of a reluctance to engage with RUSI that did Fisher no good; it was under his aegis that a belief grew among many junior officers that contributing to the *Journal* might well be regarded as a blot on their careers. In 1902, this was raised in the Annual Report and it was agreed that some 'friendly approach' should be made to the Admiralty to sort out whatever was the problem. It was suggested that giving the Russian M Jean de Bloch space at RUSI in 1901 had put a number of noses out of joint, given Russian mischief-making during the recent war in South Africa. The problem persisted for the next two years when there was a noticeable lack of naval input for the Prize Essay competitions, despite adopting a policy of encouragement. Indeed, in May 1906 it was revealed in the Commons that on two occasions serving naval officers had been refused permission to deliver papers at RUSI, while the Annual Report again noticed the reluctance of naval officers to take part in discussions at the Institute as late as 1909.[109] Getting naval pictures for the frontispieces of the *Journal* from the Admiralty also seemed to be something of a problem; only three were prised out between 1897 and 1906, whereas the Austro-Hungarians were happy to supply five in all, as were the Chileans (two), the Chinese (one), the French (thirty-three), the Italians (six) and the Germans (thirteen). The most modern and revolutionary design of them all,

HMS *Dreadnought*, never featured at all, although the Institute did try to get in on the naval design debate with the Gold Medal Prize essay of 1906, 'What is the Relative value of Speed and Armament, both Strategically and Tactically, in a Modern Battleship, and how far should either be sacrificed to the other in the Ideal Ship?'. The *Journal* also reprinted 'The Inherent Qualities of all Big-Gun One-Calibre of High Speed and Large Displacement and Gun Power' from the US Naval Institute's *Proceedings* in 1907.

Co-operation did not dry up entirely, however, and the Institute was still reckoned a valuable conduit by parts of the Admiralty; in 1907 the director of naval intelligence supplied 'Artillery Development in the United States Navy; Battle Practice' in 1907, which he had garnered from the German military press.

Preparations for War

The problem for Fisher and the naval lobby was that as a continental war appeared more likely, the question of what the navy was *for* began to loom large. The obvious answer was to defeat the German navy, and secure a command of the seas which would allow it to protect food imports and commerce while denying them to the enemy: Trafalgar and blockade duty. The problem with this was that it would not stop the German army marching on Paris, and if the Kaiser gained the industrial resources of France and added to them the ports of Holland and Belgium, then the Royal Navy's triumph would be short-lived indeed. Fisher and Wilson, his successor, never thought beyond gaining command of the sea and tended to ignore arguments that diminished the blockade as a weapon. They also tended to ignore the army and the Committee of Imperial Defence and had little faith in war planning as an activity. After the Second Moroccan Crisis in 1911, however, the army and the Committee began to take decisions that effectively relegated the role of the navy to one of escort duty for the BEF's journey to France and the protection of commerce. In the Committee meeting of 31 August 1911, it was

General Henry Wilson's vision of a commitment to France rather than Admiral Arthur Wilson's impractical plans for raids against the German coastline that prevailed. Germany would have to be fought on land as well as at sea, but it would be on land that it would have to be defeated.[110] As the military historian and *Journal* regular Spencer Wilkinson put it, 'Great Britain's battles must be fought and won on enemy territory and against an army raised and maintained on the modern national [mass conscription] principle'.[111]

The intellectual life of the Institute reflected fears of the coming war and in this respect Colonel E Gunter late of the East Lancashire Regiment made an important contribution by translating German military literature for the *Journal* between 1899–1913, while other officers translated articles from both the Russian and Japanese military presses after the Russo-Japanese War, often communicated to the Institute by the General Staff. Major tactical debates were often aired; but more mundane subjects in the form of such basics as wirecutters (Sir John MacDonald, 1911) were not below the Institute's attention, and there was also space given to the emerging possibilities of motor transport (Captain Hayter, 1910) – by 1910 the government had introduced a scheme to subsidise commercial vehicles as long as they could be requisitioned in time of war. Wireless was investigated; bicycles; the use of aircraft for attack (1909) and casualty evacuation; X-rays (the title 'The Working of the Roentgen Ray in Warfare', 1898, might be mistaken for science fiction) and military skiing.

There were also the more eccentric ideas to enjoy; 'The Art of Breathing as Applied to Physical Development' (1894), 'Kites: Their Uses in War' (1895), 'Lime Juice: A Few Centennial Remarks' (1896), 'The Sondenfield Cyclist Company's Winter of 1904' (translated from the Swedish, 1905) and 'The Phonograph and its Application to Military Purposes' (1893).

Military history remained popular – too popular, according to the librarians plagued by requests for help in compiling 'that utterly low debased form of literature called British Regimental Histories

(Laughter)',[112] while John Knox Laughton – a prominent British naval historian – spoke on maritime affairs (including a pioneering lecture that arguably gave birth to naval history as its own field).[113]

Other lectures focused attention on 'Improvised Armies of the Nineteenth Century' (1911), or 'Lessons to be drawn from the leading of imperfectly trained troops in the American Civil War 1863' (1911), as debate still ranged around the subject of the effectiveness of the Territorials. More forward-looking articles looked at how a long war might affect the civil population – 'The Internal Condition of Great Britain during a Great War' (1913), and the impact of 'The Press in War' (1913). International recognition was won: the Japanese armed forces bought 100 copies of each *Journal* and, in 1910, it won the Great Gold Medal Diploma at the St Petersburg 'Exhibition of Latest Inventions' as the best naval and military journal in the world.[114] On the whole, the Institute could be satisfied with its work and could comfortably escape the later judgement of the armed services that 'with their hierarchical rigidity, generally low level of education, dull garrison life, emphasis on sport and conformity tended to prevent anything but disaster in the field from breaking the iron ring of prescribed thought'.[115]

As 1914 opened, the Institute was hungrily eyeing next-door Gwyndyr House, which belonged to the Department of Trade, as it sought to expand still further and proposals were being made for a centenary exhibition based around Siborne's Waterloo model (there had been a similar Trafalgar Exhibition in 1905). The usual troubles with the cataloguing of the collections continued: Lonsdale-Hale had complained in 1909 that all his hard work had been undone by cleaners moving his carefully piled books back into their storage boxes to get on with the important job of swabbing the decks. Curiously enough, while the Institute developed an electrical fault necessitating plans for the building to be re-wired, across the road in the Foreign Office, Sir Edward Grey was also watching the lamps go out – across Europe.

Failure

In 1914, the army went to Belgium with seven divisions – about fifty short, according to the Director of Military Operations, Henry Wilson.[116] Thus, despite all the efforts of the defence establishment; all the improvements in naval equipment and deployment; all the concerns over imperial defence and the provision of expeditionary forces from Australasia and Canada; all the heated debates over National Efficiency, compulsory military service, military education, strategy and tactics; despite popular interest and enthusiasm for the armed forces; Britain went to war prepared to fight to the death – of the last Frenchman.

The BEF was undoubtedly a well-trained force, though not perfect, and during the – one is almost tempted to say, inevitable – retreat from Mons it held up very well and played its part. But without the French Army, it was nothing. Britain did not save France from the Schlieffen Plan, but rather the French saved the British Army from annihilation through their counter-attacks on the Marne. Again, this was no fault of the army or the defence establishment; RUSI had moved defence issues out of the officers' messes and onto the public stage. But, still, the politicians would not prioritise defence over potentially unpopular tax rises, even when the army and the navy were at an apogee of popularity in Edwardian Britain. RUSI and other parts of the defence establishment continually despaired at the Treasury and the politicians who, they felt, never seemed to understand that low taxation and efficient defences were incompatible – income tax never went above approximately 5 per cent between 1854 and 1915.[117] As a frustrated Wolseley exclaimed to Ardagh in 1892:[118]

> In our mob ruled country where honesty of purpose is now the worst quality which any ambitious man can now possess … 'Jaw' is now king and the man who can flatter the crowd most effectively is he who obtains the privilege of being its well paid servant. As yet there is no decline in the manly powers of our soldiers and sailors … it is only the quality of

our rulers, the fibre of our ministers that has undergone a change for the worst: they have conformed to the democratic system of the day … We want rulers but are told to look for them in some howling fellow who for the time being is in the front rank of the most ignorant of our people.

The cost would be paid in terrible bloodshed before the Battle of the Somme, in 1916, showed that Britain could indeed raise and train a mass army to exert sufficient military force capable of breaking the back of another army.

IV. THE CRUCIBLE
1914–45

It may be reasonably assumed that most of the necessary qualifications for a military people, such as patriotism, unity, discipline, tenacity are inherently characteristics of the British race, but the circumstances of our history were such that it was never thought necessary to weld them into a 'national will to war'. No one ever imagined that one day such a process might be necessary. Consequently, Great Britain remained until 1914 a non-military nation. It was not surprising therefore, that the revolutionary character of the Great War ... came as somewhat of a shock to the conservatism and excessive complacency of the British people. Yet the amazing way in which they adapted themselves ... was an accomplishment without parallel in our history .... The people of this country were ready to give full expression to the 'will to war' as long as the dangers to their country and their cause were apparent.

(Captain K P Smith, 1938)[1]

On 31 July 1914, the Home Fleet was declared ready for war at its base in Scapa Flow, while Admiral Wilson conceded the primacy of the army in the coming war at the War Council meeting of 5 August 1914 when the decision, ratified by the Cabinet the next day, was taken to send the BEF to France. There was no talk of amphibious assault. The job of the navy was to convoy the BEF and keep the nation supplied, and this could be achieved by doing not very much at all.

Despite all the hyperventilated panic of what the German High Seas Fleet might do, the reality was that the lion's share of German funding had gone to its army, leaving it with thirteen dreadnoughts, six pre-dreadnoughts and only five battlecruisers to take on the twenty-one dreadnoughts, eight pre-dreadnoughts and four battlecruisers exercising at Scapa Flow and the nineteen pre-dreadnoughts holding the Channel at Portland. Until this disparity could be rectified, the High Seas Fleet was told to stay safely behind the minefields and forts in the Heligoland Bight where the British could not reach them. Holding the entry points to the North Sea from Portland and Scapa Flow effectively established a 'distant' as opposed to a 'close' blockade, which meant that the navy could patrol the ocean highways without risk of loss and thus ensure that the disparity in strength would remain. The Battle of Jutland in 1916 changed nothing, whatever the claims of the Germans to a tactical victory. The strategic victory belonged to the Royal Navy and Germany slowly starved. Similarly, German surface commerce raiders proved to be no more than a momentary panic as the mixture of coastal defence works and wireless communications denied them access to fuel and removed the anonymity they needed to survive. Most were sunk or bottled up within the first few months of the war.

The great surprise of the war was the emergence of the submarine and torpedo as a potential war-winning combination when, on 22 September 1914, the armoured cruisers *Aboukir, Hogue* and *Cressy* were sunk by a single submarine. From that point on, Admiral Jellicoe proved extremely reluctant to put his ships to sea and, most controversially, turned the Grand Fleet away at Jutland to avoid a torpedo attack by German destroyers. For many observers, this was the death knell of the battleship, as it made little point to build something as large and as expensive as a dreadnought when it could be sunk by a cheaper 'stealth' weapon. The rapid expansion of the German U-boat fleet after 1916 and the devastation it wreaked on British merchant vessels – 38 per cent of the 1914-sized fleet – meant that Britain was, almost, starved into submission before the convoy system was revived. The navy never did get its dreadnought 'Trafalgar' moment, and the surrender of the High Seas Fleet in 1918 – the table on which the surrender was signed is now in the Council Room of RUSI, next to the table on which the Crimean Armistice was signed in February 1856 – was an empty victory, a point made most forcefully when the Germans scuttled at Scapa Flow rather than hand over their ships. More ominous still for future naval supremacy was the creation of a large new battle fleet in the US and the loss of effective supremacy in the Pacific and the Far East to Japan. The Washington Naval Conference of 1921, which conceded parity in naval force to the US and placed the Japanese navy higher than the French, ended Britain's weakening sole command of the sea.

The British experience of the land war was quickly characterised by trench warfare, the rapid expansion of the New Army and the grim learning curve that led from the battles of 1915 up to the Somme and beyond into the 1918 Hundred Days Offensive. The cost in casualties came as a great shock but, overall, the efficiency of the army with its solid staff work, determination to learn from mistakes, and integrate new technologies into a combined arms force of remarkable power, kept the butcher's bill below that of its enemies and rivals. Its concern for the welfare of its troops also kept morale up long after that of the Russian, French, Italian, Austro-Hungarian and German armies cracked in mutiny, revolution or collapse. In the end, the abandonment of dreams of cavalry breakthroughs and the application of 'bite and hold' operations that never outran their artillery support allowed the Allies to break their way through the Hindenburg Line, and after Ludendorff's last offensive failed in March 1918 the way to Berlin lay open. When the Kaiser, removed from any semblance of control of his government after 1916, abdicated and fled into exile, Hindenburg surrendered to save what he could of the German Army: there were more than a few soldiers in the British Army who thought that the Armistice had come too soon and that the basis of the subsequent peace, Wilson's Fourteen Points, was deeply flawed.

Out in the Empire, the record had been a mixed bag. The Indian Army had served magnificently on the Western Front before being thrown away at Kut in Mesopotamia; and naval hubris, in continually overestimating its ability to engage forts while simultaneously disdaining too much co-operation with army pongoes, brought on the disaster at Gallipoli. Even so, Allenby pulled the irons out of the fire in 1917 and mopped up much of the Middle East to finally achieve complete security for the route to India. For many, however, this was beginning to look like an irrelevance; the over-recruitment of Indians in places like the Punjab had strained loyalties to the limit and independence was really beginning to look like it might become practical politics in the very near future. In a similar vein, the mopping up of German colonies in Asia and of much British business by the Japanese – the Bolton Volunteer Artillery manning the Suez defences wet their whistles on Asahi lager – indicated that British power in the East was clearly on the wane. In Africa, the Union of South Africa took over the endless empty deserts of German South West Africa, while the Australians took over German colonial swamps in the Pacific. Perhaps the most pointless conflict of all took place in German East Africa, where Von Lettow-Vorbeck's guerrilla campaign tied up far too many troops and resources to protect a handful of unpleasant colonists in an unprofitable colony.

The War Years

What does a military think tank do during a war? How can it justify its existence when the lessons being learned are not being debated in a lecture theatre in Whitehall, but in a muddy hole surrounded by the sound of the guns? This was a question that paralysed the Institute for much of the First World War, to the point that publication of the *Journal* was seen as a waste of time. Printing was suspended from

November 1915 until the following year, and what was published was a series of rather stale articles on military history and filler items like 'Casual Rambles in the RUSI Museum' (1915). There was an attempt to provide a general narrative of events gleaned from the press and official communiqués, but this was done baldly and without much elucidating comment. It was only after 1917 that the *Journal* began to shake off its paralysis with the publication of several quite curious and revealing articles.

The first was 'The Knife in Trench Warfare', by Colonel Sir John MacDonald, which, in its candid discussion of the best design for a knife useful in a trench raid, is, in its way, as shocking as pictures of Vietnamese children scorched by napalm. Arguing for a short, sturdy stabbing blade (it came with a diagram) carried in a scabbard under the left armpit, MacDonald, who had clearly learned by experience, gave the advice that:[2]

> The jab in the face is the most flabbergasting stroke that can be given and the back handed stroke the most powerful .... The true purpose is not to kill but to put out of action – a wounded man being much more troublesome to the enemy than a dead one. The true purpose is to disable and demoralize for the time.

The second was 'An Open Letter to the Very Young Officer' (1917), by the nearly anonymous 'CNW'. This was a strange article written with a mixture of cynicism and wisdom aimed at new officers who had not had the benefit of a public school education. The advice was very good then, and remains so today. CNW's first rule was that an officer should know his job thoroughly, should not bluff and should not expect his sergeant to do it for him. On leadership, CNW felt that 'power to command = strength of character + determination + tact'. 'Tact' meant that on no account was an individual soldier to be humiliated in front of his comrades, but this did not mean that a unit might not need to be spoken to harshly if they were not

performing. His last rule was also sound; if officers wish to get drunk
or use prostitutes, then they should not do so in a place where their
men might see them – apparently both these pastimes were resorted
to often, as Cecil Lewis made clear in his account of the Royal Flying
Corps in *Sagittarius Rising*. Two German articles were included in
the 1917 *Journal*, the first being a translation of Captain Schiebe's
experiences at Jutland while the second, 'Report on the Defence
of Gommecourt on July 1st 1916', came from the War Diary of
the German 55th Reserve Infantry Regiment. This was a detailed,
objective, professional analysis of one sector on the bloodiest day the
British Army had seen since Waterloo. The conclusion was that 'it
must be acknowledged that the equipment and preparation of the
English attack were magnificent'.

By 1918, the *Journal* was once more becoming a forum for debate
as people began to look beyond the looming end of the war. 'The Army
after the War' by 'Clericus' argued that a large standing army would
be maintained because no one could ever have faith in Wilson's idea
of a League of Nations. This would be based on universal service in
the Cadets for boys aged sixteen to eighteen, followed by enlistment
in either the Regular Army for service overseas (six years with the
colours, six years in the Reserves) or two years compulsory training
with the Territorials. That this was a hopeful prospect was pointed
out almost immediately by Lieutenant Colonel King of the London
Rifle Brigade in 'The Army after the War: Another View', who read
the politicians more accurately. He predicted that the army would
be cut as soon as the war ended because Wilson's ideas, however
ridiculous, would catch on, and that the only hope for future security
would be the creation of a large Territorial Army based on almost
universal service.

The Institute itself was bundled out of the way of the war effort
in 1914 as the government requisitioned the building to use as a
press centre. For the duration of the war, only the Secretary's Office,
the Banqueting House, part of the Crypt and the Library were

retained while journalists and press officers smoked, scribbled and spilt coffee in a place where not even a genteel cup of tea had been allowed before. When they left in 1920, the Board of Works had to be called in to repair the damage and clean up the mess, but a major redecoration was still necessary at the Institute's expense. Those left in guardianship, led by the Secretary (since 1913, Sir Arthur Leetham), did their best to keep the Museum going by training the staff to be more informative, encouraging visits by school groups and soliciting up-to-date donations for the collections. The 1st Battalion, The Lincolnshire Regiment loaned a German field gun that they claimed had been the first one captured by the British Army. Not surprisingly, the war generated more interest in the museum and in 1915 over 53,000 visitors paid to enter. This, combined with the rent paid by the government for the press bureau, left the Institute's finances in such a healthy state that despite rising costs caused by wartime inflation, they were able to suspend payment for membership. By the end of the war, capital investments stood at £20,000 with an excess of income over liabilities of over £7,600[3] with a membership of 4,980. Most grievous, however, was the loss by 1919 of 434 members killed in action.

The Interwar Years

'Everything that you think you know about the First World War is wrong', was the view of a young curator at the National Army Museum in 2004. 'It's down to those bloody English teachers'. This is a view that is hard to challenge. *Journey's End, Up the Line to Death, Testament of Youth, Oh What a Lovely War* and *Blackadder Goes Forth* have been the staples fed to successive generations of English students to the point that the myth of the useless slaughter of patriotic Pals Battalions by malevolent 'upper class twits' is so far ingrained that it will take major surgery to remove it. Inconvenient truths like the fact that Haig was feted, not reviled, after the war and when he died in 1928 his body lay in state in Edinburgh where 100,000 people came to pay their respects, or that Wilfred Owen's poetry sold a measly 730 copies in 1920 and needed until 1929 to sell another 700, are simply dismissed or ignored. That surgery has begun among military historians – very notably by Gordon Corrigan in his *Mud, Blood and Poppycock* (2003), Gary Sheffield, a regular contributor to the *Journal* and John Terraine, a RUSI stalwart and founder of the Western Front Association, dedicated to debunking myths about the First World War – but it will be a long time before a thorough revision will be effected. 'Lions led by donkeys' was an outrageous calumny visited on the First World War generals, largely by politicians eager to absolve themselves from charges of culpability for not funding the armed services properly in the first place.[4] In a similar vein, it is always difficult to assess any issue after 1919 without the hindsight of 1939 clouding the view. We even call this period the 'interwar years' as though the Second World War was indeed inevitable.

Our condemnation of the Versailles Settlement for being neither Carthaginian enough nor conciliatory enough ought perhaps to be tempered by the scale of the task facing the peacemakers – there was scarcely a peaceful state or functioning government between Paris and Tokyo in 1919 – but there is always Foch's judgement to trump any such reassessment. He was right, too: it was, indeed, just an armistice for twenty years. It is even harder to come to a calmer judgement because appeasement raises such hackles among those who blame that flawed policy on the 'guilty men' of the Right or the pacifists and disarmers of the Left. The knowledge of the utter miseries inflicted on the world consonant to the failures of the 1930s adds another level of emotion to our judgement. It is impossible, for example, to ask the question whether it would have been better to ally with Nazi Germany (either before or during the war) against Soviet Russia rather than vice versa without raising a storm of indignation, even though – on simple numbers alone – Stalin was more brutal than Hitler. What is true, however, is that few policy-makers would not do things differently if they were given another chance.

This, then, raises the question of how well RUSI fulfilled its mission to 'guide through rational debate ... the future course of the army'[5] (and, by extension, the navy and the newcomers of the RAF), and so inform the political leadership of the opportunities and risks that they faced between the wars. Did the Institute give adequate warnings and advice during those two fateful decades? Could it have made its voice heard more loudly and have had greater effect than it did before the First World War? It would be a tall order.

Back to Clausewitz

> Politics have nothing to do with these questions, they ought to be put entirely on one side.... the less we mix politics up with great events ... the better for every body concerned.
>
> (The Duke of Cambridge, RUSI annual report, 1900)

Before 1914, the Institute had resolutely ignored Clausewitz's dictum about war being the pursuit of politics by other means and had concentrated almost exclusively on technical issues of strategy, tactics and technology, with a leavening of military history thrown in. For them, 'politics' meant the often unedifying spectacle of MPs engaged in aggregating public perceptions and opinions into policy decisions that looked, to their jaded eyes, as the pursuit of MPs' careers and self-interests rather than the honest debates of committed public servants. Repington thought them to be 'Tadpoles and Tapers shivering for their shekels ... [a] rabble seeking office and rewards'.[6] If they had to deal with politicians, it was only because they controlled the purse strings and duty required they swallow their natural disdain. Even politicians favourable to defence causes were looked on as rather tiresome; Hugh Oakeley Arnold-Forster, a long-time supporter of the Institute, was seen as an amateur who was not really qualified to occupy the post of Secretary of State for War, as he did between 1903 and 1905, however enthusiastic he might be. For them, the unprecedented raising of Lord Kitchener to cabinet rank while still retaining his military rank was both natural and sensible, however constitutionally dubious. After 1919, however, the Institute quickly understood that politics and the military were intimately connected and that they had indeed entered a world radically different from that of 1914:[7]

> We live in times when the world is being governed mainly by phrases, most of them meaningless, and I have little reason to suppose that the voice of reason will prevail against the charm of a phrase.

The astounding unity of the Britain that went to war in 1914 was not shattered by the war itself, but was quickly dissipated by the opportunities and disappointments of peace. The empty promises of Lloyd George to provide 'Homes for Heroes' and Eric Geddes's 'Squeeze the German lemon until the pips squeak' quickly led to disillusionment among the mass of working-class voters, a deep distrust of Liberal politicians and a class-based hatred of Conservative ones. The assault on aristocrats' privileges by Lloyd George before the First World War, followed by the enfranchisement of the working class, led large numbers of them to abandon the traditional *noblesse oblige* expected of them, and choose exile, gentile decay or hedonistic dissipation like the characters in *Brideshead Revisited*.

The literary world turned increasingly bitter towards the Victorian values they saw as being responsible for the slaughter in the trenches, and Hampstead intellectuals and Bloomsbury sceptics began to develop pacifism and a determined anti-imperialism as part of a vague but alternative value system. Lytton Strachey's *Eminent Victorians* was a poisoned pen portrait of the most revered of Victorian heroes; George Orwell's *A Hanging* (1931) and *Burmese Days* (1934) showed imperial rule in a bleak light indeed; Erich Maria Remarque's *All Quiet on the Western Front* was as overtly pacifist as the 1933 vote of the Oxford Union that indicated that the future leaders of Britain would not fight for king or country. 'The hackneyed catchphrase that the War had been fought to end war was taken up by our people … and they naively entrusted the consummation of their theories to the newly constituted League of Nations', was how Captain K P Smith put it in 1938. The 1934 Peace Pledge Union attracted 135,000 members; produced a petition against war with a million signatures on it; canvassed a 'Peace Ballot' with several million votes for collective, rather than imperial, security; and campaigned against air raid precautions in 1938 and conscription in 1939. The 1924 Empire Exhibition's most popular attractions were the funfair and the football stadium (which became Wembley Stadium), but even then it still lost money.

Organised labour espoused international socialist solidarity while a shameful collection of literary and political tourists paid homage to the worker's utopia in Russia and poured scorn on those who doubted. More sinister was the widespread exploitation of utopian Communist believers by Soviet Intelligence and the 60,000-strong Communist Party of Great Britain to build effective networks in both Britain and the US.[8] Incredibly, the Labour Party sent Harold Laski, its deputy leader, to Berchtesgaden to persuade Hitler of the benefits of pacifism and to Moscow to persuade Stalin of the benefits of parliamentary government. The period between 1919 and 1939 was a time when a tidal wave of ideas, idealism, hopes, visions, theories, concepts and brave new worlds swamped reality like a skiff in a hurricane and common sense and reasonable caution were washed straight overboard. Anyone who suggested that the most powerful vision of utopia – communism – was actually the most appalling dystopia was dismissed as a blimp or a follower of those other utopian fantasies, Fascism and Nazism. European democracy survived only in pockets outside Britain, while France collapsed in slow motion in a state of virtual civil war from 1934 onwards.

In short, the defence establishment in Britain as it existed before 1914 was gutted, hollowed out and treated with disdain at a time when most of Europe progressively adopted governments committed to Social Darwinist militarism, Mackinder's theories, racial purity, class war or even more bizarre mystic notions of 'blood and soil', runic occultism and the re-founding of the Roman and Holy Roman empires in one form or another. Within what was left of Britain's defence establishment, there were also some worrying signs that influential parts of it had swallowed the notion that the army should not simply serve the society it came from, but should actually run it. J F C Fuller ended up in the British Union of Fascists after a long association with Aleister Crowley's *Argentum Astra* magical society. George Sydenham Clarke, who had done such good work in promoting the interests of defence in the Colonial Defence Committee, the Hartington Commission, the Esher Committee and the Committee of Imperial Defence, embraced an increasingly bizarre set of notions during the 1920s regarding an international Jewish conspiracy (Brahmanism, Zionism, jazz, modern art, Bolshevism and German militarism were all linked, apparently) while his wife organised the British Fascists' children's club. Admiral Domville, winner of the RUSI Gold Medal in 1906, Director of Naval Intelligence 1927–30, Institute Council member and Vice-Admiral commanding the War College 1932–34, slipped into anti-Semitism, attended the 1937 Nuremburg rally and set up 'The Link' to promote Anglo-German friendship. He spent the Second World War interned in Brixton Jail. Captain Archibald Ramsay, ex-Coldstream Guards, set up the anti-communist United Christian Front in 1937 and the Right Club in 1939, which earned him the dubious distinction of being the only MP to be interned during the war.

The first thing to be ditched – the practice of balancing foreign policy interests by negotiations based on self-interest – was ejected in favour of a revival of Gladstone and Bright's worthy internationalism. Ententes and alliances were out and collective security in the form of the League of Nations was in; everyone would disarm because no-one could possibly want or see advantage in war as an instrument of policy; and because the spirit of goodwill could not be resisted, there would be no secret diplomacy. In October 1919, the first post-war *Journal* carried Lord Eustace Percy's lecture on the virtues of the new organisation, which argued strongly that collective security was rooted firmly in the British national interest and that 'there can be no healthy internationalism that does not spring directly from the needs of national policy'. Prefacing his defence of the League by characterising his audience as 'men whose business in life is to deal with facts', and who were naturally suspicious of 'idealistic oratory and pacifist polemic',[9] many of those present agreed with him, but not all were convinced. The historian and military theorist T Miller Maguire, who had himself lectured at RUSI in 1897 and 1905, was almost speechless with rage as he thundered:[10]

> There has been no improvement in foreign politics since … 1914 …. We were then assured by a gentleman sitting where the noble Lord sits that there could not be a war at all, and that the notion of a war in the 20th century was preposterous and monstrous …. Why? Are there no villains left, are they all converts, have they all joined the Salvation Army? Not likely …. Why is there to be no more war … Because of the Hague Convention? He assured us of that and I laughed with all my heart …. Stick to the old track, become military Britons and not an international constabulary …. the league of Nations [*sic*] is a mockery.

This was a devastating critique, but Maguire was battling the *zeitgeist* and losing. In 1920, Major General Louis Jackson remarked that he had been mocked for even proposing a paper entitled, 'Possibilities of the Next War'. 'Ah, my dear General', he was told, 'If you would only talk of the impossibility of the next war'. This did not stop him from pointing out that, 'Germany has not refrained from telling us through many mouths that she hopes for revenge some day', and that, 'war is an inevitable accident of human existence'.[11]

> People cry aloud for disarmament ... the temptation to yield to them ...
> is great ... but if we do ... I say that we will be exposed to even greater
> dangers.

Colonel John Ward MP put it in rather blunter terms:[12]

> We shall never be such a society of Angels that we can do without the
> hangman and the prison ... because there are always a certain number
> of lunatics who think they are sane.

The Gold Medal Prize Essay for 1921 re-stated the central
message of RUSI – *si vis pacem, para bellum* – after its brief flirtation
with the League, when Flight Lieutenant C J Mackay compared it
to 'a small boy put into a cage of hungry lions to teach them how to
eat politely', and argued that official parsimony and unpreparedness
were the prime causes of wars.[13]

This was in tune with most of the nineteenth century issues of
the *Journal*, but sadly out of step with the economic realities that
produced the Ten Year Rule. Indeed, if a reminder that politics and
the military were intimately connected were needed, then the decision
taken by Lloyd George, Bonar Law, Austen Chamberlain, Churchill
and Walter Long to proceed on the assumption that there would be
no war for a decade provided it in spades and *sinus bellum pecuniam
est* became the tag of choice. There simply was not anywhere near
enough money for defence – as late as 1932, servicing the war debt
accounted for every penny of income tax and all the death duties –
and, as Keynesian economics had not yet replaced Victorian thrift as
financial orthodoxy, defence cutbacks were inevitable. It also meant
that the government had little choice but to fall back on the abilities
of the Foreign Office to predict trouble long enough in advance and
stave it off long enough for precautions to be taken. This in itself
required an act of faith; in July 1914, the Foreign Office had said that
there would be no war that year.[14] The stock market, that supposed

barometer of informed opinion, was also taken by surprise in 1914. For RUSI, this meant that an interest in politics and international relations had to be cultivated because these were now, as never before, the determinants of defence issues. From 1927 onwards, the *Journal* would carry updates on international affairs as a matter of course.[15]

Resuscitating RUSI

The comfortable financial position that the Institute enjoyed at the end of hostilities rapidly collapsed with the financial uncertainties of peace. Stock market uncertainties knocked 40 per cent off the value of the investments – down from £16,812 to £9,208 by 1920 – while taxes and rates were hiked up to £2,000 pa. By 1921, the Institute was running at a loss, having had to cash in almost 25 per cent of what stocks remained to meet running and redecoration costs at a time when visitors to the museum halved in number. At this rate, the Institute would shortly be facing bankruptcy. In 1922, the deficit stood at £1,500 and in 1923 at £1,200, largely due to the burden of taxes. Cutbacks were inevitable and the *Journal* was the first casualty, being kept at its wartime size of 200 pages rather than its pre-war size of 320 pages. In 1923, the editor, Colonel H C Wylie, resigned and a part-time replacement was advertised for on a reduced salary of £50 pa – about £2,000 in modern currency, and a paltry sum even then – and there were major difficulties in finding contributors to the *Journal*.[16] Receipts from visitors to the museum fell by 10 per cent in the year 1922–23, the membership remained static at around 5,500 despite the vast expansion of the armed forces during the war, while the burden of rates and taxes raised concerns about the viability of the Institute.[17] It was even mooted that the museum should close and merge with the new Imperial War Museum – a suggestion that was dismissed out of hand.

Leetham showed real resourcefulness here in managing not just to get an exemption from income tax in 1925, but also to wring a rebate out of the Treasury. The City of Westminster Council proved a tougher nut to crack, however, and refused his attempts to get an exemption from the rates and thus pull off a financial hat-trick. Leetham responded by including a Bankers Order in each issue of the *Journal*, which members were expected to use to persuade others to join[18] and renewed his efforts to pester Westminster into a rates cut, which finally paid off in 1926 (although Westminster Council tried to go back on the deal subsequently but lost to the Institute in the High Court in 1939).[19] The benefits of this coup were short-lived, however, as the central heating system now needed to be replaced at the cost of £900. Leetham also persuaded the RAF to pay £100 pa towards the upkeep of the Institute, only to see the Treasury reduce the contributions made by the army and navy by a corresponding sum.

What made matters infinitely worse was that the assistant secretary and accountant, A H Pinhey, had managed to embezzle £2,035 4s 9d between 1923–28 from under Leetham's nose, compounding his poor post-war investment strategy. Leetham was devastated and offered to make good the sum from his own pocket, an offer that was generously refused. Pinhey was sacked (and spent a year in jail) and replaced by *Miss* E G Bickell – a revolutionary development that did not pass without comment.[20]

Leetham's efforts did pay off. By the time he retired in 1927 after twenty-five years' service, the Institute was in the black (just) to the tune of £28 14s 1d, which he had achieved by selling off capital assets, increasing *Journal* sales and subscriptions and mounting a special exhibition of ship models which pulled in 8,000 extra visitors to the museum and £1,427 12s 6d to the till. He also had the foresight to begin planning for when the lease on the Banqueting House ran out in 1972. The Institute was right to give him a testimonial; he had saved it.

Leetham was succeeded by Captain Edward Altham RN as both editor of the *Journal* in 1922 and then secretary in 1927. His arrival marked a change of course. Altham had served on the Dover patrol

during the 1914–18 war and had then commanded the Archangel
River Expedition against the Bolsheviks in 1918–19. Mentioned in
dispatches no fewer than nine times and awarded the Tsarist Order
of St. Vladimir, he had been demobilised by the Geddes Axe and
had thus turned to journalism, contributing the chapter on naval
aviation for Brassey's *Naval Annual* in 1924, before marrying the
aeronautically named Joyce Dick in 1927. In 1929, he was doubling up
his duties at RUSI with editing the naval aspects of the *Encyclopaedia
Britannica* (Liddell-Hart edited the military aspects), and in 1938
he would write a biography of Jellicoe. Altham was assisted by a
deputy editor, Lieutenant Colonel De Watteville, a staff officer
of the Royal Garrison Artillery who had served in the War Office
Intelligence Branch 1903–05 and then in coastal defence during the
war.[21] Altham would build on Leetham's financial reorganisation of
the Institute by achieving charitable status in 1930 and increasing
the professionalism of the staff by introducing a pension scheme and
calling himself 'Chief Executive Officer'. The staff even got a pay rise
in 1937. Civilians were permitted to join the Institute from 1931,
whereas previously the only people admitted without having served
in the armed forces were cabinet ministers (although 'distinguished
strangers' had been admitted to lectures since 1927). It was also a
further indication that RUSI was expanding its horizons. By 1937,
the Institute was able to afford a refurbishment of the lecture theatre
– the podium was opposite to today's arrangements – and its balance
sheet revealed a net worth of over £100,000. This did not end
worries over the lease, however, and as late as 1939 the government
was eyeing the Banqueting House with a view to repossession,[22]
especially as the government was already developing what was left of
Whitehall Gardens, now the site of the present Ministry of Defence,
into a huge complex for the civil servants of the Board of Trade,
Ministry of Labour, Ministry of Transport and the Air Ministry.[23]
Indeed, in 1938, the Ministry of Works made a determined attempt
to use the Banqueting House for a proposed reception for the

president of France, which the Institute saw as a stalking horse to regain possession. Pointing out that this would mean sawing up the Trafalgar and Waterloo models, an enormous effort at packing and the construction of a temporary building to act as a kitchen, which it did not currently possess, the Institute appealed to the King, but without success. It was only when the Ministry of Works realised the cost – £7,000 plus six months' compensation to the Institute for closing the museum – that the plan was abandoned.[24]

The museum continued to receive donations and to develop its activities. Lord Kitchener's Field Marshal's Baton was donated in 1916 to add to those of Earl Roberts, the Peninsular veteran Sir John Fitzgerald and Sir Garnet Wolseley in 1920. A piece of one of the bells of Ypres cathedral appeared in 1916 and in 1922 both the Royal Dublin Fusiliers and the Royal Munster Fusiliers donated items (a silver statuette and a VC respectively) which were, it was understood, to be given back if ever these regiments were reformed – and indeed, the mess plate of the 2nd Battalion Inniskilling Fusiliers was returned on its reformation in 1938. In 1934 the model head of a German soldier, painted by the war artist Sir William Orpen and used as a target by Canadian snipers, arrived. An exhibition of polar exploration was mounted in 1933 which included the journal of Ernest E Joyce's part in the Shackleton expedition of 1907–09 – the only book published, to date, in Antarctica.

More remarkable still was a slab of Captain Cook's desiccated soup; a sprig of holly from the plum pudding eaten on the Christmas Day of Scott's 1902 expedition; and the sextant which Shackleton used to navigate the 750 miles from Elephant Island to South Georgia. The RAF had its turn with a 1934 exhibition of aircraft models while the museum staff had to turn down the offer of a swap of one of Sir Philip Broke's swords in return for a piece of the Chesapeake flag. Frederick Hitch VC's finest hour was commemorated by the donation of a Zulu pipe retrieved from the battlefield at Rorke's Drift and his General Officer Commanding, Lord Chelmsford, was remembered in a 1937 diorama of his final defeat of the Zulus at Ulundi in 1879. Items of rather more remarkable provenance included locks of both Nelson and Wellington's hair, Nelson's baby clothes and Wellington's pencil, plus three chairs sat on by Napoleon. In 1938, Miss C E Landor donated a pair of Charles I's gauntlets while the wits of IX Corp HQ donated Pigeon No. 2709, which had died of wounds after heroic service on 4 October 1917. More underhand was the decision to keep Captain Marchand's flag, taken from him by Lord Kitchener during the Fashoda Incident of 1898 and the subject of a campaign to return it to him. The Institute would have nothing to do with giving this up and hid it in the safe.[25] There were also the sensitive souls who found the display of a cat-o-nine tails in the Institute's windows too much to bear to be placated – 'the public conscience was offended'.[26]

In 1939, the International Tin Research and Development Council requested help for an exhibition on 'Historic Tinned Foods' – apparently opportunities for entertainment in London were becoming sparser in 1939 – which the Institute was able to meet by providing two 114-year-old cans, one of veal and one of carrots, which Sir Edward Parry had taken with him on his 1824 expedition to find the North West passage. Remarkably, the resultant paper, 'The Examination of Some Tinned Foods of Historic Interest', ran to two editions. The success of the museum in attracting these donations meant that by 1936, the old problems of space were beginning to appear again and approaches were again made to the government to acquire Gwydyr House next door, now that the Board of Trade was to be so generously accommodated elsewhere.[27]

Altham's greatest achievement, however, was the redirection of the *Journal*'s editorial policy in 1927. He wanted the *Journal* to be an officially recognised medium for 'the higher study of war, the better understanding of Imperial Defence, and a closer relationship between the doctrines, tenets and activities of the three services'.[28] He also advertised the 'unique privilege of receiving the active support and assistance of the Naval Staff, the General Staff of the Army and the Air Staff,[29] and pointed out that the council members also had valuable contacts in the Historical Section of the Committee of Imperial Defence, the Naval Staff College and the Army Staff Colleges. The *Journal* would remain committed to its encouragement of professional debate and the promotion of new ideas from younger officers, but it would now include articles dealing with 'the economic and commercial life of our nation which vitally affect our powers of defence'. 'Scientific developments in relation to weapons' would also be investigated, as would 'the military situation … in disturbed parts of the world', whereas historical pieces would only be accepted now if some concrete lessons could be drawn from them. There would also be colour pictures.[30] The modern *RUSI Journal* was born.

Imperial Defence in the 1920s

We know now that the First World War served a notice to quit on the British Empire and there could be no clearer indication of this than the independence of Ireland. Held as an English possession since the Middle Ages, its strategic significance came into focus after the Reformation and the religious wars that followed up until the end of the English Civil War, when Cromwell put down independent Catholic Ireland for the next 150 years. Ireland was the Catholic back door into Protestant England. Wolfe Tone's rebellion in 1798 was similarly put down, this time with fear of French intervention at the root of English concern – as such, the *Journal* had contributions on Irish regiments in French service in 1905 and 1914 and on French landings in Ireland in 1909. Throughout the nineteenth century, there had been an uneasy relationship between England and Ireland, as an influential Home Rule lobby was balanced by the economic relationship between the two islands and the opportunities for military service in the British Army that Irishmen took up with enthusiasm – about 33 per cent of the British Army in the nineteenth century was Catholic and Irish.

The First World War brought about the Easter Rising of 1916 and the resultant post-war rebellion and civil war produced a divided Ireland of Catholic south and Protestant north, with the south effectively independent. Its ruling class took power in bitterness and took care to foster that bitterness enshrined in the old saying: 'England's danger is Ireland's opportunity'; they maintained a shameful neutrality against the Nazis, even when it was clear that the fall of Britain would mean the fall of Ireland and despite the fact that thousands of their own citizens had enlisted in the British Army to fight the common enemy. The legacy of this mutual distrust festered on both sides of the Irish Sea until the 1990s and it became a commonly held belief in the northwest of England that the lights of Dublin had been left on during the Blitz so that the Luftwaffe could navigate to Liverpool and Manchester. When British troops were withdrawn from the Ship Street Barracks in Dublin in 1923, they donated a weathervane in the shape of a gunner firing a cannon from the roof – which was placed on top of the Institute[31] – symbolic of the first retreat from the second British Empire. The weathervane still exists in a display case, often visible in the third-floor Reading Room.

Less obvious, but perhaps more significant, was the assertion of independence by the Dominions of Australia, New Zealand, Canada and South Africa, who made it clear that they would retain control of their armies from now on and would expect a greater say in imperial foreign and defence policies. This did not mean that the empire was about to disintegrate; the realities of power meant that all the Dominions were, in the final analysis, dependent on British power for their defence and would remain so until 1942 when Japanese victories shifted Australasia into the American defence orbit. What it did do was to end any ideas of imperial federation based on an imperial parliament. Strong ties would be maintained, but they would be voluntary and on the basis of negotiations between very near equals. As if to symbolise this change, the Royal Colonial Institute changed its name in 1928 to the Royal Empire

Society and, still with a healthy membership of 15,596, built a new sixty-room hotel, library, lecture theatre and assembly room for empire visitors on Northumberland Avenue in 1935.[32] In 1931, the banker Frederick Craufurd Goodenough built London House for postgraduate students visiting London from the empire – it still functions as the Goodenough College – and its main hall is rich in imperial symbolism that belied any idea the empire was in danger.

There were indeed plenty of people in 1919 who believed that they had just witnessed a major imperial victory. The acquisition of the German colonies and the mandates in the Middle East seemed to usher in a new era of imperial splendour, whatever the Bloomsbury sceptics might say. The route to India and the Far East was now firmly under control and a Cape to Cairo railway on an all-red route was now a possibility. The straits of Constantinople were firmly guarded by a revived Turkey and Britain's traditional imperial rivals, France, Germany and Russia, were simply too weak to challenge it, while the newer ones – Italy and Japan – were not yet strong enough. True, naval parity had been conceded to the Americans, but then America had retreated into isolation. All in all, things looked rather rosy, if the question of cost could be ignored.

As a result, the *Journal* continued to reflect concerns about imperial communications, imperial federation and the protection of trade in articles that could have been written seventy years earlier. The 1925 winner of the Naval Gold Medal Prize Essay was 'The Communications across the Oceans of the World being essential to the Empire, how best can they be safeguarded?',[33] while in 1924, Captain Wilkinson of the Bombay Pioneers argued that the main fleet should be based at Singapore, it being the geographical centre of the empire.[34] And the question of cost could be ignored because the new RAF claimed that they could both defend and police the empire on the cheap; the 1921 Gold Medal (RAF) went to Flight Lieutenant C J Mackay for 'The Influence in the Future of Aircraft upon problems of Imperial Defence'.[35] Eager to defend their status

The Old Egyptian Campaigner: sailor and scientist, Captain William Henry Smyth's letter (below) in the *United Services Journal* called for RUSI's creation.

Sir,—Though I cannot flatter myself that an anonymous suggestion can effect " a consummation devoutly to be wished," yet you may perhaps be inclined to give it insertion, coming, as it does, from one who anxiously hopes to see the United Service Journal become the medium of rational intercourse between the retired and the efficient members of the Services.   Others, who, like myself, can no longer draw their swords in the service of their country, may occasionally serve it by the contributions of their pens.

It has long been a favourite idea of mine, that officers of the Navy and Army have it in their power, from the frequent opportunities presented to them on service in almost every part of the known world, to contribute to the promotion of science and art, but more particularly in the department of natural history. The experience of nearly forty years has proved to me that a taste for reading, for information, and for general literature, has grown up rapidly in the army.   I speak only of that service with which I am best acquainted.   We have too many proofs *in print* of the scientific progress made by officers of the Navy, to require any other testimony of improvement, " *pari passu,*" amongst the " blue jackets."

Now my proposal is, that to give a tone of science to the character of both services, it would be a desirable point to set on foot a Museum, to be formed, conducted, and maintained, solely by the military, medical, and civil branches of the Royal Navy, the King's Army, the Hon. East India Company's services, and their connexions : to be called the *United Service Museum.*

I should hope this Museum, if patronized by His Gracious Majesty, as the head of the Army, by His R. H. the Duke of Clarence, and the actual heads of the Navy, would soon attain an interesting character, reflecting honour on the nation, raising in public estimation the individual contributors to and support-ers of it, and finally proving that the two professions have entered the lists of science, and are ready to contend for honours " *tam Artibus quam Armis.*"

I am, Sir, yours,
AN OLD EGYPTIAN CAMPAIGNER.

The Thatched House Tavern (exterior, right): here, in St James's, the Institute held its early meetings. It shared the venue with a number of other dining clubs, including the Dilettanti Society (pictured below).

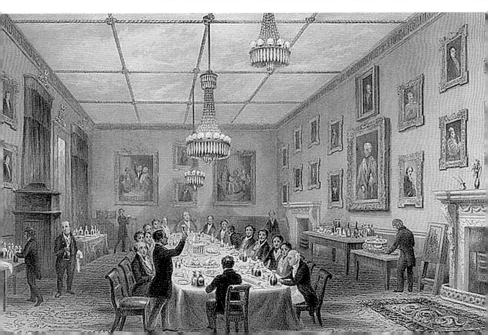

Present at the creation: Major General Howard Douglas (left), a noted soldier-scholar, was the first secretary of the Institute.

Friends in high places: General Henry Hardinge (left) was a crucial backer of the enterprise and forwarded the initial motion founding what would become RUSI. He would go on to become Viscount Hardinge of Lahore.

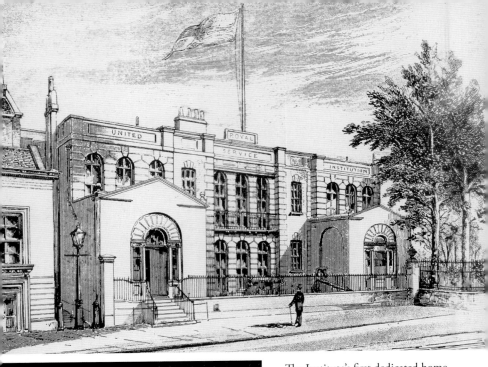

The Institute's first dedicated home (above), Vanbrugh House on Whitehall Yard, pictured here in 1886.

The impressively named John Charles Ready Colomb (left), a ubiquitous and influential member of the Institute in an age of imperialism.

A RUSI committee (bottom, opposite page) poses in Banqueting House for a photograph during the 1893 'Fancy Bazaar' fundraiser for the Institute's proposed new building. Pictured are (from bottom left, clockwise): Captain Malton, Sir A Jephson, Sir G Chubb, Colonel A Lonsdale Hale, Sir Augustus Webster, Captain Holden, Captain S M Eardley-Wilmot, Lieutenant General Goodenough, Sir G Willes, Prince Edward of Saxe-Weimar, General G Erskine and Lieutenant Malby.

Victorian *Kriegsspiel* (above): the war game 'Polemos' is played at the Institute — an event worthy of this full-page lithograph in this 1888 issue of the *Illustrated London News*.

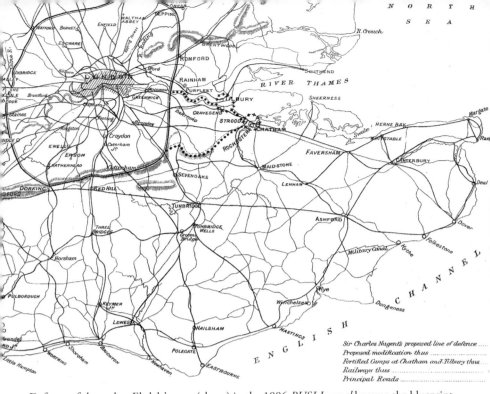

Defence of the realm: Elsdale's map (above) in the 1886 *RUSI Journal* became the blueprint for the War Office's plans for the defence of London.

Interwar public diplomacy: the procession of King George VI and the Queen passes RUSI during their return from the 1939 royal visit to Canada and the United States.

Eager crowds pack into the RUSI museum, Banqueting House (above), to wish the new queen well at her coronation, 2 June 1953.

Peace breaks out: a historic moment at the Institute (below) as the Commander-in-Chief of the Warsaw Pact, Petr Lushev (left), shakes hands with the NATO SACEUR, John Galvin (right), at RUSI in May 1989 – the first time the two counterparts had ever met.

British security in an age of terror: President George W Bush and Director of RUSI, Rear Admiral Richard Cobbold (top), at Banqueting House in 2003; US General David Petraeus giving a keynote speech at the 2010 RUSI Land Warfare Conference (middle); and Prime Minister Tony Blair (bottom) gesturing in front of a RUSI audience on the HMS *Albion* in 2007.

as a separate service, one might be forgiven for thinking that the RAF put as much effort into bombarding RUSI as they did into putting down rebellious tribesmen. In the 1927 and 1928 volumes alone, there are no fewer than twenty-two articles on air power and 'A Flight to Abyssinia' by Squadron Leader J L Vachell reads as well as any *Boy's Own* adventure, while at the same time making the point that the RAF could reach into the most inaccessible parts of the world.[36] This was all wishful thinking, however. Within the Colonial Office there was a growing feeling that it was time to get rid of the empire[37] and active ways were being sought to turn the Colonial Office into a development agency which would prepare the way for self-rule. Marking this change in emphasis too, the Royal Empire Society declared that its aim was 'to enlist the services of youth in the cause of good will between the peoples of the Empire and mankind generally'.[38] At the same time, developments in Germany meant that the issue of imperial defence was being pushed aside to make way for the possibility of another German war.

This in turn prompted B H Liddell-Hart, military historian and *Times* correspondent, into advocating a return to what he saw as a 'British way in warfare'. Arguing that the decisive factor in the defeat of Germany was the effectiveness of the naval blockade, he hankered for a strategy based on blockade and armoured expeditionary forces, rather than the large-scale pitched battles of the First World War as the way to beat Germany. Presenting his case at RUSI in 1931, Liddell-Hart seemed to be looking for a way to avoid the bloodshed of the Somme, while still achieving a victory through a repetition of the strategy that had defeated Napoleon. This was an understandable desire, but unless an army could be found to play the part of the Austrians, Russians and Prussians in 1814, the 'British way in warfare' would be doomed to failure – especially if he hoped the weary, divided France would provide it.

New Technology

Armoured Warfare

The arrival of tanks and aircraft on the battlefields of Flanders naturally caused much discussion in the immediate post-war *Journal*, even though there were still those who clung to their horses. Lieutenant Colonel Poudret was, incredibly, still willing to argue that a massed cavalry charge was a potential battle winner[39] and as late as 1932 there were those willing to argue that the horse would always be more reliable than motor vehicles.[40] There were still an embarrassing number of troops on horses in 1936 – but the balance of interest was firmly pointed towards mechanised warfare. In 1920, J F C Fuller began his attempt to apply the lessons of the First World War to the development of armoured forces for the future in 'The War on Land: The Application of Recent Developments in the Mechanics and Other Scientific Knowledge to Preparation and Training for Future War on Land', for which he won the Gold Medal Prize Essay in 1919.[41] He followed this up in 1925 with the 'Progress in the Mechanicalisation of Modern Armies'[42] in the *Journal* while in 1932 Major McLeod summed up the increasing use of automatic weapons, radio, armoured vehicles and air power as nothing less than a 'mechanical revolution' in which smaller, armoured forces would become many times more effective than larger, slower moving armies:[43]

> The machine and not the man has become the dominant feature on the battlefield – in the attack, the tank, in defence, the machine gun.

This was prescient stuff and in the best traditions of the nineteenth century *Journals*. The problem was that the development of an effective British mechanised force was hampered by the lack of investment in research and development – possibly because the research effort went into building better aircraft. It can certainly be argued that Britain never developed a decent tank until the appearance of the Centurion, which first saw combat in Korea. When Major Edwards wrote about the 'endurance, mobility and firepower'[44] of the tank in 1935, we need to be aware that he was talking about the British five-ton, machine gun-carrying Mk VI and the 2pdr armed A9 'cruiser', with effective speeds of 15 mph and a range of 100 miles. German armour was based on the six-ton Panzer II, while the Italian Fiat Ansaldo 1933 model weighed under four tons and neither had so much as a half inch of armour. This article also pointed out the lack of a viable doctrine of mechanised warfare and referred to the Royal Tank Corps exercising on Salisbury plain 'like battle squadrons at sea'. As opinion was divided between whether tanks should support an infantry attack or act independently, no resolution was reached and two different types of tanks would be produced to fulfil two different roles – heavier 'infantry' tanks like the Matilda and Churchill, and lighter, faster 'cruiser' tanks like the Covenanter and Crusader.[45] This was in stark contrast to the development of a combined-arms fighting force being developed by Guderian in Germany.[46]

Still, the *Journal* did make an effort to study current developments in armoured warfare and reprinted 'Infantry and Tanks in the Spanish Civil War' in 1939 from the French *Revue Militaire Générale*. In this article, Commandant Andriot made several interesting points regarding the folly of relying on Maginot and Siegfried lines, largely because 'defensive lines, however strong, cannot compensate for deficiencies in the training of the troops'. His well-argued dismissal of the value of light tanks in combat, and his prescient assertion that the mortar integral to the infantry unit was the best weapon for dealing with the enemy in close contact, was undermined by the rather complacent comment that medium tanks 'would appear to have great possibilities',[47] but he did point to the necessity of large medium tanks working in co-operation with well trained infantry as the way forward. Mechanised infantry he dismissed as too vulnerable to air strikes if they were simply carried in commercial lorries.

Not every article was of this standard, however; Lieutenant Warringa of the Dutch infantry completely misinterpreted German doctrine in a piece entitled 'Tanks in the Attack'.[48] Backing the French idea that tanks were primarily an infantry support weapon, he argued that German tank tactics would fail because they intended to attack in depth without infantry support, an assertion which was simply untrue.

Lieutenant Colonel Hilton, who had served in both the RAF and the Royal Tank Regiment before joining the Royal Artillery, offered a comprehensive anti-tank strategy in 'Anti-Tank Tactics', based on indirect fire directed onto forming-up areas by aerial reconnaissance looking specifically for tank tracks heading into wooded areas (still a give-away today) – air attack was discounted as the bombs available were too feeble and inaccurate to do much damage – followed by indirect fire brought down on the supporting infantry to detach the tanks from their supports. Deploying anti-tank guns among the infantry would be the next step, but the difficulties of concealing the flash of such a weapon would be so great as to render it an obvious target for enemy tanks, machine guns and artillery. Some form of light, hand held anti-tank weapon was called for – but Hilton could only offer the idea of 'spraying some blinding preparation' over the apertures of the tank, which even he admitted was 'fantastic'. The Panzershrek and Bazooka were still some way off, obviously. In the event of a breakthrough, all artillery types would be required to concentrate their fire on tanks which, as they became detached from their infantry, would become ever more vulnerable. The RAF would spot for the artillery, ideally, and so some form of air-ground wireless set ought to be issued to the artillery. This was revealing in itself about the state of Army-Air Force liaison. Only Brigadier Wilson seemed to have worked out that for tanks and infantry to work together, the infantry would also have to be mounted in armoured vehicles[49] – a decade after Guderian had been exercising his troops on that premise.[50] *Achtung*

– *Panzer!* was not translated into English before 1939.[51] Hilton
finished his piece by arguing that:[52]

> Tank attacks in mass will have decisive effects on the battle; *if* the
> opposing air arm has been adequately blinded; *if* the opposing artillery
> has been adequately neutralised; *if* adequate continuous fire support is
> provided so that anti-tank guns can be knocked out directly as they
> open fire; and, finally, *if* the infantry holding the opposing defended
> localities have been adequately shattered or cowed by bombardment or
> other action so that they no longer have the spirit to resist tanks at close
> quarters.

As a description of what Guderian had in mind, this is hard to beat.

Death from Above

The development of the aircraft during and after the First World War
engendered an excitement that sometimes bordered on 'Dorking-ist'
hysteria. Here, it appeared, was a wonder weapon that could win wars
by devastating an enemy's industrial base or terrorising its population
into surrender, transport troops around the globe at unprecedented
speeds, police the empire, while also being able to dispose of fleets and
break up tank attacks before they could get going. This was mostly
wishful thinking – to be set alongside contemporary plans for aircraft
carriers made out of icebergs, aircraft launched from submarines and
glue guns for blinding tanks – but no bar to pacifist beliefs that an
International Air Force would be strong enough to deter aggression,
a proposal that was witheringly dismissed by RUSI:[53]

> Is it really necessary to write, much less to read, a whole book – even
> a small one – to show that the idea of an international air force is
> impracticable? .... To pacifists – especially of the belligerent brand – to
> internationalists and idealists who look to Geneva to give birth to the
> millennium, we commend this painstaking analysis of an academical

proposal: but we fear that those are the very people who avoid reading anything which tends to demolish their pet theories and castles in the air.

The author of the book under review was J M Spaight, one of the most prolific writers on air power and a senior civil servant at the Air Ministry. Even the professionals were taken in for a while; the 1930 RAF exercise report concluded that there would be such a collapse in civilian morale after only three nights of bombing that Britain would have to sue for peace.[54] 'The next war in view of the progress of scientific invention [poison gas bombs], might end in a few days in the annihilation of a whole people',[55] was typical of the inflated claims made by the protagonists of air power. This particular claim was countered in 1937 by Professor Haldane's 'Science and Future Warfare':[56]

It has been pointed out with perfect truth that ten tons of gas would render the atmosphere poisonous over an area of several square miles if rightly distributed, but it is also true that a ton of bullets would destroy the whole British Army if they were rightly aimed. The question we have to face is what is likely to happen in real life because it is quite certain that a hostile air force would not be allowed to drop its bombs wherever it wished without interference.

A more measured appraisal was presented by the French Inspector-General of the Air Force, who argued that air superiority was important as it could be used to deny an enemy strategic surprise and attack his concentrations; and that to this end, air attacks should be concentrated against enemy airfields in the first instance. The result would be that 'sooner or later every operation will degenerate into a frontal attack, with the result that the defence remains the stronger'.[57]

Perhaps the best analysis came again from Brigadier Wilson, who pointed out the practical difficulties of delivering enough TNT, gas or chemicals to mortally wound a city – the small town of Ypres had provided an existence 'not too uncomfortable' for the thousands of soldiers who lived in it during the First World War. He was also right about the effect of air raids on cities – people would exhibit dogged determination, essential services would be maintained by expedients and the existence of even the most basic road, rail and maritime infrastructure would be enough to prevent the appearance of a 'maimed and maddened population'. He was, after observing the behaviour of ordinary Japanese during the Tokyo earthquake, convinced that 'persons who argue like this have no comprehension of the exigent demands of war or of the grandeurs to which it raises ordinary humanity'. More importantly, the co-ordination of a big enough air strike would probably defeat the organisational capacities of any air force without substantial previous experience and, what was more, the key to success in an air war would not be the existence of a mass of machines, but the supply of pilots. In short, he dismissed the idea that the aeroplane was a war-winning weapon on its own, but did endorse its value in conjunction with other arms. He could not have known that his final judgement on air power would be proved true within a very few years:[58]

> It is when a nation is exhausted by the struggle and tottering towards its ruin that ... aircraft will possess the power summarily to end the agony by independent air action.

The idea of a massive strategic bombing force was, however, probably guaranteed to survive largely because Lord Trenchard, the first head of the RAF, believed in it, and he had chosen so many like-minded officers. His spiritual successor, Arthur 'Bomber' Harris, was able to realise these dreams during the Second World War when he unleashed the campaign that would raze most of Germany to the ground.[59]

Fears of what air power could do at sea were aired in the Gold Medal Essay (Air) for 1936: 'The effect of the development of

air power on British interests in the Mediterranean', by Wing
Commander Cochrane, argued that air power would make life very
difficult for the navy in the Mediterranean in the event of war, and
that the air defences in that theatre needed upgrading immediately
with the provision of an airfield for Gibraltar (the result was the only
runway in the world with a traffic light on it). Not only that, he
argued, but the Cape route should be prepared as the main convoy
route to Egypt and further east. The Eardley-Wilmott Prize Essay
for 1936 also dealt with 'Changes in Naval Warfare owing to New
and Modified Weapons', in which Lieutenant Commander Brock
RN argued that air power and its application at sea generally would
be the naval challenge of the future. There were also those officers
such as Lieutenant Commander Young of the Fleet Air Arm who,
in an article examining the best way to attack a warship, pointed
out that the technical limitations of the available aircraft ruled out
many of the claims made for them; their bombs just were not big
enough.[60] This, again, was substantially true at the time, in 1936:
the fact that in less than a decade, a B-29 Superfortress would drop
a bomb powerful enough to destroy an entire city should not blind
us to the feebleness of such existing designs as the Fairey Battle,
the Boulton Paul Defiant (which could not fire forwards) and the
Blenheim bomber. The success of the Swordfish biplanes – outdated
by war's start – of the Fleet Air Arm during the raid on the Italian
fleet at Taranto was as miraculous as it was improbable. It might also
allow us to forgive the decision to build HMS *Hood* with a teak deck
– but not the decision not to repair this mistake before she was sent
out against the *Bismarck*.

Similarly, the debates as to whether an air force should be primarily
a tactical support to the army, or a strategic asset to destroy cities,
still had the power to baffle experienced practitioners like Hermann
Göring, who built a tactical air force for the support of an armoured
blitzkrieg and then tried to use it as a strategic bombing force for the
destruction of London. What was not in doubt was that cities would

indeed become targets; in 1936, H A Jones reviewed *The War in the Air* for the *Journal* and, commenting on the effect on governments of popular clamours for revenge, wryly remarked that 'Democracies, perhaps, get the wars that they deserve'. For him, all moral or civilised conduct would be swept aside when the peoples' war came. Wilson agreed; 'In the savage struggle to win, war will be as relentless and frightful as the ingenuity of man can make it … All-in war will be the order of the day, and every man woman and child of the warring nations will be concerned in it'.

As in armoured warfare, there was still a great deal of uncertainty as to the use and effectiveness of aircraft, which was made ever greater by the rapidity of technical developments; in 1935, the Luftwaffe was still flying HE 51 and HE 60 biplanes, but three years later they were in ME 109s. In 1923, Trenchard had concluded that bombers were more versatile than fighters and thus should be built in the ration of two bombers for each fighter, but in 1934, this priority was revised in favour of building fighters. Similarly, during the 1920s it was felt that aircraft had such a vast cubic space to manoeuvre in that the only way to cope with aerial bombardment of cities was to retaliate in kind, but by 1937 the *RAF Quarterly* was championing the view that bombers should be attacked in the approach, while bombing and on their return journey by aggressive fighter aircraft relying on speed to avoid the bomber's defensive armament. Again, during the 1920s, there was a strong view that bombers were virtually indestructible because their defensive armament was greater than the armament of fighters, but by 1937 it was beginning to be suspected that they would have to be escorted by their own fighters if they were not to be annihilated – there were views expressed to Chamberlain by the RAF before Munich that Germany could not be bombed effectively.[61] There was even a suspicion that bombers might be used as bait to lure up enemy fighters, which would then be pounced upon by escort fighters.[62] In the end, the progress of the RAF in creating Fighter Command with its sophisticated system of radar and command and control, and the

arrival of fast, single seat, monoplane fighters after 1936 was the most
powerful antidote to fears of moral collapse brought on by air power.
What was particularly curious about this debate, however, was its
insularity; there was little talk of tactical ground attack in support of
the army. The *Stuka* never seemed to enter the consciousness of the
RAF.

Reaction to Germany

> A great people intoxicated with an idea might perpetrate harm
> which would take a great deal of bother to put right.
>
> (Brigadier B T Wilson)[63]

Faith in the ability of the League of Nations to preserve the peace
bled away steadily during the 1920s and then haemorrhaged at
the beginning of the 1930s. Whereas in 1919 many people were
willing to give the League a chance – and that included many RUSI
members – by 1933, the rise of Hitler, and Japanese designs in the Far
East, meant that the Locarno Honeymoon, Spa diplomacy and the
Kellogg-Briand Pact were increasingly regarded as prime examples of
wishful thinking. In 1930, British defence policy was still based on
the Ten Year Rule, the assumption that there would be no war with
Japan, and great hopes for the Geneva Disarmament Conference
scheduled for 1932. Prime Minister Ramsay MacDonald was also
firmly of the opinion that the economic depression meant that the
financial threat to the country far outweighed any military one and
that another dose of Victorian thrift was required; defence spending
reached its lowest figure in 1932–33 of 2 per cent of GNP.[64] The
Japanese invasion of China in 1931 galvanised the chiefs of staff into
demanding the removal of the Ten Year Rule, which was formally
abandoned in March 1932. This did not end wishful thinking among
politicians, however; Stanley Baldwin was still trying to work out a
way to abolish capital ships, heavy weapons and bombers. Germany

walked out of the Disarmament Conference in October 1932, even before Hitler came to power (once Chancellor, he formally withdrew Germany from both the conference and the League of Nations).

In 1934, the Defence Requirements sub-Committee recommended the completion of the Singapore naval base, an expansion of the navy, an expansion of the RAF and the reconstitution of the BEF, but the Chancellor of the Exchequer Neville Chamberlain felt that this was ruinously expensive. His alternative proposal was to freeze work on Singapore, *halve* the size of the army but *double* the size of the RAF, as it was both cheaper and (influenced by the inflated claims of the air power 'Dorking-ists') apparently more effective. The services began to mutter about the Treasury being less concerned about fighting a war than being able to pay the indemnity after losing it. Both Baldwin and Chamberlain justified the cuts on the grounds that public opinion was so determinedly pacifist that they would lose the 1935 general election if they attempted to rearm; Clement Attlee and the Labour Party gave notice that they would indeed oppose any attempt at rearmament. Political leadership was at a premium in the early 1930s.[65]

The concern with Germany was reflected in the *Journal* in 1932 when Major Reynolds, who had been resident in Germany for most of the last decade, wrote that, 'the German mind is in a state of chaos: they are unable to see any way out of the present quagmire … consequently it is difficult to say what they are likely to do'.[66] Major Polson-Newman was under no illusions in 1933 that Hitler intended to rearm and then revise the Treaty of Versailles. 'The International Situation: The European Crisis' identified the four main strands of instability as being German-Polish ethnic tensions in Danzig, the Polish corridor and Silesia; the Nazi accession to power; the economic depression; and the failure of disarmament. At the root of this crisis was the relation between disarmament and Versailles Treaty revision. In short, he argued, no-one wanted to disarm or revise the treaty, but the Germans would insist upon it and as the disarmament conference was something of a job-creation scheme for diplomats, there was nothing for it but to either insist on maintaining the treaty as revised at Locarno in 1925, or give in to German demands. As the guarantors of Locarno were Britain and Italy (rather than the League of Nations), it seemed clear that only a direct threat of force could ultimately restrain Germany; yet, given the state of the British armed services, that force would have to be Italian, and, as Italy wanted treaty revision in the Adriatic, this was not likely to occur. By 1934, while the *Journal*'s 'International Situation' briefing was quoting *The Times* on 22 January 1934, giving detail on German plans as 'the choice is no longer between disarmament and re-armament but between open re-armament ... and secret re-armament',[67] 'German Aviation' in the *Journal* noted a 160 per cent increase in spending on the Luftwaffe.[68] In the next issue, Lieutenant Colonel Dunlop noted that:[69]

> There is arising a conception even among the most ardent advocates of international concord, that stability in international relationships may have to be backed by the use of force.

It was, therefore, with some considerable satisfaction that the *Journal* for May 1935 reproduced edited highlights from Ramsay MacDonald's statement in parliament, in response to Italian aggression in Abyssinia:[70]

> Hitherto ... public opinion in this country has tended to assume that nothing is required for the maintenance of peace except [the League of Nations] and that ... navies, armies and air forces ... are no longer required. The force of world events has shown this assumption to be premature ...

> The National Government can no longer close its eyes to the fact that adequate defences are still required for security ...

This did not result in any increase in spending immediately, but it was an indication that change was on its way and the new prime minister, Stanley Baldwin, immediately abandoned his opposition to rearmament on winning the 1935 general election. The rapid defeat of Abyssinia – which the *Journal* noted had occurred despite both moral force and economic sanctions[71] – and the German reoccupation of the Rhineland in 1936 moved the chiefs of staff again to warn the cabinet that they could not defend the empire against Germany, Italy and Japan with the forces then at their disposal. This again resulted in a limited commitment to naval rearmament, a vastly expanded RAF and again demands from Chamberlain that there could be no question of a BEF; the Labour opposition attacked even these modest proposals as undermining the League and collective security. Even then, the RAF would not be ready until 1939 at the earliest because many of its favoured designs were still on the drawing board. Responding to Winston Churchill's increasingly vehement warnings about the German threat, Chamberlain claimed that increased spending on defence would result in:[72]

A feverish and artificial boom followed by a disastrous slump, and finally the defeat of the Government and the advent of an ignorant, unprepared and heavily pledged Opposition to handle a crisis as severe as that of 1931.

With hindsight, this looks like an opportunity missed, if we consider Churchill as the opposition. When it became clear that rearmament would take place, Chamberlain again tried to hamstring it by proposing that it should be paid for by a loan – thus violating the principle that expenditure should be financed by taxation – and thus deliberately provoking parliamentary opposition. In 1937, when he replaced Baldwin as prime minister, he then fielded the Admiralty request for a renewed two-power standard navy by instituting another defence review which did not report until December. By

1938, all confidence in the League had evaporated, a point made after the *Anschluss* when RUSI declared that any attempt to involve the League would simply 'add to that body's humiliations'. Captain Smith also noted that the attitude of the public towards preparation for war had greatly improved to the point that all political parties now admitted the need for at least some 'passive' measures.[73] Even Chamberlain began to accept the need for more expenditure on arms, but then turned down the Admiralty request for another battleship. After the occupation of Czechoslovakia in March 1939, in defiance of the Munich Agreement, the May 1939 'International Situation' consisted of a forthright damning of the League of Nations as a 'Tower of Babel' for its idealism, 'that prince of idealists' Ramsay MacDonald for disarmament and Hitler for his violence. There was little doubt that war was on its way. Plans were announced to double the Territorial Army to twenty-six divisions, conscription was announced in April 1939 and in July the navy was given *carte blanche* for its building programme. Finally, the services, helped along by the Institute, had pushed the government into action.

Preparation for War

By 1936, RUSI was under no illusions that war was coming and commissioned three major articles which aimed to dampen inter-service rivalry by 'making each service better known to the other two'.[74] The Royal Navy offered a brief outline of its administrative history, the various types of ships in the fleet and, most importantly, its mission: blue-water control of the sea to ensure commerce and troop movement, achieved by bringing the enemy's main fleet to action. The army was rather more tentative in giving an indication as to what its mission was and, again, betrayed its poor grasp of armoured warfare when it revealed that the one anti-tank weapon deployed by a platoon commander – the remarkable Boys anti-tank rifle – was held in a truck at Company HQ.[75] A later article by the same author claimed that barbed wire would stop a tank and the 2pdr anti-tank gun, now removed from the control of the infantry and handed over to the artillery, was equal to any known tank – a dubious prospect when faced by Panzer IVs.[76] As to a tactical concept, the army was again way behind Guderian. Tanks were compared to battleships; the overall concept of an encounter battle between armoured car reconnaissance, followed by attrition and break-in by infantry, infantry tanks and artillery, and a breakout by 'cruiser' tanks, could have been drawn from the 1870s by merely substituting 'cavalry' for 'armour'. Although there was much talk of the different arms co-operating and supporting each other, there was no understanding of combining different arms within the same formation, as in the Panzer Division, which contained armour and infantry as organic components. This was a major failing for a nation that prided itself on such hybrid innovations as Mounted Infantry and the Royal Naval Air Service Armoured Car Regiments, and especially so when the existence of Panzergrenadier units was known.

Here again though, it had been the financial stringency imposed on the army by Chamberlain and the Treasury that was to blame. The army really was a Cinderella service in the last years before the war and as late as February 1938 could only scrape together two infantry and one 'mobile' division for service (probably) in the East. General Henry Pownall, director of military intelligence, thought this was all nonsense and absolutely refuted the idea that the British could simply lend air and naval power to supplement the French Army dug in on the Maginot Line – but it was not until January 1939, when a rumour got about that Hitler was about to seize Holland, that a BEF was authorised. Four Regular, four Territorial and two mobile divisions were quickly cobbled together for service in Europe. As far as the RAF was concerned, presenting an administrative history was rather difficult and the author had to make the dubious claim that the RAF was a direct descendant of the Royal Engineers Balloon School established at Chatham in 1879. The author of this contribution, identified only by his initials, preferred not to talk about strategic bombing, but tended to emphasise the flexibility of the RAF. He also managed to avoid any mention of the RAF's most important weapon – radar.[77]

Radar was, of course, top secret and the Institute took great pains during these years to ensure that its discussions over it did not result in any breach of security. It was already the practice that serving officers submitted their contributions for clearance by the service ministries, and several articles were felt to be too sensitive to be given publication or a hearing. There was a proposal to exclude the press and general public from certain sessions, but, even then, 'The Employment of Aircraft in the Defence and Attack on Seaborne Trade' was ruled out by both the navy and the RAF.[78] Similarly, the 1932 and 1936 Naval Gold Medal essays were censored, but published in confidential Admiralty papers, and, probably less wisely given what was to happen four years later, 'Combined Operations at Singapore' was dropped in 1938.

Altham also gave thought as to what role the Institute would play during the war and approached the government with a proposal that, as in the First World War, the buildings might be utilised as a press or censorship office. In September 1938, the Institute was formally taken over by the HQ Postal and Telegraphic censors. Altham no doubt thought that the financial future of the Institute had been assured, but in May 1939 the government went back on the deal. The building would remain in the Institute's possession throughout the war and although it would emerge in 1945 in reasonable financial shape, there was no prospect of the 1918 bonanza. An expectation that the Institute *would* survive the war was revealed when in October 1939 Altham reminded members to be on the look-out for 'relics of the present war'[79] and hired two extra nightwatchmen to guard against incendiary bombs.

The War, 1939–45
On the whole, despite the sometimes patchy performance of RUSI between the wars, its efforts were irrelevant to the early war catastrophe of France 1940, even if one rules out the failure to develop

a coherent doctrine of armoured warfare. It could fulfil its mission to debate, warn, experiment and advocate, but it could not alter the dire strategic and economic circumstances that imprisoned the political leadership and placed Britain in such peril. More importantly, in the end it could not do anything much to dissuade from war those 'certain number of lunatics who think they are sane'.

Further, the old jibe about generals preparing for the last war holds no water at all, and the Institute can take a great deal of credit for supporting the services in their age-old struggle against the complacency of politicians, the delusions of idealists and the parsimony of the Treasury. To its great credit, in the same way that RUSI had not been seduced by preatorianism in the late nineteenth century, the various fascist utopias on offer during the 1930s had failed to distract it from its overwhelming desire to defend the realm. The fact that the Institute had allowed the German Ambassador to Britain to give a vision of Nazi Germany as a workers' paradise – apparently the function of concentration camps was to teach errant employers how to treat their employees properly – in 1938, did not mean that they believed him; especially the part where he envisaged sending large numbers of young Germans to visit foreign countries in the near future in order to increase 'respect for other nations and their accomplishments'.[80] Similarly, J F C Fuller might well have enjoyed being a guest at Hitler's birthday parade in April 1939, but he was certainly not there to represent RUSI.[81] Instead, the Institute held hard to the British warrior's belief that the prosaic delights of Saturday afternoon football, golf, gardening, Sunday lunchtime in the pub and a pipe and slippers represented a better vision of utopia than a boot stamping on a human face forever.

The Phoney War
Given the fears of a mass bombing campaign, the Institute had begun the war in 1939 by packing up its books and sending them off to Baron Newborough's country house, Glynllifon, Caenarfon in

North Wales. The museum was closed and those items that could not be protected in the heavily sand-bagged crypt were evacuated to Lord Desborough's Taplow Court, while the Reubens ceiling went to Hall Barn in Buckinghamshire[82] – but not before the workmen had damaged the Waterloo and Trafalgar models in removing it. The machine guns, rifles and pistols were confiscated by the police.

However, it was decided from the outset that the Institute would not go into the type of shock that gripped it at the start of the First World War. Exhibitions would be held in the Lecture Theatre and the Library would continue to lend books on application – and Gwydyr House was still being considered for annexation. *Journal* sales increased as demand grew with the rise in the number of units mobilised and the Trench Gascoigne Prize was still to be awarded. As in 1914–18, the membership saw no great increase in size, indeed fifty-six casualties contributed to a slight decrease from 6,068 in 1939 to 5,823 in 1940,[83] but the work of the Institute went on. From 1941, it would even admit women for membership (as long as they were in uniform). The noted war artist Laura Knight – who exhibited *In For Repairs*, a picture of WAAFs mending a barrage balloon, at the National Gallery in 1942, and *Ruby Loftus Screwing a Breech-Ring* (perhaps the model for Norman Rockwell's *Rosie the Riveter*) at the Royal Academy in 1943, and who later went on to record the Nuremberg trials – was also found a place in the Institute. Her painting of WAAF controllers during the Battle of Britain remains among the Institute's treasured possessions. Captain Altham went to work at the Postal and Telegraphic Censorship Department, handing over to the popular librarian Colonel Hughes and Captain Parker, while Colonel F E Talbot took over the acting editorship from Colonel Armstrong; however, Altham still remained the directing influence by continuing to occupy his position as chief executive officer.

An optimistic picture of Wellington bombers raiding Kiel on 4 September 1939 and pulverising the *Scharnhorst* adorned the February 1940 issue of the *Journal* and, in the Trench Gascoigne Prize

Essay of 1939, Cadet Captain E G Mandeville Roe RA confidently repeated the conviction of the RAF that they had blown the KMS *Gneisenau* in half (they had not). The 'International Situation' in the same issue hopefully reported that the resistance of Finland to Soviet attack would lead to the collapse of Bolshevism while the 'Navy Notes' looked forward to the launch of two new Dutch cruisers in 1941. Even more comforting was the claim in 'Air Notes' that not a single British fighter had been shot down, while suitable swathes had been cut through enemy Messerschmitt and Heinkel forces, and the news that the Royal Lofts at Sandringham had been turned over to the National Pigeon Service. In 1938, the *Journal* had carried a profile of the French general Gamelin, which described him as having 'been born under a lucky star'; to this they now added a eulogy of Admiral Darlan in May 1940. The *Journal* of May 1940 also carried 'Is Mobile Warfare in the West a Myth?', in which Captain Lind dismissed the whole idea of a mobile war in France, resolutely ignoring the Polish experience, and calling for an armoured personnel carrier to get over No Man's Land after the artillery barrage lifted. The Phoney War was in full swing indeed.

Collapse in Europe

It was a punch-drunk Institute that watched the subsequent disasters in Norway, Belgium and France in the spring and summer of 1940. The reasons for the collapse of the French armies that year caused such controversy after the war that the relevant French archives were kept closed until the 1980s. This was largely due to the very deep divisions that existed in post-war France over the responsibility for the defeat. In short, the Left blamed proto-fascist *Ancien Romans*, while the Right blamed decadent *Jeune Cyclistes*, a mirror of the debates about guilty men and pacifists in Britain. Muddying the picture further was the creation of the myth that Charles de Gaulle had predicted defeat and been ignored for his pains. For very many historians, the argument was framed in terms of whether France was defeated by its internal interwar divisions more than the Panzer divisions. Martin Alexander's argument that France had more tanks than Germany and that they were concentrated in the path of the attacking panzers, rather than doled out in penny packets, is particularly telling here. For him, it was the lack of a doctrine rather than the shortage of equipment that was crucial. When the tanks did attack, they did not do so in a co-ordinated strike which guaranteed defeat in detail.[84]

It can hardly be doubted, however, that the political chaos of the Third Republic prevented both French industry and the armed forces from gearing up for war – the Left thought that De Gaulle's idea of a professional army was praetorianism, while the trades unions' insistence on a forty-hour week priced many businesses out of the rearmament market. There is also a strong argument to say that the refusal of Belgium to allow French and British troops onto its territory before the invasion created a strategic situation that fatally handicapped any chance of defeating a German attack. To cover Brussels, assuming that Germany would initiate another Schlieffen Plan, allied forces would have to pivot on Sedan and advance to the River Dyle as soon as the Germans crossed the border. This was something that the Germans understood, and thus feinted through Holland and Belgium before punching through the pivot. What looked like the Schlieffen Plan initially was actually something much more lethal, a *Sichelschnitt* to cut off and destroy the BEF and the best of the French armies in Belgium before turning south. Neither the divisions within the French General Staff, nor the competence, equipment or training of the BEF, 1st and 7th French Armies, could compensate for the political decision to go to the aid of Belgium – even when General Ironsides and Lord Gort both warned against the plan.[85]

As far as the British armed forces were concerned, no-one has ever really disputed that the German attack represented as complete a defeat as anyone could wish for, or that Dunkirk was as lucky an escape as anyone could wish for. From the French perspective, however, there is one major charge that has always been ducked – that Britain did not take the war seriously and made a completely inadequate contribution in terms of its troop numbers. This is substantially true. The BEF was among the best trained and equipped of the allied armies, but it was still far too small and only a fraction of the size of the French or German army. The implication is that had Britain mobilised half a million soldiers in 1939–40 instead of a mere ten divisions-worth, then even the Panzers would have been swamped. That Britain did not was due to its straitened economic circumstances, but also because the political leadership of Britain was ambivalent about the desirability of preparing for war. Chamberlain and Halifax were too decent by half, while Harold Laski, deputy leader of the Labour Party, was a pacifist who still thought he could dissuade Hitler from war as late as 1942. With this sort of leadership and the very great internal strife experienced in France after 1934, it could be argued strongly that the armies were beaten before the first shot was fired.

When the BEF washed up on the beaches of Sussex the Institute was reduced to reflecting the defiance that the country felt, but could not turn into much action at that moment in time. 'The operations of the BEF in Belgium and Northern France' (August 1940) could only offer a crumb of comfort by blaming the French and Belgians for the defeat and adding to the completely untrue boast that 'tactically our troops mastered the enemy whenever they encountered him in the field'. The 'International Situation' offered a brave piece about Britain being less a beleaguered island than an advanced base, but did offer the reassurance that an invasion could not be attempted without air superiority being achieved – a theory that was at that very moment being put to the test over Kent. The sense of humour and stiff upper lip inside the council also asserted itself, as this entry in the minutes of 2 July 1940 shows:

> The Council noted that the resignation of Major-General JRM Minshull-Ford been received on his appointment as ... GOC ... Guernsey and Aldernay [sic], but in view of the subsequent termination

of that appointment, they decided that General Minshull-Ford should be invited to withdraw his resignation.

Minshull-Ford refused to see the funny side, however, and remained resigned.

In the spring of 1941, 'The Air Battles for Britain' gave an officially sanctioned version of the Battle of Britain, which discussed the command and control of the Spitfires and Hurricanes but, as in 1938, made no mention of radar, while the 'International Situation' of February 1941 seemed to draw hope from the fact that neither the USSR nor the US was in the war as yet. Hitler was compared to a businessman who has expanded his assets but not yet claimed a dividend and Germany, argued the Institute, 'has yet to learn the lesson that territory without trade is a liability and not an asset'. In August, the frontispiece showed French balloons attempting to invade Britain in 1805 as if the *Journal* could now allow itself a little mockery as fears of an Operation *Sea Lion* receded.

The stunning news that Germany had invaded Russia was met with a certain ambivalence. Three articles on the Red Army were published, but little positive could be concluded from their early performance while the 'International Situation: The New Ally' of August 1941 speculated as to why Hitler should ever want to commit the folly of fighting a war on two fronts, but could not quite welcome the long-hated Bolsheviks into the fold. The motive for the German invasion was felt to be the oil fields of the Caucasus, but this would be futile as the infrastructure to carry it to Germany did not exist, argued E M Friedwald in 'Germany's Oil Supplies'.[86] In the autumn, there was a further burst of confidence with the resumption of the lecture programme, which even the attack on Pearl Harbor and the fall of Singapore could not permanently dent.

The *Journal* also began to sharpen up its intellectual edge again in 1941 by reproducing a lecture given by General Wavell at RUSI in 1936, in which it set out a blueprint for 'The Higher Commander'[87] needed for the present war. He argued that professional armies would be replaced by 'the hastily trained but better educated citizen' and that a commander would need to understand the media in order to reach out to them – Montgomery, MacArthur and Patton would certainly take these lessons to heart.

The most important tactical lesson for a commander was to be able to understand the other arms available to him and to this end he proposed that it be a prerequisite for promotion in the army that an officer spend time with the RAF – he was also an advocate of early responsibility for junior officers. Modern warfare, argued Wavell, also demanded an ability to understand and get along with politicians. This was something that Wavell found more difficult to practise than to preach after Churchill ordered him to aid Greece, invade Lebanon and secure Iraq – and thus ensure his defeat in the Western Desert. He would then have to face it all over again when the Japanese swept over Southeast Asia and Wavell was transferred there to salvage an impossible situation. His later relations with Gandhi as Viceroy of India were also fraught with difficulty as first Churchill, then Attlee undermined him; he had at least some revenge with his poem *An Indian Jabberwocky*.[88] Wavell and his contemporary, Claude Auchinleck, did their best in impossible circumstances, but never really enjoyed laurels for their role in holding an empire with the inadequate forces bequeathed to them by Chamberlain, Laski and Attlee. Nevertheless, the promotion of the debate about the nature of generalship was a major success, leading one later study to conclude that:[89]

> RUSI ensured that the generals of this later war knew of their predecessors' errors and the expectations they were to meet. That service alone was more likely to help bring far more soldiers home alive than had been the case in their fathers' generation.

The 1941 *Journal* also printed the 1940 Trench Gascoigne Prize Essay on 'How have the Lessons of the War of 1914–1918 been confirmed or modified by the Experiences of the present War to date?' Here, Major Frederic Evans MC RAMC enunciated twelve lessons that were being digested under the circumstances of the present war and drew some conclusions accordingly. The mechanisation of infantry and the introduction of the tank seemed to point to the development of smaller armoured forces rather than larger infantry armies, as J F C Fuller had recommended, and added enormous significance to the security of oil supplies. The development of air power meant that civilian morale had to be considered seriously, but perhaps more importantly, Britain needed an aircraft that could operate with the army, as the *Stuka* did for Germany. The importance of command of the seas remained unchanged. The use of propaganda in the sense of a clear statement of war aims was vital. The emergence of total war and the impossibility of a limited war meant that Germany would continue to push into the Balkans – the attack on Russia was not considered yet – and Japan would not forego the oil supplies of the Dutch East Indies. The necessity of defence in depth, rather than linear tactics based on fortifications, had been proved by the fall of the Maginot Line; the importance of attacking on a narrow front rather than employing a general advance meant that defence in depth based on 'tank destroyers' and the defence of localities would be necessary. The impotence of naval force against land fortifications meant that bombardment was probably pointless. The need for self-contained forces built up in each theatre of war and able to act without dependence on reinforcements would give Britain an enormous advantage because of its imperial spread. However, no mention was made of overstretch. The importance of diplomacy as a strategic weapon seemed to place Britain at a disadvantage because she had tended towards ethical positions which prevented it from buying off Russia, Italy or Japan by acquiescing in their aspirations – here the author could only hope that 'British honesty' would triumph in the end. This was all not a bad analysis for 1940, but the author wanted something more than a sober reflection on lessons learned.

He wanted a much-needed victory to galvanise British arms because 'the outstanding lesson of the last war which applies to this, as to all wars, is that "nothing succeeds like success."'

The Tide Turns

By 1943, the three victories at El Alamein, Stalingrad and Midway had created a belief that however long it took and whatever setbacks were ahead, the alliance of Britain, the US and USSR was going to win the war. Before that, however, there would have to be a landing in Europe and this would have to be kept an absolute secret if it were to succeed. As the south coast of England became an armed camp, Operation *Mincemeat* dropped corpses on Spanish beaches with forged papers, and the Operation *Fortitude* deception programmes were put in place – and even the *Journal* agreed to be censored from 1942. The administration of the Institute went on apace however, and the row over the storage of the Library in late 1943 over Lord Newborough's desire to get more rent for Glynllifon by letting it to the USAAF resulted in a decision to bring the books back to London at the earliest opportunity – the work being carried out by temporary librarian Sergeant J O'Connor and three boy scouts. The RAF was also beginning to scent victory and in February 1943 renewed its attempt to get itself included in the Institute's Royal Charter, only to have the request turned down on the grounds that the taxman would use the change of the title as an excuse to attack their rates exemption again.[90] They also tried to get the RAF emblem put on the crest of the Institute in February 1944, but this was again refused.

In early 1944, in the interests of Anglo-American relations, the Institute invited the company of the Irving Berlin hit musical *This is the Army*, then on tour in London, to tea. The film version would star Lieutenant Ronald Reagan and this turn very nearly had him in the stage cast, but Berlin always seemed unable to recognise Reagan. (Berlin had the compliment repaid when Churchill invited him to lunch under the impression that he was Professor *Isaiah* Berlin).[91]

In May 1944, the 'Salute the Soldier Week' exhibition saw a staggering 42,378 visitors to the newly re-opened museum. The *Journal* was also thriving with articles submitted in 1944 on technical issues such as 'Jet Propelled Aircraft', 'The Future Development of Self-propelled Gun Mountings', and 'The Flying Bomb'. Bomber Harris and Air Marshal Keith Park (who had played a key role in the Battle of Britain and the defence of Malta) supplied articles on air strategy, 'Boy' Browning on airborne forces, Leo Amery on 'Mountain Warfare' and the first article written by a woman appeared, the gloriously unselfconsciously titled 'Universal Service – The Woman's Part'. Dame Helen Gwynne-Vaughan of the Auxiliary Territorial Service was clearly not a fan of D H Lawrence.

Looking Post-War

What was not clear, especially after the Red Army went on the offensive in 1943, was what the place of Britain would be in the post-war world. Indeed, British foreign policy from 1943 onwards began to look increasingly threadbare as the enormous power of the US and USSR became apparent. The certainty of Indian independence after the war seemed to indicate that interests further east would become ever more vulnerable, while possession of the Middle East began to look like a white elephant. Despite the massive mobilisation of imperial resources, South Africa, Australia and Canada were all drifting out of the British orbit and it had been long realised that what remained of the African empire was not worth the candle. In many ways, Britain seemed unwilling to face up to these realities and subsumed its future fears in one overwhelming goal: winning the war. The Institute reflected this refusal to think about politics by dropping the 'International Situation' from the *Journal*, possibly because Altham temporarily gave up the position of secretary between 1942–45, and possibly because the future looked so awful. When the feature did return in 1945, it limited itself to bald statements that read like an official communiqué. The

Yalta Conference and the dropping of the atomic bombs drew no real comment at all.

What did elicit comment was the Beveridge Report, which called for the founding of a welfare state after the war as both a reward for the commitment of the working classes to the war and a step on the road to a socialist utopia. Awed by the success of wartime state planning in the US, USSR and the British Empire, a broad consensus across parliament was entranced by the possibilities of extending this into the post-war world. The New Jerusalem so long sought by liberals, Fabian socialists and the Labour Party seemed to be within grasp; but their enthusiasm for social welfare schemes, a National Health Service and an expansion of educational opportunities meant that the tough question of how to pay for them was given insufficient attention. What was more, the Education Act of 1944 carried more than a whiff of social engineering, introducing as it did selective grammar schools, secondary technical schools and secondary modern schools. As far as the Institute was concerned, this was all wishful thinking unless 'The Buckler of the New Order' (1943) was kept in good shape:[92]

> While the steps to be taken to ensure sound social and economic conditions for this country after the war are being widely discussed, hardly a word has been uttered with regard to the future of the fighting forces.

Just as the Institute had pondered the future of the armed forces at the end of the First World War, so it began to think about them as the end of the Second World War seemed to be in sight. As before, it thought in terms of conscription and short service for a home army, and a long service, volunteer army for service abroad. The 1943 Trench Gascoigne Prize asked for an answer to the question 'Is Compulsory training in National Defence desirable for the youth of this country after the war?' In 1944, three more articles appeared on post-war army reform.

All in all, the Institute had done itself proud both in the lead up to and the duration of the war. It remained a forum for informed debate without giving away any secrets, kept the Museum and Library going and consistently obtained good articles for the *Journal* from informed commentators. If there were weaknesses in its coverage, for example of Japan and the Far East throughout the 1930s and 1940s, and a reluctance to attempt to plumb the politics of the post-war world, this could be explained by lack of correspondents in the first case and, in terms of the looming Soviet menace, an unwillingness, that ran throughout British society in 1944–45, to criticise an ally. Nor had it lost its sense of what was right; in June 1945 it loaned Wellington's sword to Eisenhower when he was granted the Freedom of the City. In terms of doing its duty, the only time the council cancelled a meeting was the one scheduled for 8 May 1945 – which was perhaps excusable.

V. COLD WAR, DECLINE AND REVIVAL

1945–89

The thirty-five years that followed the end of the Second World War saw a collapse in British power so profound that a whole new discipline was invented to explain it – declinology. Beginning with Indian independence in 1947, Britain then pulled out of Africa as fast as decency would permit – in some cases faster – and finally withdrew from the Gulf and Far East between 1968 and 1971. Ties of sentiment with Australia, New Zealand and Canada remained as emigration sent new colonists to old dominions – 'The Case for Planned Mass Migration from Britain to the Dominions' was an article in the 1952 *Journal* – but they no longer looked to Britain for their security needs. South Africa explicitly rejected the British tie with the election of a National Party committed to Apartheid, while the influx of settlers to Rhodesia complicated an already ambivalent attitude in Britain to the realities of power in southern Africa. The entry of Britain into the European Economic Community (EEC) in 1973 produced yet another level of ambiguity and confusion; was Britain's role to lead the Commonwealth, to subsume itself in Europe or become part of a transatlantic community, or all three? Or none? There was also a profound economic collapse. The war had virtually bankrupted Britain and the spending commitments that Clement Attlee's welfare state entailed meant that financial failure was a major possibility. This in turn meant that the temptation to stave off financial failure by reducing defence spending was too often just too tempting for the pressed politicians of the time.

Perhaps the most profound and unsettling of these changes was the
growing realisation that Britain was now, for the first time in its
historical memory, dependent on another country for its security. As
Lewis W Douglas, the US ambassador to Britain, noted at RUSI in
1949:[1]

> I suppose that in no similar period of historic time have there been
> shifts in the centre of international political gravity and re-directions
> of national attitudes towards international affairs, breaches in the
> social, political and economic traditions comparable in size, sweep and
> intensity ... with those of the last decade.

For most of the nineteenth and early twentieth centuries, the
focus of British foreign policy had been on reacting to threats and
finding allies to help deal with them. Now, according to Professor
Brogan, 'there is far more serious thought ... about the duties of the
United States than there is about our duties'. Foreign policy would
be as much about managing the transatlantic relationship as it would
be about managing the communist threat; no doubt there were some
well-thumbed copies of Thucydides' *History of the Peloponnesian War*
being handed round the Foreign Office, with the passages on the
Melian Dialogue heavily underlined. 'Everything the United States
does is news', argued Brogan. 'It is more than news; it is, in fact, a
policy for the rest of the world'.[2] The reality that economic decline
was relentlessly undermining British power was also noted by the
Institute, as was the dependence on Middle Eastern oil first noted in
the post-war period after Suez with presentations by Sir John Glubb
and R G Searight in February 1957. Glubb's expertise was called
upon again in 1958, while in 1959 Sir Tom O'Brien MP submitted
'A History of Trade Unions and their Functions Today' to the *Journal*.

The turning point came with the Macmillan years (1957–63),
when the decision was made to try to reinvigorate the ailing British
economy by cutting defence spending and using the resources thus

freed to produce a consumer boom. Nuclear weapons were to provide 'more bang for the buck' than a large conscript army spread around the globe and Duncan Sandys' 1957 Defence Review saw defence spending reduced below the 10 per cent minimum of GDP that it had absorbed since 1939. The manpower of the services was to be reduced from around 700,000 to around 400,000 with the abolition of conscription, overseas garrisons reduced and replaced by aircraft carriers and, most controversially, the replacement of fighter aircraft by anti-aircraft missiles – Sandys had been an air defence gunner during the war. The British Army of the Rhine (BAOR) was also reduced to an almost skeletal 55,000 – well below what Britain had agreed to provide to European defence – while the Thor intermediate range ballistic missile was deployed to make up for this downgrading.

The problem with this review was that substantial overseas commitments were retained without much thought going into how they might be secured. This mismatch of commitments to resources was to be a continuing problem and drew the *Journal* editor's comment that 'we weaken ourselves everywhere ... instead of being strong where it matters'.[3] Sandys' attempts to rationalise the British aircraft industry have also been blamed for bringing it to the brink of ruin. In 1959, Mr Shenfield, economic adviser to the Federation of British Industries, wrote 'The Impact of Reductions of Defence Requirements on British Industry', in which he argued that the aircraft industry had had 'a severe shaking' and that research and development had been especially hit in the radio industry. However, he added that on the whole, the manufacturing base would remain because, as Macmillan wanted, industry would go over to producing more consumer goods. Vice Admiral Longley-Cook was rather nearer the mark in the discussion which followed when he contended that:[4]

> [After] more than 20 years of preaching to labour that they can have more money for less work ... I do not believe that we are sufficiently

competitive at the present time. We have got to realize that the rest of the world does not owe us a living.

In 1965, the editor again asked the question of 'What are we trying to do East of Suez?' If the answer was to protect trade and prevent communist influence in the Indian Ocean, then it was perhaps time to reduce the expensive commitment to BAOR as Britain was, in effect, doing its bit for Western freedom in warmer climes.

The Institute had no love for Sandys and the Conservative Party of Harold Macmillan, and not just because of their desire to cut spending while still enjoying the pomp of an imperial role. Indeed, Sir Gerald Templer was once said to have remarked that Sandys was 'so bent that if [he] swallowed a nail, [he] would shit a corkscrew'. It was, perhaps, for this reason that the *Journal* gave a sympathetic view of the Labour Party defence policy in the 1965 volume, written by the Fulbright scholar, Charles Stevenson, who argued that, under then Defence Secretary Denis Healey, a lesser dependence on nuclear weapons and a more rational approach to both conventional forces and commitments would be realised. 'Historically', argued Stevenson with real accuracy, 'the most disastrous defence decisions have been made on economic grounds'.[5] This was a motto that should be hung over the Treasury door.

When Healey came in as Minister of Defence in the Wilson government of 1964–70, the pressure of economics continued to bite and added to the growing pressure from the left of the Labour Party to disarm in favour of more social spending. There was also a growing lobby in favour of unilateral nuclear disarmament, which had succeeded in getting a motion passed on this issue at the Labour conference in 1960. Frank Cousins, who was behind the motion, now sat in the Cabinet as Minister of Technology. Between 1964 and 1968 a series of cuts were made, which included the amalgamation of the service ministries into the Ministry of Defence, the halving of the Territorial Army to 45,000 men in 'cadre-ised' units of notional existence, the abandonment of the aircraft carrier-building programme and ultimately, the decision to withdraw from east of Suez. For the Institute, grittily rooted in reality, it was the Six Day War of 1967 that tolled the death knell of British power in the world:[6]

> Dreams die hard. For two centuries the reality of British naval power worldwide was a fact upon which British statesmen could build a foreign policy that commanded respect throughout the world ... If they have done nothing else, those six days of war in early June have presented Britain with an electrifying view of her impotence to control, or even influence, the flow of events outside her own immediate waters. Argue or gloss how one will, this remains, the stark, unpalatable fact.

In general, the Institute supported the withdrawal to Europe as the only realistic option for British defence,[7] but the crumbling economy and the inability of Healey to defend his department against repeated attacks on its budget were regarded with real alarm. The cuts left Britain, in the opinion of the Institute, with defences that had now been run down below minimum safety levels. There was also a growing note of frustration in the declarations that, 'when money gets tight, the nation's defence is the first target for emasculation' and that 'there are very few politicians indeed with sufficient strength of character to throw away a political dividend when it stares them in the face'.[8] Continuing in the delusion that Britain could play a global role without effective armed forces would result inevitably in 'the last vestiges of international respect [being] very rapidly ... shredded away'.[9] In fact, Britain still had a long way to fall in 1968.

The 1960s also witnessed the emergence of a popular counter-culture which saw itself in opposition to an ill-defined 'system' or 'the Establishment' and which elevated the ramblings of pop stars to the status of social and political wisdom. At what was arguably the premier popular cultural event of the late twentieth century, the Woodstock Festival, the band Sly and the Family Stone declared that war was good for 'Absolutely Nothing' without noticing that it had been rather effective in ending slavery and Nazism. Simultaneously, the expansion of social and political science education resulted in the widespread acceptance of Marxism among the new intelligentsia, which saw in it both an explanation for the world and a blueprint for its re-making. It was true that this intellectual dominance was being increasingly challenged, but its influence was still visible enough in 1958 to convince Major Gwynne Jones that the ideological struggle for the West represented a greater danger than nuclear weapons: Moscow was 'the dynamic centre of an idea that can destroy us all without a single megaton explosion'.[10] This in itself was remarkable, for while Nazism had died in the bunker in Berlin, communism in its various permutations survived all attempts to equate the two. The behaviour of the Soviets in Hungary in 1956 and Prague in 1968 hardly dinted Marx's popularity (if not the Soviets'), producing at best a plethora of Trotskyite groupings and 'fellow travellers' who held the incredible view that all would have been well with the communist ideal had Trotsky, rather than Stalin, succeeded Lenin. What was worse, according to the editor of the *Journal* in 1974, was that an increasing number of those social scientists, 'especially sociologists', who chose to write on defence issues, did so without bothering to consult people in uniforms and exhibited 'a degree of dislike or suspicion of all applied violence which ... is extended to those actually in the military business'.[11] Admiral Plunkett-Ernle-Erle-Drax drew the conclusion from this state of intellectual debate and economic decline that 'any nation heading for trouble will decay from within before it is smitten from without'.[12]

No doubt there was an element of post-colonial Blimpishness abroad in the Institute during these years, but it remains the case that the declining number of people who had contact with the military through either experience or family connection was beginning to open an increasingly wide gap between the soldier and large parts of civil society.

The realities of the post-war world took a while to sink in, however, and in 1945 Britain still thought of itself as an independent, global power, a member of the 'Big Three' and with an imperial role to play. The Suez debacle of 1956 and the inability of Britain to afford its own nuclear weapons put paid to these pretensions; decolonisation and dependence on the US followed hand-in-hand, whatever the lingering dreams of using the Commonwealth as the basis of continued power and status.[13] The social and intellectual shifts that began on the university campuses quickly made it clear that large sections of the intelligentsia had an active revulsion to imperialism in any form and a marked aversion to military commitments of whatever nature. Even in Parliament, an interest in defence issues was usually confined to a handful of Conservatives and, unless it was concerned with nuclear disarmament and decolonisation, was an anathema to most Labour MPs. The Vietnam War also acted as an enormous catalyst to the growth of anti-Americanism in Britain, which fitted conveniently into the anti-capitalist/imperialist/ establishment zeitgeist of the times. This meant that by the end of the 1970s, there were substantial elements within the Labour Party prepared to see a Socialist Republic of Great Britain, devoid of its nuclear weapons, withdrawn from NATO and resolutely opposed to anything that might make Britain look like, in the popular phrase of the times, 'the 51st State of the US'. The 1983 Labour election manifesto brought this process to its nadir (or apogee, depending on one's point of view) when it committed the party to unilateral nuclear disarmament, abolition of the House of Lords, the establishment of a centrally planned economy and withdrawal from the European Union.[14] This reality was, it is fair to say, met with a certain amount of dismay within the Labour Party itself – Gerald Kaufman, then a Labour shadow minister, declared it to be 'the longest suicide note in history' – and produced both the defection of the 'Gang of Four' to form the Social Democrat Party (SDP) and, a little later, the genesis of the New Labour project.

The shifts in the political and social landscape of the 1960s and early 1970s greatly complicated the problems that those actively involved in defence strategy had to address. Any strategic or tactical debate was now likely to involve a much wider input from civil society than ever before, much of which was actively sceptical of military perspectives, and which thus attracted attention that often felt onerous to the military thinkers. Of course, the most important challenges came from the existence of nuclear arms and the vast weight of the Red Army on the Inner German Border, but there was still Britain's dependence on the sea and the security of its trade to consider. It was also the case that Britain would continue to fight wars that looked very like the small wars of Victorian times, but this time the aim was to contain Soviet imperialism or prevent its encroachment into newly independent states.

Nuclear War

The fact that humanity now had the means to annihilate itself in a very short time indeed entered into the mainstream of popular culture and consciousness during the 1950s, when it became clear that the Hiroshima and Nagasaki bombs had elevated strategic bombing to a new level. Science fiction authors quickly seized on the plot possibilities of a post-apocalyptic world with *There Will Come Soft Rains* (Ray Bradbury, 1950), *The Chrysalids* (John Wyndham, 1955) and *A Canticle for Leibowitz* (Walter M Miller Jnr, 1960). This established a genre that would eventually result in such Hollywood blockbusters as *Mad Max* and *Waterworld*. Nevil Shute's 1957 *On the Beach* remains a classic, as does Stanley Kubrick's *Dr Strangelove* (1964), while Spike Milligan's *The Bed-Sitting Room* (1963) is hard to beat for its sheer eccentricity. Popular music could not resist the theme either and Tom Lehrer contributed 'We Will All Go Together When We Go' in 1959, Bob Dylan gave us 'Talkin' World War III Blues' in 1963 and Don Maclean recorded 'American Pie' in 1971. Nor was the basic premise of being bombed back into the Stone Age in a general nuclear exchange fanciful; the highly secret US National Security Council Net Evaluation Subcommittee expected as many as 150 million US casualties after a 'Massive Intercontinental Nation Killing Attack'.[15]

What was debated, however, was the likelihood of a surprise 'first strike' and the measures necessary to survive it and deliver the crushing retaliatory blow that guaranteed a deterrent effect. The plethora of weapon systems that followed, whether MRBM, ICBM, SLBM, ALBM, MRV, MIRV, follow-on bombers and ABM, were all designed to do no more than ensure that enough nuclear warheads survived this first strike. The willingness of the Russians to risk the retaliation was based on an assumption that a massive attack on the US would be combined with a conventional attack on Western Europe which would leave it in control of the only viable industrial base left. That the Soviet leadership might risk its own physical survival by initiating a first strike was the great unknowable factor, but the fear was of extreme ideologues gaining control of the Politburo – more madmen who considered themselves to be sane. This would then raise the issue as to whether a pre-emptive strike to disable the Soviet first strike would become a possibility and thus pose the same questions for the Soviet leadership that the US was trying to answer. This was about as circular an argument as one could wish for and for Britain (and France), it was an even stronger argument for maintaining their own independent nuclear weapons in the event that the Soviets demanded London, Paris, Rome and Bonn as the price of not blowing up New York, Boston, Los Angeles and Washington. The great advantage of an independent deterrent was that whatever the escalation in the size of nuclear arsenals, they did not negate the force of a smaller one, so awesome was the power that they contained. 'One sword keeps another in its scabbard' was a new maxim for RUSI in 1950.[16]

Britain's decision to build its own atomic weapons was taken in October 1946 after the US decided to end co-operation with Britain in this area. The tough Labour foreign secretary, Ernest Bevin, whose experience of dealing with communists in the trade union movement had taught him a real hatred for them, understood quickly that Stalin was going to push his advantages to the limit and decided that for both the long and short term, Britain would need both US support in Europe and its own atomic weapons if Soviet expansionism was to be contained. Despite the instincts of much of the Left of the Labour Party to seek a friendly accommodation with Stalin, there were sufficient numbers on the more pragmatic right of the party who saw no difficulty in being both a socialist and an anti-communist. By 1952, Britain had developed its own A-bomb, and by 1957 it had tested the Hydrogen bomb which was to be carried by the new V-bomber force. Building a bomb was one thing, but it was the cost of the delivery system that became the real stumbling block and the cancellation of the Blue Streak missile underlined Britain's inability to pay for them. Extending the life of the V-bombers by buying the US Skybolt missile was thought to be the next best option, but, when this programme was scrapped by the US, Macmillan took the plunge and bought both the weapon and the delivery system 'off the shelf' from the US. Britain's independent nuclear deterrent was now based on the American SLBM Polaris, which raised questions as to just how independent it actually was. This was a point that was discussed in the 'Editor's Notes' of February 1963 in the context of the Cuban Missile Crisis, which had been resolved without reference to Britain, but which would have drawn Britain into war had things gone otherwise. The fact that the 'special relationship' was not an association of equals was realised very early on at RUSI, however hurtful the concept was to national pride.

Strategy

How to cope with the threat from the Soviet Union without risking a general nuclear exchange provoked some interesting debates too. In 1959's 'How Strong is Russia?', Brigadier Davidson-Houston, late military attaché in Moscow, argued that the huge commitment to its armed forces entailed serious problems for Russia in the future. Over-manning, inefficiency, centralised decision-making, bureaucracy and the absorption by the military of vast amounts of educated talent meant that civilian industry and agriculture were starved and thus Russia was weakened in the long term. Russia's commitments overseas contributed to overstretch and its support for anti-colonial independence movements would rebound when Eastern European nationalism revived – as Davidson-Houston was confident it would. What was more, the intense propaganda of the regime would, in the end, be rejected by people whose everyday experience belied the 'achievements' of the Soviet state. The implication of this was that all the West had to do was hold on long enough and the Soviet Union would collapse under its own weight.

With hindsight we can see how accurate this analysis was but at the time no-one could tell just how long this might take, or if a reformer like Khrushchev might actually succeed. In a similar vein, a rising star of the Institute, Michael Howard, argued that strategic nuclear weapons were really unusable, as their deployment would represent a national suicide that could not be justified by reference to any vital interest and that neither side would therefore be prepared to use them. Throughout the 1960s this became RUSI orthodoxy, and the run-down of conventional forces was criticised largely on the grounds that it brought the nuclear option ever closer. The rather cavalier attitude of Senator Barry Goldwater to nuclear weapons exhibited during the 1964 US elections ('Let's lob one into the men's room in the Kremlin') sent a shiver down the spine of RUSI in this respect.[17] What would be a threat was 'limited' war, as identified by another rising star, Henry Kissinger, in which communist states, believing themselves to have time – and indeed history itself – on their side would gradually try to sap away at the will of the West to resist; Britain's defence policy should, Howard argued, rest on greater conventional weapons deployed as a flexible response to Soviet 'limited' aggression.[18]

The Red Army: Conventional War in Europe

The potential of the Red Army to mop up the ruined states of Western Europe just as they had those of Eastern Europe began to exercise thinkers in Britain and the US even before the war against Germany had been won. The problem was that both France and Italy contained substantial communist parties which, despite oft-repeated protestations to the contrary, were far more inclined towards the Soviet Union than towards the US. Yet the thought of using the Wehrmacht to fight the Soviets while still in the process of killing it would need a public relations effort of Orwellian proportions to convince the British people of its necessity. This was especially the case when the Labour Party was preparing to campaign on a platform of rapid demobilisation. Nevertheless, Churchill had asked for a report on the prospects of resisting a Red Army advance in May 1945 in Operation *Unthinkable*, in which the prospects of a quick blow to liberate Poland were assessed. Churchill noted the 2:1 numerical advantage that the Red Army enjoyed over British and American forces. The Joint Planning Staff noted that a quick blow might succeed, 'but it might not. That is for the Russians to decide. If they want total war, they are in a position to have it'.[19] Nevertheless, it was quickly understood by all sides in the immediate post-war world that Russian aggression would result in a nuclear strike followed up by an invasion of Eastern Europe. The answer to the question as to how that might be achieved meant that Britain would need to maintain an army on the continent as part of the collective security arrangements that produced NATO. This was a revolutionary development in British foreign policy and the permanent basing of the BAOR in Germany represented an unprecedented continental commitment. It also meant that there would be no rapid demobilisation of Britain's armed forces in the post-war period and conscription was reintroduced in the form of National Service in 1948 and not ended until 1960.

In the first decade after the war, military strategy considered war with the Soviet Union in terms of its experience in the Second World

War, with victory going to the side with the most effective blitzkrieg. As Germany joined NATO in 1955, this idea was reinforced by the understandable reluctance of the Bonn government to yield territory to the Russians: during the 1961 Berlin Crisis, the Germans were talking of forcing a way into the city overland. Nuclear weapons would be used to prepare the ground in front of the attacking forces, but after the development of Soviet tactical nuclear weapons, this idea had to be given up because NATO offensive concentrations would simply be blown apart before they could strike. This moved NATO onto a defensive 'tripwire' strategy in which the overwhelming wisdom was that NATO ground forces would have to conduct a fighting retreat as far back as the Rhine and then, if the politicians could not arrange an equitable ceasefire or if the forces could not impose a 'pause' in the Soviet advance, deploy tactical nuclear weapons to defeat the Red Army. What that meant for escalation was anyone's guess; the pessimists felt that a general nuclear exchange was inevitable, while the optimists thought that the leadership of both sides would pull back from the brink having had a foretaste of what was possibly to come. There was a corresponding worry that Western political leaders, assumed to be less ideologically driven than their communist counterparts, would not authorise the use of nuclear weapons and thus accept defeat, dictatorship and the gulags as the price of human survival – giving rise to the phrase 'Better Red than Dead'. This, in turn, would expose them to endless nuclear blackmail.

At the operational level there was a great deal of debate about how to actually fight the Red Army in the field. Would it, for example, be better to dig in on a newer version of the Maginot Line, attack the more numerous but technologically less-advanced Soviets with mobile forces or go straight to an invasion of Eastern Europe? In 1951, Lieutenant General Giffard Martel took the view that twenty armoured divisions based around a twenty-ton tank would be enough to beat the Red Army – which was remarkable given the appearance of the T-34-85 medium and JS III heavy tanks in the Soviet armoured

forces. Martel had been involved with the development of armour
since 1916, had commanded the Royal Armoured Corps and headed
the British military mission to Russia where he had observed the
Battle of Kursk first hand in 1943. But Martel remained convinced
that the Red Army was a paper tiger. Its armoured forces were, he
argued, only a 'circus' to frighten foreign representatives, 'impressive
but merely a shop window with nothing much behind it'.[20] This
was an overstatement and went directly in the face of much of the
Wehrmacht's experience. Major General F W Von Mellenthin, who
had also been at Kursk, held the view that Soviet armoured forces
took a long time to develop, but by 1944 were truly formidable. He
argued in his memoirs *Panzer Battles* that:[21]

> Today, any realistic plan for European defence must visualize that the air
> fleets and tank armies of the Soviet Union will throw themselves upon
> us with a velocity and fury far eclipsing any blitzkrieg of WWII.

J M Spaight came out of retirement to offer his thoughts on the
tactical air war and argued that massive use of air power against the
Red Army's lines of communication would do much to stop it. Martel
argued that the Red Army's logistic arrangements were so poor that
they would rapidly break down;[22] Mellenthin again argued that it
was an army that did not need anything like the logistic support
expected in the West. What Martel had done, however, was to start
a long-running debate about the effectiveness, or lack thereof, of
the Red Army, which would lead to longstanding (and traditional)
accusations that the generals were talking up the threat in order to
gain more funds.

The tactical debate was also visited often in the *Journal*. In 1951,
Lieutenant Colonel Carver was arguing in 'Tanks and Infantry: The
Need for Speed' that the lessons of the last war were being forgotten
as infantry and armoured regiments reverted back to their separate
training schedules after having operated together inside armoured

brigades throughout the war. He argued that the practice of training
for the 'set-piece' infantry attack and the armoured 'pursuit' ignored
the experience of 1939–45, which saw many operations that had
elements of both types in combination. What was worse was that
the time taken to 'marry up' units (familiarising standard operating
procedures and communications equipment) would fatally slow any
response to a rapid armoured thrust by the enemy. He particularly
criticised the long 'O' groups, which substituted meticulous planning
for the initiative of junior leaders. In short, Carver was hinting at the
vital importance of what would become Battle Group training and
C3I – Command, Control, Communications and Intelligence.[23]

> Speed on the battlefield ... depends most of all on speed in acquiring and
> disseminating information, making decisions, issuing and transmitting
> orders and, most of all, transmitting them into action.

In 1954, Major General H E Pyman, who had lately commanded
11th Armoured Division BAOR, gave his views on how armour would
be used in conjunction with nuclear weapons in 'Armour in the Land
Battle' and concluded that they would be an excellent way to destroy
either enemy concentrations or 'shatter sectors of defensive systems
to a considerable depth *in an instant*' and thus create the conditions
for a (British) armoured breakout constituted from dispersed forces.
At this stage the nuclear weapons under discussion were Hiroshima-
type weapons, and so this was a good contemporary analysis. What
was perhaps disturbing was the lack of distinction made by many
authors between 'nuclear' and 'conventional' weapons as representing
different orders of violence in this and other analyses; Pyman assumed
that 'we can be certain ... that in the event of another great war
atomic weapons will be used by the contestants'.[24] Both Carver and
Pyman made the point, hammered away since 1918, that infantry
needed to be in armoured personnel carriers (APCs) and not rely on
hanging onto the back of a tank or jolting along in lorries as they

had, for the most part, in the Second World War. There would be progress in this area with the introduction of the Saracen in 1952, but the British Army would continue to lag behind other armies on this issue.

With the appearance in 1955 of the Corporal surface-to-surface guided missile in American units, the debate then moved on to just how tactical nuclear weapons might be used. In 1962, the historian and journalist Anthony Verrier challenged the ability of tactical nuclear weapons to impose a 'pause' after observing the BAOR exercises of late 1961 in 'Strategic Thinking in Europe: Reflections on "Spearpoint" and "Bootjack"'. In Exercise *Spearpoint* the attacking forces had feinted so well and attacked so quickly that the nuclear strike went completely awry – a 47 kiloton strike on a supposed HQ only 'killed' a single despatch rider because the HQ was 40 miles away. He also made the point that BAOR *did not have any tactical nuclear weapons* and therefore any decision to deploy them would be a political decision dependent on the Americans and thus, inevitably, the strike would be delayed even further. This was not a problem that was resolved when BAOR did get tactical nuclear weapons like the 1960s' Honest John and 1970s' Lance missile because there was still uncertainty over who actually controlled the warheads. There was also a massive upgrading of Soviet equipment during the 1960s which, to a certain extent, left NATO forces standing as all Soviet mechanised infantry divisions were converted to Motor Rifle Divisions. The introduction of the T-72 to counter European tanks such as the Chieftain and Leopard 1 sparked a debate about whether the superior quality of NATO tanks could match the sheer numbers that the Warsaw Pact could field – and the gap in quality looked to be narrowing rapidly. In 'Shield-72', a study of Warsaw Pact exercises, the view given was that the Soviets would use tactical nuclear weapons from the outset and follow this up with an armoured offensive which featured the seizure and creation of river crossings by amphibious and airborne forces.[25] Crucially, they had introduced the BMP-1 infantry fighting vehicle (IFV) in 1967, which would allow infantry to fight in an NBC environment and which was more than a match for the US M-57 and the British AFV-432, which clung to the old concept of an APC being a 'battle taxi'. Likewise, the wheeled BTR-60 APC was a vast improvement on the Bedford Four-Tonner (more formally known as the Bedford MK) for moving troops around the battlefield.

In the air too, Soviet forces seemed to be narrowing the quality gap at the same time as producing quantitative superiority with the introduction of the MiG-23 Flogger and MiG-25 Foxbat fighters and the Mi-24 Hind helicopter gunship, which, as a flying IFV, had no Western equivalent. By the early 1970s, the concept of the 'pause' was looking increasingly beleaguered as Soviet conventional forces took on an ever more formidable aspect.

Sea Power

The continental commitment demolished any lingering hopes that there could be a return to a 'British way' in warfare, of relying on naval strength for its security and avoiding the bloodshed inherent in pitched battles and long campaigns. The fact that air power, as demonstrated by the Japanese sinking of the *Repulse* and *Prince of Wales* in 1941 and by the Americans at the Battle of Midway in 1942, was now deadly to any fleet in the North Sea, English Channel and most of the North Atlantic raised the question of what a navy could actually do in a European war. Lord Granville, president of the Navy League, thought more battleships were in order,[26] but Montgomery declared in a lecture given at the Institute in October 1954 entitled 'A Look Through a Window at World War III'[27] that aircraft carriers (and by extension, all large ships) were now obsolete for use in European waters.

The reality was that the army, backed up by tactical air support, was now the main guarantor of British security and the future would require the senior service to give up the sort of independence that Sir John Fisher had claimed for it before 1914. This was a hard pill to swallow and Captain Pelly hung on to the notion that the protection of commerce would be the basis on which a future war would be won 'in exactly the same way as it was in 1942'.[28] This was simply untenable; the war would be won or lost long before Britain would be starved out. Soviet Russia's decision to build an ocean-going navy, made plain in Admiral Gorshkov's *Red Star Rising at Sea* (1974), emphasised the fact that the Royal Navy was no longer capable of winning a naval battle against the Russians except in conjunction with the US Navy or with massive support from the RAF. In 1965, Commander Clarkson argued that the defeat of Soviet submarine forces – estimated at 400 strong – had to be the navy's top priority and that the naval building programme should concentrate on anti-submarine and mine-sweeping vessels. This was challenged by Admiral Gretton, who argued that any mass submarine attack against trade or the navy would only come as a result of all-out war and that the ultimate decision would be made by nuclear forces. The corollary was that the navy should produce 'commando carriers' for use in the Indian Ocean and the Gulf where British power would still need to be projected to resist communist encroachment and protect the oil supply.[29] It was a long way from Trafalgar and Colomb, but it was still a sensible concept. Indeed, the previous year, the commando carrier HMS *Bulwark* had been deployed to East Africa to put down a series of mutinies brought on by the incompetence of one of the doyens of the new post-colonial Africa, Julius Nyerere. In reality, the navy was entering some dangerous shallows: it could not affect the outcome of the battle on the Rhine, was increasingly vulnerable to air power and was probably a sitting duck against the Russian submarine force. Unless it retained its power-projection capability it would inevitably face redundancy. Without Polaris and an expeditionary capability, the navy was looking increasingly vulnerable. Macmillan's decision to buy the SLBM did indeed give the navy a reinvigorated role but its surface fleet would suffer death from a thousand cuts until the 1982 Falklands war emphasised the need to retain an expeditionary capability.

Small Wars

Despite the withdrawal from India and Palestine in 1947, the Soviet takeover of Eastern Europe and the triumph of the communists in China meant that American desires to see the end of the British Empire became muted as the realisation grew that Britain might well be a useful ally in the policy of containment. British success in confronting a communist insurgency in Malaya, plus its major bases in Singapore and Egypt ensured its value as a member of both SEATO and CENTO even as decolonisation progressed and Britain maintained a strong presence in the Far East and the Persian Gulf until the early 1970s. This meant involvement in several wars in what became known as 'out-of-area operations', which were designed to halt communist insurgencies or to protect the fragile new states that were emerging from the wreck of the Empire. In conducting these wars the British had a wealth of imperial experience to draw on, which they would develop to become, arguably, the leaders on counter-insurgency warfare (COIN) in both theory and practice for the next five decades.

From the beginning it was realised that 'it is no good crying them [the guerrillas] down as gangsters, terrorists, communists and so on',[30] and that a proper strategy had to be put in place if the armies sent to fight them were not to be paralysed. Lieutenant Colonel Oatts defined the main characteristic of a guerrilla as someone fighting on his own territory with a fair degree of support among his own people; the forces were irregular in size but drawn from and adapted to their own localities. They were also centrally directed but permitted wide initiative and did not respect the rules of war as understood by conventional forces – they would freely surrender, claim that they had been pressed and then desert back at the earliest opportunity. Nor would the guerrilla stand up and take casualties in a 'fair' fight, but would always consider discretion to be the better part of valour and so live to fight another day. Attempting to send in small groups of regulars to fight fire with fire was a short road to disaster, argued Oatts; and defeating the guerrillas through 'the slow laborious occupation of the country', as had been used in the South African war, was impractical because the communist guerrillas had no desire to enjoy peace for its own sake. This was hinting at the concept that a professional revolutionary did not see peace and war as separate states but interwoven ones; one could be a farmer one moment and a fighter the next without the Western transition from 'civilian' to 'soldier' status.

Oatts believed the best counter was to recruit one's own guerrillas from the local population, which, again, tackled the important concept that guerrilla wars were not only fought against an external occupier, but also against internal competitors for power. As such, they were as much civil wars as wars of liberation from external occupation. This seemed to discount the development of special forces to act in small groups against insurgents that had been a feature of Britain's long imperial experience and more recent employment of groups like the Long Range Desert Group, Special Air Service, Special Boat Squadron and Special Operations Executive during the 1939–45 war. A year later, in the *Journal*'s 'The Campaign against the Terrorists in Malaya', Air Vice Marshal Francis Mellersh underscored the primacy of civil action in combating insurgency:[31]

> This campaign is not, in the strict sense of the term, a military operation. It is a problem for the Civil Administration and it is, first and foremost, a Police affair.

Mellersh correctly isolated the basic problem that a large, disaffected, poor, immigrant Chinese population was watching to see 'whether Communism is going to swamp Democracy' and that however successful military operations might have been in 1949, they would ultimately fail unless the civil administration did better. The Briggs Plan of 1950 aimed to defeat the insurgents by more effective administration for the entire population, appealing to the Chinese population in particular in order to cut the insurgents off from their sources of supply. Gerald Templer's subsequent success in defeating the Malayan communists by appealing to 'hearts and minds' was largely based on this approach; his masterstroke was an insistence on full citizenship rights for the immigrant Chinese. It was the realisation that insurgencies required a political solution supported by force of arms that distinguished British success in Malaya from the French disasters in Vietnam and Algeria – and in those years the French army was nothing like the broken sword of 1940.

When the Americans took their turn in the counter-insurgency fight in Vietnam, the results were nothing less than disastrous. In the topsy-turvy world of 1960s popular culture and protest, the dictatorship of Ho Chi Minh was turned into a heroic opposition to American 'imperialism', while poor leadership and a perverse system of maintaining a permanently inexperienced army in Vietnam through the rotation of both individuals and units led to the virtual internal collapse of the American army. Public opinion in the US was also undermined by a largely unrestrained media on a scale never before experienced – to the point where returning troops were rejected and treated with contempt by many. One only needs a cursory reading of the first parts of Norman Schwarzkopf's *Storm Command*, with its picture of lieutenants in red shorts and beards alongside colonels who never exited the bunker, to get a feel of how bad things became. But this need not have been the case; indeed, in a lecture presented to the Institute in 1965, Colonel Marion C Dalby USMC showed a very full understanding of Viet Cong tactics and what needed to be done to win hearts and minds there.[32]

> The basis of everything is the peasant, who needs social and economic conditions which will permit him to make a decent life for himself .... the Viet Cong have made the security situation so bad ... that he has little hope of finding this decent life .... The soldier must hold a sort of protective umbrella over the countryside while schools are built, teachers

trained, agricultural methods are improved .... These are actually as much a part of the soldiers' mission as military combat.

Dalby also pointed to one of the main advantages that the Viet Cong enjoyed: the initiative. With secure bases in North Vietnam, large covert units in South Vietnam and virtual control over those areas of Laos and Cambodia that constituted the Ho Chi Minh trail, they could choose to strike whenever they pleased and could then retire away from effective US retaliation. What was depressing was that neither of these pieces of wisdom was acted upon with sufficient vigour as discipline began to break down in substantial parts of the US forces. In October 1972, Sir Robert Thompson, the doyen of British COIN theory and practice, lectured at RUSI on 'The War in Vietnam: Reflections on Counter-Insurgency Operations' – arguing that the war was still winnable and that there was still a lot of life in the South Vietnamese Army. This, however, was wishful thinking. The follow-up came in 1973 when Professor Donald Cameron-Watt gave a blistering critique of what went wrong in 'Lessons of the American Defeat in Vietnam' in which he argued that a 'self-seeking intellectual elite' based in the universities and military believed that sociological and political doctrines put into practice in Vietnam could transform it into a modern prosperous democracy and thus undermine communist influence. Unfortunately, they did not understand local conditions and failed to counter the Viet Cong's ability to assassinate the lower and middle leadership of Vietnamese society who were supposed to bring about this transformation. This led them into a situation of denial which finally resulted in 'internal deceit and external misrepresentation'. The situation was then compounded by both the television coverage and returning veterans who exposed the rotten state of the US military in Vietnam and undermined any claims of 'a civilising mission and general humanitarianism' and allowed opponents of the war 'to lead American opinion to ignore completely the crimes, massacres and brutalities committed by their

Vietcong enemy'. Defeat was hard to stomach of course but, argued Cameron-Watt:[33]

> What America's European allies have to ponder and worry over is … the weakness of the American machinery of state … to control and command public support in any but the most short haul of military efforts … and to hope that it does not result in a new withdrawal from a wicked, alien and un-American world.

This was a remarkably good analysis of both the failure of the US military in Vietnam, but also of the dangers of the unrestrained anti-Americanism present in the British and European popular imagination.

The Banqueting House Disaster

Digging up the pavements outside the Institute in 2009 revealed the foundations of the Tudor palace of Westminster, more properly known as York Place, but even in Tudor times popularly known as Whitehall. The Institute was formerly the site of a suite of offices used by the Lord Keeper of the Great Seal, looking out onto the Privy Garden, which stretched as far as Downing Street, with a bowling green beyond. Opposite were the Treasury offices, tennis court and cockpit on a site which sprawled across the present Dover House and the Cabinet Office buildings. It was never one of Henry VIII's favourite palaces – he preferred the rural surroundings of Hampton Court or Greenwich and used Bridewell, by Blackfriars Bridge, if he really had to stay in the city. This might have been the result of a guilty conscience proceeding from the fact that he had stolen Whitehall from Cardinal Wolsey in 1530. He did find it convenient on one particular occasion, 6 November 1540, to use it for the purpose of meeting his councillors to decide what to do with his fifth wife, Catherine Howard. She, being young, attractive and athletic had appetites that the older Henry was not entirely able to cope with and she had, therefore, sought out extra company in the foolish belief that it was possible to keep secrets in a Tudor court. On 13 February 1542, she was executed at the Tower of London after one lover, Thomas Culpepper, had been beheaded and another, Francis Dereham, had been 'hanged, castrated, disembowelled, beheaded and quartered'.[34]

James I had intended to redevelop the palace at Whitehall after a fire had ripped through it in 1619, but he had got no further than the building of the Banqueting House in 1622 by the noted architect, Inigo Jones. His son, Charles I, employed Rubens to paint the ceiling between 1630 and 1634 but probably wished the thing had never been built in the first place because it was from a first-floor window that he was carried out onto the scaffold in 1649 for his decapitation at the end of the English Civil War. Miserable from the January cold, he had asked for two shirts so that the regicides would not mistake his shivering for fear. What remained of the Tudor palace was then destroyed by two successive fires in 1691 and 1698, which left only the Banqueting House standing. George I designated it the Chapel Royal, also known as the Whitehall Chapel, and it remained an under-used white elephant until the Institute took it over in 1893. As already mentioned, this acquisition was regarded with a certain ambiguity in political circles and the Institute had to fight several battles before 1945 to retain control of it. Within a very few years it would have to fight another more serious eviction attempt, and this time, it would lose – to another headless man.

This was a great tragedy because the Institute came out of the Second World War in good shape, both intellectually and financially, having made £2,000 despite the extra expenses of moving the Library and Museum. The *Journal* continued to provide a wealth of interesting material looking forward to the changed conditions of warfare, drawing on the lessons of the last war and looking back into history. In 1948, there were articles on 'Atomic Energy', 'Australia's Experimental Rocket Range', 'The Strategic Bomber Campaign against Germany' and 'The Home Fleet in the War' and 'Army Doctors in the XVIIIth Century'. Current affairs were also covered with articles on Palestine, Pakistan, India, Korea and Berlin, while the eccentric was not forgotten in 'Toasts in the Army'. There were also articles which carried on the long tradition of bringing to light issues that were unlikely to get an airing anywhere else, including 'Ireland's Naval Policy', 'Mercenaries' and 'Physiological Aspects of High Speed Flight'. There was even a note of post-war hedonism in the proposal to open a bar in the Institute (a proposal that was quickly quashed),[35] while the RAF again felt that it had now done enough to get its badge included on the Institute crest (they had not). Still, at least smoking would now be allowed.[36] Donations to the Museum continued to arrive, too. In 1951, the commander-in-chief of the newly independent Indian Army, General K M Cariappa, presented a collection of British–Indian Army cap badges to the Institute, which remain on display today. There was, however, a blow to be suffered with the death of Captain Altham in 1950.

The change of the guard did allow for a reorganisation of the management of the Institute with the separation of the duties of the secretary and the editor, now Lieutenant Colonel P S M Wilkinson and Major General R E Vyvyan respectively. For many, Altham's domination of these two posts had been irksome, especially as he began to gain a reputation for being 'difficult' and it is possible that his part-time editorship of the *Journal* had produced the sometimes lacklustre insights into international affairs that were a feature of the later wartime editions. The Institute also began to suffer financial problems once again. Austerity Britain meant that there was little spare cash for museum outings and by 1958 the low subscription rates meant that the Institute would run out of cash by 1962 unless something was done. In October 1958, the decision was taken to appeal for a government grant to keep the Museum afloat. This, however, provided the opportunity that the government had been seeking since 1890 – they wanted the Banqueting House and they were now in a position to force the Institute out of it. Duncan Sandys, minister of defence in the Macmillan government, had had his eye on the building since 1945 when, after visiting the Institute in his role as minister of works, had suggested that the Banqueting House might be traded for Apsley House.[37] In 1950, the Museum had been forced to close temporarily so that the Rubens ceiling might be restored in time for the 1951 Festival of Britain and by 1951 the chairman of the council was convinced that 'certain government officials' were plotting against the Institute again and that it was time to consider the 'best line of defence'.[38]

There were questions in Parliament about the Museum again in 1953, while the claim of the Institute to be the repository of the nation's military and naval history was increasingly undermined by the establishment of the Imperial War Museum after the First World War, the National Maritime Museum in 1934 (a project that the Institute had supported since 1906)[39] and the National Army Museum in 1960. Unable to resist the opportunity, a campaign was led by the traitor Sir Anthony Blunt (one of the Cambridge Five) in his guise as director of the Courtauld Institute of Art to evict the Institute from the Banqueting House on artistic grounds.[40] The blow fell in July 1960 when Lord John Hope, minister of works, made it clear that the Institute was to be blackmailed into eviction with the offer of a confirmed lease of the extension until 2000 if they went quietly.[41] He also insisted that this offer was entirely off the record and when the Institute tried to appeal directly to the prime minister, threatened to 'rack rent' them out.[42] The prime minister and Minister of Defence Duncan Sandys turned down the Institute's appeal and, despite a last minute plan to relocate to the Tower of London, the fate of the Museum was sealed. 'The prospect of State banquets and entertainments presented such a dazzling picture' to Macmillan, Sandys and Hope that they ignored the reality that the Banqueting House was completely unsuitable because it had no catering facilities.[43] At an Extraordinary Meeting on 15 January

1962, it was announced that the Museum was to be closed and its collections broken up. Closing the Museum doors for the last time in September was the worst day the Banqueting House had seen since 1649. Duncan Sandys, who could have saved it, was at that point involved in an affair with the Duchess of Argyll – his part in which he managed to conceal when it became public in 1963 because the photographic record of a group sex session involving himself, the Duchess and Douglas Fairbanks Jnr revealed him only from the neck downwards.[44] A headless man had decapitated RUSI.

As if to add insult to injury, the charity commissioners in next-door Gwydyr House decided to repay the Institute's attempts to annex their building. In a completely unnecessary intervention, they decided to oppose the sale of museum artefacts on the grounds that they were charitable donations and therefore not disposable to the financial credit of the Institute. This was no more than 'legal mumbo-jumbo'[45] and served only to delay the sale for a year and increase the level of frustration already experienced. There was no shortage of takers either: the Glenbow Foundation of Calgary, Canada, backed by the Canadian government, offered to buy the whole of RUSI Museum outright for £100,000. Sotheby's was interested in the complete set of Hakluyt Society publications which raised £861 when sold, while several private collectors were interested in the ship models. Siborne's Waterloo models went to the National Army Museum, while the dioramas of Ceasar's landing in Britain, Crecy, Blenheim, Waterloo and Balaclava went to Canada; *Marston Moor* went to the Castle Museum at York; *Flers 1915* and the *Normandy Landings* to the Imperial War Museum; *Hastings* went (naturally) to Hastings Town Hall and *Queen Elizabeth I at Tilbury* went to Thurrock Museum, Tilbury. Altogether they had cost £7,500 to install; Sotheby's valued them at £1,275. The government would offer no compensation, however, and only grudgingly agreed to pay £5,000 to cover removal expenses. If this was not bad enough, the Banqueting House would be re-opened to the public on 22 September 1964, but:[46]

As water supply is very difficult and it is impossible to install large kitchens, any idea of large entertainment was quickly abandoned though not mentioned. The complete absence of ante-rooms, powder rooms, cloak rooms etc had perhaps also been overlooked. It will be exhibited redecorated but empty and it is proposed to charge visitors a shilling a head....

One can only trust that the empty Banqueting House will be as popular with the public as it was when it housed the well known military collection of the RUSI.

This turned out not to be the case, and even today caterers have to bring everything with them. 'The most beautiful building in London is almost entirely ignored by Londoner and Tourist alike', according to *The Times* in 1970.[47] Still, the controller of the Plant Variety Rights Office got to use it for his seedlings once. The only consolation for the Institute staff was that they would in time witness a further eviction – of the charity commissioners from Gwydyr House, to make way for the Welsh Office.

Re-orientating RUSI

There could be no disguising the blow that the Institute had suffered in terms of prestige but more important was the loss of a major source of revenue derived from museum receipts. In 1962, the *Journal* decided to step up its advertising efforts to try to fill this gap but this was never going to be enough in the face of Macmillan and Sandys' hostility. Michael Howard, serving on the *Journal* committee feared a 'national disaster' if the Institute failed,[48] especially as there was a growing hostility towards the Institute from 'shadowy figures'[49] in the Ministry of Defence, who saw it as an unnecessary rival to the educational courses being taught in the staff colleges and obstructed the publication of articles by serving officers in the *Journal*.[50] They also wanted to use the buildings as a luncheon club.[51]

This was at a time when, in the opinion of the US Naval Institute's *Naval Review*, the *Journal* was 'believed by some to be the best in the world'[52] – not bad considering the RAND Corporation employed forty times the number of staff. Over the winter of 1963–64, the secretary (now 'director') Brigadier J Stephenson brought together the chairman of the council, Air Chief Marshal Sir Claude Pelly, now working on weapons development at the Atomic Energy Authority, and Lieutenant General Sir John Cowley, recently retired as Master General of the Ordinance, to consider what the future of the Institute was to be. Their conclusions were blunt: the Institute would be out of business long before the present lease ran out in 1972 unless the government increased its grant. In order to persuade the government to do this, they would have to offer something valuable in return and this something would be a research institute able to take on government work.

The idea had already been floated in the letters page of the *Journal* in 1963, when it had been suggested that a 'British institute for strategic affairs' should be set up under the aegis of RUSI to bring together academics, government planners, industry and the services into a wider forum which recognised that 'the scientist, the economist, the sociologist and the industrialist all have their part to play'.[53] It should become the 'Royal United Services Institute for Defence Studies'.[54]

This was easier said than done. When the proposal was developed and presented to the Ministry of Defence (MoD) in September 1964, it was rejected; the MoD felt its own research unit would be preferable to shouldering the £40,000 per year cost of RUSI.[55] However, a confidential Joint RUSI-MoD working party was set up in May 1966,[56] which pitted the author Admiral Royer M Dick, Professor Michael Howard, the finance officer Brigadier J A Longmore and Director J Stephenson representing the Institute against Sir Henry Hardman who, despite being a retired air chief marshal, had little sympathy for RUSI. The Institute's proposals were again rejected. Not deterred, Dick and Stephenson managed to get a meeting with the Secretary of State for Defence, Denis Healey, on 9 February 1967 which promised to be more productive because Healey understood the value of research institutes, having served as a councillor for the Royal Institute of International Affairs and co-founded the International Institute for Strategic Studies with Michael Howard. Stephenson got Healey to agree in principle that RUSI would be funded to the tune of £50,000 per year and a working party was set up to see which studies and research tasks the Institute might undertake.[57] It was a golden moment: the Institute had again been rescued from financial meltdown. It was a shame that Brigadier Longmore could not share in it; filling the role of finance officer for twenty years had broken his health in December 1966.

The conclusion of the working party was that the Institute needed a complete reorganisation and a comprehensive expansion of both its activities and its staff. The Institute was now to have a dual role, providing information to an informed public through lectures, seminars, discussion groups and publications as it had always done, but also running a research department tasked with investigating subjects at the request of government. The government would pay the bulk of the Institute's costs but, in order to maintain its independence, it would still be expected to raise funds elsewhere. The membership was to be widened from a narrow service base to include more academics and more representatives from industries involved or interested in defence technologies with a new class of corporate membership to be introduced. There would also be the appointment of a director of studies supported by two research teams with access to classified information amidst a general expansion of staff numbers (with a pay rise) from ten full and four part-time staff to twenty-six full time. All would be overseen by a director-general, 'a man of established reputation and outstanding personality' who would 'enjoy the confidence of all concerned including the services and industry'. The whole aim was to provide 'a national institution outside of government in which the problems of Britain's overseas and defence policy can be objectively studied and discussed on a multi-disciplinary basis'.[58]

In effect, by widening the activities of the Institute from providing a forum for informed debate, the dissemination of ideas in the *Journal* and a lecture programme into active research, the modern Institute was born. A special general meeting was held on 12 October 1967 to agree the changes and the following year Air Vice Marshal Stuart 'Paddy' Menaul, lately the commandant of the Joint Services Staff College, became the first director general, with Hugh Hanning as the editor of the *Journal*. Hanning was a naval officer, a historian and journalist who believed that military forces ought to be used more for peacekeeping than fighting and, after leaving the Institute in 1970, did much to promote the cause of disaster relief.[59] The director of studies post had to wait a while to be filled but a strategic studies research wing was immediately set up to look into 'Britain's Armed Forces in the 1970s', 'The Relationship between Industry and the Armed Forces' and 'Future British Naval Strategy and Britain's Reserve Forces'. The driving forces behind this wing were, amongst others, Professor Michael Howard and Professor Bryan Ranft of the Royal Naval College, Greenwich.

The importance of an appeal to industry was clear (a fundraising campaign went ahead in 1968) in the first seminars held at the Institute: 'The Application of Space Technology to Defence Studies' and 'Military Aircraft Procurement and its Effect on the British Aerospace Industry'.[60] The Library had another reorganisation and the map room went – its contents were sold to the British Museum for £45,000 – in order to make room for the strategic studies wing.[61] The 'civilianisation' of RUSI was perhaps the most notable change in outward appearance of this reorganisation but, even then, Hanning was emphatic that 'the changes ... should not be allowed to give a misleading impression: the RUSI and all it has stood for will remain untouched. The changes will be additions not subtractions'.[62] By

1969, Hanning was convinced that the new Institute had recovered
its balance and was now on the way to confirming its place as *the*
British institute for defence studies; *Journal* sales were up 20 per cent,
young officers were contributing, the seminar report *Vietnam* (Sir
Robert Thompson had attended) had sold 300 copies in the US,
there was interest in the mainstream press and the study on 'Britain's
Reserve Forces' had drawn criticism from the government. MPs
were joining the Institute in growing numbers and a real dent had
been made in the ignorance of defence issues among the country's
influencers.[63] In 1970, in addition to the *Journal*, the range of
publications included contributions from the historians M R D Foot
and Anthony Nutting, the Bishop of Norwich, Anthony Farrar-
Hockley, Sir Frank Roberts from the Foreign Office and eleven MPs
amongst others equally distinguished. In 1971, Brigadier Shelford
'Ginger' Bidwell took over as editor and revamped the *Journal* to be
more lively – coloured covers were introduced – in an attempt to
move it away from being too closely associated with purely academic
publications. Bidwell was an artillery officer and military historian
of wide experience and a brusque manner – 'wet enough to shoot
snipe off'[64] was a favourite epithet applied to those he disliked –
but he was committed to widening the appeal of the Institute and
unafraid of expressing strong opinions through his editorial column.
The Institute thus entered the 1970s rejuvenated and reinvigorated –
which was more than could be said for the rest of the country.

Winds of Change

It could be argued that the Cold War reached its crisis during
the 1970s as it became increasingly apparent that the *détente* that
Western leaders had hoped for since the Cuban Missile Crisis looked
more like a one-way street. Soviet foreign policy remained aggressive
as it expanded its influence in Africa, the Middle and Far East
while keeping its iron grip on Eastern Europe. The Strategic Arms
Limitation Treaty processes took on a note of surrealism because

neither side would ever give up their ability to launch a devastating strike, while Soviet intelligence continued to support virtually any and all organisations that they thought might hurt Western defence. Such organisations ranged from the radical chic of Baader-Meinhof and the Brigado Rossi, through the frontline states of Black Africa (sub-Saharan Africa) and into the British Campaign for Nuclear Disarmament, whose governing body had a Stasi agent on it – an economics lecturer from Leeds University. West German Chancellor Willy Brandt found one in his private office, too, in 1973, which raised eyebrows at just how much influence Brezhnev had over his attempts to find a German rapprochement in his *Ostpolitik*.

American confidence was still in a state of collapse, brought on by the defeat in Vietnam, while the corresponding collapse of the British economy under the combined weight of the 1973 oil crisis and the continuing conflict with trade unions more interested in constructing a new socialist order, gave many the impression that the liberal democratic Western world was indeed staring defeat in the face.

Despite the Conservative's decision to try to reverse the destruction of the Territorial Army by the previous Labour government in the years 1970–74, the Labour government's Mason Review of 1974 saw a further cut to the armed forces, with expenditure dropping below 5 per cent of GDP with both manpower and overall spending to drop by 11–12 per cent over the next decade. The army lost its reserve division, the RAF had its transport fleet halved, airborne forces were sliced by two-thirds and amphibious forces were also punished. In 1976, a further Sterling crisis forced the final withdrawal of the last posts at Singapore and Gan in the Indian Ocean. Neither the Prime Minister Jim Callaghan or his increasingly beleaguered chancellor, Denis Healey, could do anything to resist the growing power of the Left of the party – now led by Michael Foot, a man whose sartorial elegance was a perfect metaphor for the state of the economy, and Tony Benn, regularly satirised by *Private Eye* as wearing a saucepan on his head and smoking a pipe through his ear. Both men were prepared to entertain notions of unilateral nuclear disarmament and withdrawal from NATO. With inflation rates as high as 16–24 per cent between 1974 and 1979, the intervention of the IMF and the endless absurdities of demarcation disputes, secondary picketing and pay differentials, it was clear that a crisis was approaching. As the uncollected rubbish piled up on the pavements and the bodies went unburied in what would become known as the 1978–79 'winter of discontent', it seemed that Britain had reached a true nadir.

There were, however, signs that change was in the air. From the mid-1970s, there was growing evidence that British university campuses were perhaps not as left-wing as had long been thought. The student unions might well have been dominated by groups of activists, but the main body of students were beginning to acquire an increasingly opposite view. The satire of left-wing politics in Monty Python's 1979 film *The Life of Brian* (for example, the People's Front of Judea spitting vituperation at the Judean Popular People's Front, and the absurd discussion about 'What have the Romans ever done for us?') would probably have fallen flat a very few years earlier. It was also the case that a growing number of university history, politics and international relations departments were beginning to turn out a growing number of students who had undergone some systematic study of war, strategy and foreign policy and were no longer necessarily willing to accept that history was on the side of the socialists and Soviets. Indeed, there would be a revolution, but it would come from the Right rather than the Left. The incredible popularity of the American soap opera *Dallas*, which began in 1978, also indicated that large numbers of British people aspired to a greater degree of conspicuous consumption and wealth than was on offer under consensus politics and nationalised industries. The 1990s stereotype 'Mondeo Man' was already in gestation during the 1970s, as frustration and disgust at the reluctance of the Labour Party to deal with the unions mounted.

Return to Dorking

In the face of the Mason cuts, RUSI was forced to go back to the Dorking scenario in order to put the case for the revival of Western defences. The original 'Battle of Dorking' had, as we have seen, been produced at a certain arm's length by the Institute in 1870, but this time there would be no attempt to conceal either the authorship or the intent. Indeed, not content with a single attempt at Dorkingism, the Institute would, in 1978, be involved with two books. The first of these was *World War 3: A Military Projection Based on Today's Facts* (1978), which came from the pen of Shelford Bidwell. It also contained contributions from soon to be Director-General Rear Admiral Teddy Gueritz and *Journal* contributor Anthony Verrier.

It was, however, General Sir John Hackett, late commander of NATO's Northern Army Group, who dominated this new Dorkingism with his fictionalised *The Third World War: August 1985* of 1978, reissued in 1982 as *The Third World War: The Untold Story*, for which the Institute awarded him the Chesney Gold medal in 1985. The idea for the book had originated after discussions with Denis Healey and several leading NATO officers in 1968, when Hackett was becoming increasingly concerned that the balance between NATO and the Warsaw Pact was swinging too much towards the latter. Convinced that the public needed to be reminded that NATO conventional forces had to kept strong in order to reduce the dependence on nuclear weapons, Hackett took the unusual step of writing to *The Times* in February 1968. This caused a minor stir about whether British generals should be engaging in politics which Hackett side-stepped by claiming to be, at that particular time, a NATO general and therefore within his rights. In the then economic clime, there was little that Hackett could do to influence the Labour government and so it was not until 1977 that a publisher approached him to write a future history, possibly on the prompting of Gueritz, who might have been less convinced of Bidwell's rival scenario.

Hackett's original set-up envisaged a long war in which a Soviet attack was successful in capturing West Germany and the Low Countries in ten days, after the West could not agree on the use of tactical nuclear weapons and a French communist-dominated government refused to honour its NATO commitments. The Soviets then offered a ceasefire, which the US declined and instead began an enormous military build-up on the Rhine facilitated by a change of heart in France. This draft ended with an assault across the Rhine, the defeat of the Soviets and the liberation of Europe, but was torn up after the German general Bennecke warned him that 'if a cautionary tale is to make children behave better, it is a mistake to pitch it so strongly that it only makes them wet their beds'.[65] General William DePuy, the American originator of the air/land battle concept, also commented enthusiastically on the draft, but argued that a more aggressive defence aimed at showing that NATO could win the first battle of the next war needed to be a feature of the book. Hackett then decided to re-write his tale to show what would need to be done if NATO was to hang on by the skin of its teeth (and thus give the publisher a happy ending). The magic wand was the appearance of a second British Corps constituted out of trained reserves and deployed to Germany as a counter-penetration force. The Soviets are held – just – at Venlo on the Dutch-German border after a massive B-52 strike, but both Birmingham and Minsk are sacrificed in nuclear strikes. The book sold three million copies in ten languages, generated a major debate and established Hackett as a well-respected TV pundit. It was hardly surprising that *The Times* noted the growing reputation of RUSI for 'stirring things up a bit'.[66] More importantly, it finally posed the question that the consensus politicians had been ducking since 1957: had the defences of the country been run down below minimum safe levels – again?

On both sides of the Atlantic, with the election of Ronald Reagan (1980) and Margaret Thatcher (1979), the answer came: yes. And it was now time to do something about it. The need to do so was doubly underlined on Christmas Eve 1979, when Soviet forces invaded Afghanistan, an act that was interpreted as a strategic move in the long 'Great Game' rather than as tactical support for a fractious puppet government, but which advertised the bankruptcy of *détente*. The new attitude was summed-up in Reagan's apocryphal question: 'The Cold War – we win, right?' It was reinforced by Margaret Thatcher's determined re-conquest of the Falkland Islands in 1982, which gave notice that the medicine already served up to the mangy lion of Britain was taking effect and a little more would soon see it roaring again. This attitude was shared by RUSI's new director general 1979–80, Teddy Gueritz, a man who had survived a torpedoing in the Mediterranean, served as a beachmaster in Normandy and then risen to be commandant of the Joint Warfare Establishment. Gueritz intended to take the debate to the opposition in no uncertain terms, as did his successor Group Captain David Bolton and his formidable *Journal* editor, Jennifer Shaw.

Much of the opposition to the subsequent rearmament programmes among informed commentators was based on the idea that the Soviet Union was a paper tiger. P H Vigor of the Soviet Studies Research Centre at Sandhurst was convinced that 'no Russian leader, whether political or military, is anything but appalled at the prospect ... of fighting an all-out nuclear war' and would only do so as 'the least bad policy option open to them at a time of acute crisis'.[67] Even if they did choose to fight, the possibility of the tactical surprise that they deemed so necessary would be denied them because rising tensions would allow time for NATO to prepare and deploy. There could be no bolt from 'a clear sky'. Quite remarkably for the time, Vigor also contended that the Russian people would not support a war of aggression unless it was won in a very short time indeed and that as this could not be guaranteed, the Politburo would be most reluctant to embark on one. Furthermore, a quick victory would depend on a well-trained army designed and exercised for the purpose and the Soviet armies were not fit for this purpose, being under-trained, under-exercised and likely to be fighting in built-up West

Germany rather than the pastoral training areas in the East. There was also the question of whether the Poles, Czechs and Hungarians would actually fight and whether or not the high attrition rates expected in a massed armoured attack would not cripple the Red Army very quickly indeed. Steve Smith of the University of East Anglia argued in 'The Myth of the Soviet Threat'[68] that George Bush Snr, then director of the CIA, had vastly exaggerated Soviet defence spending since 1976 and that consequently, by the early 1980s, in countries committed to the Warsaw Pact spending was far less than that of NATO. He also argued that the Soviet military posture, both conventional and nuclear, was actually defensive and based upon repeated experience of invasion from the West. Russia's experience in the Second World War was, apparently, 'often forgotten' and a justification for its oppressive policies in Eastern Europe and the invasion of Afghanistan. This was, of course, a hopeful analysis based on a selective reading of the historical record and which ignored the very strong Byzantine inheritance among Russians that advised treating foreigners as either enemies or vassals. It was also a tribute to RUSI that it was prepared to give space to those who felt that this was just another example of Dorkingism, talking up a threat in the interests of gaining more funding rather than in the interests of the debate.

Winning the Cold War

Hackett had chosen the year 1985 for the outbreak of his fictional war on the grounds that it would be at this crucial time that the Soviet forces would need to be re-equipped if they were not to become obsolete, and thus the temptation to use them before costs escalated would be at its greatest. This was a remarkably good guess, informed as it was by the general upgrading of NATO equipment during the late 1970s as guided weapons and computer technologies began to find military applications – but it is doubtful if even Hackett really understood just how far ahead of the Soviets the quantum leaps in technology would take the West. One of the first glimpses of this truth was when Viktor Belenko defected to Japan with his MiG-25 Foxbat fighter in 1976. When the aircraft was dismantled it was found to contain avionics based on vacuum tube technology that was arguably two generations behind the emerging microchip technology. Attempts to explain this as being a deliberate design feature to make the aircraft more rugged were unconvincing.

Within the British Army the deployment of Rapier, Milan and Swingfire missiles along with the more controversial Blowpipe and Javelin guided missiles, represented a very visible improvement in capabilities, but it was what they augured for the future that counted. Western technology was becoming more versatile and applicable to areas that the Soviets had previously dominated; the cover of the June 1985 *Journal* showed the multiple launch rocket system, an answer to the BM-21 family of 'Stalin organs', which the MLRS completely outclassed. Professor Mason argued in 1984 at the Institute that emerging technologies in IT, imaging, satellites and electronic warfare stood a very good prospect of defeating the Red Army by denying them strategic or tactical surprise, allowing deep strikes by cruise missiles, and grounding their air power through electronic countermeasures. Already, he argued, the best anti-tank weapon was no longer another tank but the cheaper, guided anti-tank missile.[69] If the Soviets wanted to keep up, they would need to develop their own equivalent of Silicon Valley and this they were incapable of doing without anything approaching the efficiency of capitalism. By 1983, the editor noted that the Russians were reduced to a 'systematic and calculated effort – using both legal and illegal means – to raid the free world's technological base'.[70]

The issue of replacing ageing nuclear systems was also of concern to the Russians as, in the West, the MX replaced Minuteman, Trident replaced Polaris, and Pershing was upgraded. But these developments were not as important as the appearance of the Tomahawk cruise missile and the Strategic Defense Initiative (SDI), popularly known as 'Star Wars'. The cruise missile represented a genuine advance in missile technology, being more of an unmanned aircraft than a ballistic missile, able to fly complex mapped courses, difficult to intercept and with a high degree of precision accuracy – while the possibilities of the SDI announced in 1983 held out the prospect of making Soviet nuclear forces obsolete through computer-controlled interception of Russian ICBMs. As far as the Russians were concerned, in the opinion of the Institute, it meant that Reagan was moving America from mutual assured destruction to 'assured survival'.[71] This was very much a theoretical possibility for American technology in 1983, but a complete impossibility for the Soviets in anything like the near future. The reality was that the Soviets had lost the technological race.

Indeed, the most determined opposition to nuclear weapons upgrades came from domestic campaign groups which, although penetrated by Soviet intelligence and the Communist Party of Great Britain, and run by Marxists like E P Thompson and the Leftist fringe, nevertheless represented a widespread, genuine alarm in Britain and Europe at this apparent escalation in the arms race. Their claims to be specifically a 'peace' movement provoked revulsion among many concerned with defence, who saw only naivety in their hopes that sit-ins, vigils and passive resistance would have any effect on the granite-faced men in the Kremlin.

The Institute was as much about peace as the CND, and only differed on the means to attain that worthy goal. Julian Lewis MP, a future winner of the Trench Gascoigne prize, was to make his name as organiser of the Coalition for Peace and Security, which he described as 'basically anti-CND'[72] – and which might equally have been named 'Peace through Superior Firepower' or even '*Si vis pacem para bellum*' – while Hackett took on Bruce Kent, the religious face of the CND, in a debate at the LSE, which Kent only narrowly won.[73] Nor was RUSI prepared to take a back seat in the debate and in addition to encouraging members to appear in press debates, issued an appeal through the *Journal* for 'willing helpers' to speak in 'schools, universities, clubs and societies up and down the country'.[74]

Their task would be to combat the CND, an organisation that Jennifer Shaw believed was part of 'a well orchestrated movement at work, using individuals and societies, to undermine confidence in the basis of all efforts to maintain our national security'.[75] This would be done by refuting emotive claims that the deployment of cruise missiles would put Britain on the front line, a claim which Miss Shaw dismissed without conscious irony with the blast that, 'Where in God's name have we been since the development of zeppelins?' The reality was that NATO was not being vigorous enough in presenting its own case. Sir Clive Rose, RUSI chairman from 1983, had plenty of experience of fellow travellers when he had been involved in managing the civil contingencies response to the 'winter of discontent' and produced a book, published by RUSI, titled *Campaigns against Western Defence: NATOs Adversaries and Critics* in 1985. Rose was also involved with the Institute for the Study of Conflict, which included General Sir Harry Tuzo, a chairman of the RUSI Council, on its board. Hackett was awarded the Chesney Gold Medal in 1985 and he took the opportunity in his acceptance speech, 'The Man at Arms in the Nuclear Age', to dismiss the famous Greenham Common Peace Camp – although not without a certain amount of sympathy – as 'damp and devoted women clinging together in sagging tents and dismal weather' with no hope of success. Gueritz appeared on the TV programme 'Christians Under Fire' in August 1987 to insist that all had a right to self-defence, including one that had a nuclear option attached to it. There was also a concerted attempt to dispel the notion – and in reality this was and remains a very widespread notion – that the Soviet Union, which had managed to take territory from just about all of its neighbours since 1917, was not a predatory power and that if NATO disbanded, the Warsaw Pact would follow suit.

The second strand in the Western strategy for revival was the reinvigoration of the capitalist system. 'Reagonomics', with its emphasis on a freer market for business, through the removal of regulation and the weakening of the trade unions – the breaking of the air traffic controllers' strike in August 1981 was the keystone in this policy – was matched in Britain by Margaret Thatcher's denationalisation and deregulation programmes, reform of the tax system and the breaking of the miners' strike in 1985. Both leaders were strikingly successful in reviving the economies and the confidence of their countries, and neither was afraid of proclaiming their successes. This was particularly significant because it became increasingly clear to the occupied peoples of Eastern Europe and to the people of Russia itself that capitalism was the future and that the sacrifices they had made to 'build socialism' had been utterly futile. These were the years when parties of Western schoolchildren would visit their counterparts in Eastern Europe and come home with pockets bulging with unspent cash, having sold every pair of jeans and trainers that they could stuff into their suitcases for bundles of Zlotys, Forints, Lev and Deutschmarks. When the trip was made in reverse, parents were faced with the tiresome prospect of Eastern European teenagers who stayed up all night listening to pop music that was banned in their own countries. Perhaps the genius of Margaret Thatcher was to have engineered a consumer boom every bit as good as Macmillan's without undermining the defences of Britain but by hacking out the root causes of British failure – outmoded ways of doing business. The result of economic revival was that the West was able to outspend the Soviets when it came to rearmament. It was almost as though RUSI was able to mutter the phrase *nervi bellorum pecuniae* – money is the sinews of war – for the first time since 1919 without shuddering.

That the benefits of the reviving economy would be used in part for a revived defence was made clear in the 1981 Defence Review carried out by John Nott. Even when the economy was in an appalling slump, and massive demonstrations had been organised by CND, Thatcher and Nott took the decision to buy Trident, to rebuild the Territorial Army, order a replacement for the Tornado and re-equip the BAOR. RUSI's grant from the MoD also went up from £24,000 to £35,000[76] – announced by Geoffrey Pattie, a future council member and fellow lobbyist with Julian Lewis MP of the policy group First Defence. By 1990, the grant would reach £130,000. The planned reduction of the navy and expeditionary capability that was supposed to help offset the renewed commitment to NATO – condemned by the First Sea Lord Sir Henry Leach in a lecture at RUSI[77] – was quickly overturned when Argentina invaded the Falkland Islands in 1982. For the remainder of the decade, money was made available to improve the armed forces. Nor was this commitment displayed only in big ticket items that a politician could pose in front of; in 1983, decent socks were issued to the army for the first time, followed by waterproof jackets that were a considerable improvement on the antediluvian poncho.

There was also a new confidence in the armed forces which became evident in the ideas of the commander of NATO's Northern Army Group, General Sir Nigel Bagnall, hailed by many as the outstanding military thinker of his day.[78] Dissatisfied with the idea that his soldiers should simply wait to be annihilated while defending a militarily incoherent inner German border, Bagnall developed a much more aggressive concept which he called the land/air battle, which he presented to the Institute (along with Air Marshal Sir Patrick Hine, commander of the Second Allied Tactical Air Force) in May 1984, and published in the *Journal* in September. These ideas had developed in tandem with the work of the US general Donn Starry, who had commanded a corps in Germany in 1976–77 and then worked in the Training and Doctrine Command to develop the air/land concept in 1978,[79] which he discussed in a seminar at the Institute in 1981.

The underlying assumption of this doctrine was that while NATO forces might disable the first wave of attacking Warsaw Pact forces, their follow-on forces would swamp whatever defences remained and

NATO defeat would inevitably follow. The new doctrine proposed to deal with this situation by encouraging corps, divisional and brigade commanders to fight not only along the forward line of their own troops but also to disrupt the follow-on forces as they approached the battlefield through the deployment of air power, long-range artillery and special forces. Bagnall also proposed a return to attacking manoeuvre warfare rather than static defence as he believed that the superior training and flair of NATO officers and men would allow them to seize the initiative and disrupt the much more doctrinally rigid Warsaw Pact forces. There was also an emphasis on disrupting Soviet command and control, while using superior technology to gather intelligence from deep behind enemy lines.

This was fighting intelligently, rather than hoping to win a straight attrition battle against an enemy with superior numbers. It also emphasised that the war would be fought on Warsaw Pact territory, rather than on exclusively Western soil, and carried with it the unstated possibility that seizing the initiative could mean fighting a lot of it there – enough to produce questions in Parliament from the Labour Left.[80] In some cases, the unsubstantiated rumour got about that while NATO might well fight an aggressive defence on the north German plain, German and American forces in the south might take the opportunity to go for a right hook through Czechoslovakia. Needless to say, the Institute promoted the debates around the new concept with contributions on 'The Impact of Surprise and Initiative in War' from Corelli Barnett and 'The Air/Land Battle and NATO's New Doctrinal Debate' from the defence/industrial analyst Robert Gessert in June 1984.

Despite the improvements in Britain's defence position made during the 1980s, there were still some glaring gaps in both equipment and training. The lack of an IFV was perhaps the most serious before the introduction of the Warrior in 1987 – an issue covered by the *Journal* in September 1986.[81] But the fact that much of the infantry of BAOR and almost all that of the Territorial Army (TA) was unarmoured led to a very pointed debate over British defensive tactics. In 1980, General Sir William Scotter argued that infantry based in mutually supporting defended localities, liberally supplied with anti-tank weapons, could slow down a Soviet armoured attack by forcing them to deploy and fight through villages and woods to clear the anti-tank weapons that denied them use of the open ground between these points. This became known around the mess tables of both BAOR and the TA as the 'Goodwood' concept, named after a particularly tenacious German defence against a British armoured thrust in Normandy in 1944, and was widely adopted in the BAOR. According to TA Intelligence Corps Captain Charles Dick, this was a clear case of 'situating the appreciation', whereby a historical precedent had been dredged up to justify utilising a mass of unarmoured infantry, instead of accepting the financial cost of equipping them properly.[82] This was an explosive issue and it was precisely because Dick was a TA officer that made it all the more timely.

There was scarcely any armour in 2nd Infantry Division and few TA officers had much experience of exercising with or against armour. Given that much of the TA was involved in defending the rear area against Soviet airmobile forces (which included air-portable armour) and then expected to be heavily involved with armour as the regular elements of BAOR withdrew into it, this was a matter widely discussed within the TA, if less so among the regulars. Overwhelmingly, the TA was in soft-skinned vehicles and often still armed with the Wombat recoilless rifle which, with its enormous back-blast, defied any sort of concealment. However determined they were to give a good account of themselves, most TA officers understood that their chances of surviving an attack from T-72, BMP and Hind were slim and, as a result, there was a great deal of black humour in the TA about keeping the Dunkirk–Dover ferry timetable close to hand in case of war. Again, the decision to publish a major attack on British doctrine from a very junior officer in the interests of sparking a debate was very much to the credit of the Institute and several other articles followed on the subject during the mid-1980s.

Uncharted Territory

In 1983, Sir Clive Rose, a diplomat who, by his own admission, spoke Russian like a Moscow tram conductor,[83] became the first civilian chairman of the RUSI Council and oversaw another upgrade in the activities and performance of the Institute, the membership of which now stood at 7,200 – up from 5,100 in 1980. The finances were in good shape, which allowed a pay rise for the staff in 1984 and an expanded range of research activities, and in 1982 the membership rules were changed to allow associate membership to bodies normally based outside the UK. Ambassadors and High Commissioners were quick to take up this opportunity and after recommendations from the chiefs of staff that serving officers should take an interest in the Institute, the membership continued to grow. The director of the Institute from 1981 onwards was Group Captain David Bolton, a man committed to the Atlantic Alliance – in light of this, the Institute mounted an exhibition in 1984 to celebrate thirty-five years of NATO – and an influential figure in the British-America Project, which aimed to foster contacts between leaders in London and Washington and whose first conference report in 1985 was edited by the *Journal* regular, Christopher Coker.

Bolton's conviction was that the Institute should take a lead in fostering personal contacts between those with an interest in defence and those who had influence but little expertise in this area. Seminars and round table discussions which brought together participants to exchange ideas and information on a non-attributable basis were a particularly valuable feature introduced during the 1980s, especially if they engaged in attempts to peer into the future. Bolton was a believer that the *Journal* should indeed deal with contemporary issues, but that it should also strive 'to be a little more prescient'.[84] He also expanded and reorganised the research work of the Institute, shaping 'main study themes' for each year, appointing two assistant directors and creating distinct programmes for the study of the Soviet Union and Eastern Europe, technology and defence procurement, space and international security (which was sponsored by Rockwell), the Middle East and a meetings, briefings and studies support group. Four research fellows were appointed in 1983 to look into defence technology and procurement, intelligence and terrorism, emerging technologies and Soviet prospects. He also took the revolutionary step of introducing computers to the Institute in 1982 – items which were by no means common then. The aim was to provide research 'with a strong operational flavour' that would inform 'future policy options'.[85] Joint seminars with the Foreign Office, Oxford and Cambridge Universities, the London School of Economics and King's College, London were introduced, as well as high-level seminars held with German and UK politicians in Bonn.

The range of publications was extended with the introduction of the *RUSI Defence Studies and Military Power* series, which each produced book-sized contributions at a rate of around four per year. There were also joint projects with both Jane's and Brassey's Defence Publishers and the introduction of the monthly *Armed Forces,* and the *Newsbrief,* which provided analysis on contemporary issues far beyond anything that might appear in a newspaper. Indeed, one of Bolton's repeated complaints was about the poor quality of defence reporting in the mainstream media. 1985 also saw the introduction of the *Whitehall Papers*, which aimed to cover occasional research and conference reports. Lectures by leading politicians, including Michael Heseltine, Geoffrey Howe, Francis Pym and King Hussein of Jordan, became a regular feature – although the nearest the Labour Party got to the podium was in the form of David Owen, who had left the party to form a new centre-left grouping. A military history circle also flourished. As a result, the *Journal* continued to attract contributions from a wide range of military, academic, journalistic and government figures as the Institute was recognised as an increasingly influential forum which looked with equal intensity at past wisdom, current affairs and prospects for the future with 'plain speaking, clear thinking and wise judgement'.[86] This continued to be the case when Field Marshal Sir John Stanier took over from Sir Clive Rose as chairman in 1986 and initiated a research project into 'The Soviet Union and Eastern Europe: Strains and Developments'. Ironically, the main study theme chosen for 1987–88 was 'NATO and the Warsaw Pact: The Next Fifteen Years'. The events of 1989 took everyone by surprise.

Having become used to dealing with the duplicitous grey despots of Brezhnev, Andropov and Chernenko, it was not unreasonable for the West to treat Mikhail Gorbachev with a certain amount of suspicion when he took over the Politburo in 1985. As Air Vice Marshal Mason put it, would the new leader be 'Mikhail the Great? ... or The Terrible ... or the Inconsequential?'[87] The Institute intended to find out and a RUSI-Soviet Forum was quietly set up in 1986 to foster contacts on the other side of the increasingly rusty iron curtain. The caution remained despite the sacking of the ultimate Cold War warrior Andrei Gromyko in 1987 and the introduction of *Glasnost* and *Perestroika*. The Intermediate-Range Nuclear Force (INF) reductions between 1985–87, including the suspension of the deployment of the iconic SS-20 in 1985, were greeted by the Institute with a qualified welcome, lest it lead to an increase in Soviet conventional dominance.[88] A further sign of an emerging thaw came with the visit of Colonel General Makmut Gareyev, deputy chief of the Soviet General Staff, to the Institute in 1988. In many ways, the defence establishment could not really believe the evidence of their own eyes and ears when they considered Gorbachev's repeated and radical initiatives to end the Cold War, and the vast body of Kremlin watchers focused on when he would be overthrown by party hardliners rather than accepting that this was genuine and revolutionary change. In the spring of 1989, however, the *Journal* published 'Elements and Pillars of Soviet Military Power' by Admiral W J Crowe US Navy, in which he argued that 'it has become increasingly apparent that the social, economic and industrial pillars underlying Soviet military power are not in good shape'. This was an understatement indeed, but it should also be noted that at a lecture given at the Institute in February 1989 by General Hans van Sandrart on 'Defence Concepts and the Application of New Military Thinking' there was absolutely no inkling that the revolution was about to happen.

It was Gorbachev's breathtaking announcement before the Council of Europe in Strasbourg on 6 July 1989 that Soviet control of Eastern Europe was to be abandoned that opened an entirely new world order. Few people knew what to make of this initially but when Hungary opened its border with Austria, 30,000 East Germans leapt at what they believed was a once in a lifetime chance to escape their imprisonment. 'Has Peace Broken Out?' asked Bolton in the autumn *Journal* of 1989 and sounded a warning note that with this wave of change would come instability and security challenges that would need to be managed. Above his article was a photograph of the commander-in-chief of the Warsaw Pact shaking hands with the Supreme Allied Commander in Europe at the Institute in May 1989. Earlier in the year, the chairman of the council, General Sir Martin Farndale had also led a RUSI team to Moscow and Eastern Europe where they had addressed the military academy of the Soviet General Staff and had meetings with the Russian foreign and defence ministries.[89] The world was turning upside down. No-one could quite believe what was happening as attempts to contain the revolutions became increasingly futile and communist governments across Eastern Europe collapsed. The iconic moment came on 9 November 1989 when the Berlin Wall was stormed by those East Germans who had not managed to escape and by the end of the year communist rule in Eastern Europe was over. It fell to Jonathan Eyal, himself of Romanian extraction, to sound the tocsin for the Cold War in the spring 1990 *Journal*:

> How was it all possible in a system which exercised complete control over all social and economic activities, spied on its people and operated

an overlapping mechanism of security police, interior ministry, militia, armed forces, border guards and special communist paramilitary units?

The title of his article answered the question: 'We are The People: The Year of Revolutions in Europe'. The expected twentieth century revolutions had arrived, but in a different setting and a very different ending. The war was over. The West had won. History had come to a full stop.

VI. THE NEW WORLD ORDER
1990–2010

Of course, History could not come to an end. Liberal democracy may have triumphed in Europe, but it had been crushed under the tank tracks of the Chinese army in Tiananmen Square, remaining just an aspiration for many and simply not wanted in other parts of the world. Furthermore, the collapse of Soviet power released all sorts of hares as the equations of power were undermined by suppressed ethnic, cultural and religious tensions, organised crime and the possibilities of nuclear proliferation. The world was still a dangerous place and it was not long before there would be a certain nostalgia for the certainties of the Cold War and the stabilising effects of old empires detectable in the discussions around the buffet in the Institute library. But this was looking back wistfully; the Institute intended to look forward.

Even before the collapse of Communism was certain, there had been a major review of how the Institute would continue its work in the coming uncertain years and 'to respond to those fresh challenges with the development of future policy choices for those directly involved'.[1] The first challenge was to define what 'security' meant in this new world and what new technologies and defence policies would be needed for the future. There was also an early realisation that defence spending would be slashed; the military had, for far too long, experienced the resistance of politicians to the recommendations of defence experts to expect any different.

The emphasis of the immediate studies was to be on Europe – how could it not be with the re-unification of Germany? – but the rest of the world was not to be ignored. The Space and International Security programme was merged with the Technology, Industry and Defence Procurement programme in order to make way for a new Regional Security programme to look at the Pacific Rim, Africa and the Middle East, for which Dr Rosemary Hollis was recruited from George Washington University. The aim of the Institute was clear, however:[2]

> The Institute's focus is now and very firmly directed upon international security issues. It has become the professional Institute of the wider defence community and it intends to maintain that position as it seeks to further enhance its standing.

The ink was not dry on this paper before the international security issues came tumbling in.

The First Gulf War

That part of the Middle East centred on the Gulf had been an area of only peripheral interest to Britain in the nineteenth century, but Winston Churchill's 1911 decision to convert the Royal Navy from coal- to oil-powered ships moved it right to the centre of British strategic thinking. Empire in Egypt had been about protecting the route to India through the Suez Canal, but empire in the Gulf was now about supplying the Royal Navy. Two World Wars emphasised the importance of oil, but after 1945 the demand for black gold from the increasingly automobile-dependent West saw an unprecedented surge in the wealth of Iran, Iraq, Saudi Arabia and the Gulf sheikdoms. In 1973, this wealth turned into political influence as the Arab world replaced the US as the main price setter for crude oil and then choked off supplies in protest at Western support for Israel. Western economies crashed as energy prices rocketed. During the 1950s, this would probably have resulted in the removal of those governments who had taken such a drastic step – indeed in August 1953, Britain and the US had conspired with domestic Iranian elements to remove President Mosaddegh of Iran for threatening their energy security[3] – but by the early 1970s there was no stomach for such economic imperialism. Indeed, the decision by Wilson and Healy to pull out of the Gulf between 1968–71 was probably the worst foreign policy decision made in the post-war period because it created a power vacuum that drove the more vulnerable states there into positions that they would not necessarily have taken otherwise. It also ended any hope of British energy security. Fear of an Iran eager to fill the power vacuum meant that the Gulf States had to seek accommodations with the bigger Arab powers of Egypt, Iraq and Syria, the price of which was embroilment in the Israel-Palestine dispute, when they would probably have preferred the British presence to remain.[4]

This second strand of the tangled skein of Middle Eastern politics was also to bedevil the relationship between the West and the Arab states. In 1947, Bevan had washed his hands of Arab-Jewish relations in Palestine and pulled Britain out of the mandate in the firm belief that there could be no British solution there. This reflected the hopeless split in British attitudes to the dispute; one that remains to this day. On the one hand, there was enormous sympathy for the Israelis because of the Holocaust, admiration for their military victories in the Arab-Israeli wars of 1967 and 1973, revulsion at the activities carried out by groups like Black September, and fears of what might happen to the Jews if they were indeed pushed into the sea. On the other hand, there was a longstanding Arabist tradition within the Foreign Office, 250,000 British expats working in the Gulf by 1990, lucrative arms sales to the region and a growing sympathy for the plight of the Palestinians, especially after the massacres perpetrated by Israeli-backed militias in Lebanon in 1982. This lack of any consensus has compelled successive British governments to walk a very fine line between offending Arab sentiments and the risk of being seen to support terrorist acts against Israeli.

A third, more complex strand also emerged with the tales of corruption, incompetence, waste, opulence and excess that began to emerge as the oil-rich states sprouted new cities out of the sand. For many, too much of the wealth was being concentrated in too few hands and this was producing ungodly behaviour. A new form of political Islam began to emerge which was revolted at what it saw as excessive materialism, secularism and creeping westernisation, and which declared itself in opposition not just to the West, but also to the insufficiently religious governments throughout the region. In 1979, this produced the Iranian revolution and the establishment of a theocratic government hostile to Israel, the West, Saudi Arabia, the Gulf States and modernity itself. Within a year, this hostility had erupted into war with Iraq, with the Ayatollah Khomeini seeing in Ba'athist Iraq everything that was wrong with the Arab world, in addition to his personal grievances of being expelled from his exile there in 1978 and Saddam also having had his sister executed. In September 1980, Saddam Hussein, believing that his longstanding disputes with Iran over the Shatt-al-Arab and over Iranian backing for Shia agitation inside Iraq could be solved while Iran was still in a state of revolutionary chaos, launched a surprise attack across the Tigris and began a war that would last until 1988.

The Institute had, of course, maintained an interest in this vital region for many years. The journalist Malcolm Muggeridge (at that time editor of *Punch* and still a decade away from his curmudgeonly stance, Canute-like, against the spirit of the 1960s) had given 'A General Survey of the Middle East' to the *Journal* in May 1952; Colonel Smiley had contributed 'The War in the Yemen' in 1963; and Brigadier Heathcote followed this up with 'Operations in the Radfan' in 1965. The Arab-Israeli War of 1967 produced two lectures by Charles Douglas-Home, the military correspondent of *The Times* who had covered the war, and Brigadier Peter Young (a military historian at Sandhurst, also the founder of the Sealed Knot, the English Civil War re-enactment society) as well as an analysis of 'British Military Policy on Arabia' by Anthony Verrier. In 1972, 'Israeli Counter-Guerrilla Measures' were examined and in 1973 and 1974 attention was focused on the Yom Kippur War. In 1975, the Irish-born future president of Israel, Chaim Herzog, delivered his thoughts on the 1973 war at the Institute, while the Israeli Defence Force was revisited again in March 1976. The Iranian Revolution moved the Institute to hold a special seminar in 1980 on 'Holy War: Military Power and Religion', which featured a long and illuminating discussion on the meaning of jihad. It pointed out that while there was certainly an interpretation that jihad was a personal, internal struggle, the idea that it was a call to physical struggle was also a potent one. The controversial Iraqi historian, Elie Kedourie, was the main attraction here and this analysis pointed out the uncomfortable problem for both Islam and the West as to how this concept was to be accommodated without coming to blows. This was especially the case when Soviet forces invaded Afghanistan and made an alliance between Islam and the West a practical possibility; the background to this new conflict was given in 'The Soviet Military Stake in Afghanistan 1956–79' by Patrick J Garrity in September 1980, and 'The Leaderless Afghans' by the historian, journalist and security analyst, Edgar O'Ballance. He also contributed 'Arafat and the PLO' in March 1984 and in December, 'The Lebanese Sea of Trouble'. 'The Death of an Army: A Short Analysis of the Imperial Iranian Armed Forces' in June 1980 was also a timely addition to the debate.

The *Journal* also included in December 1984 a contribution from Fred Halliday, one of the most brilliant scholars working on Middle Eastern politics, with 'The Middle East, Afghanistan and the Gulf in Soviet Perception'. For NATO in the 1980s, the Islamic world, in the form of Libya, was also seen as a potential threat to the southern flank, an idea discussed in 'Danger in the Maghrib: A Growing Threat to NATO's South?' This was an idea that found its way into unit air defence training in the British Army at least. Another brilliant scholar, Anthony Cordesman, wrote on 'The Realities and Unrealities of the Middle Eastern Arms Market' in March 1987 and published a *Whitehall Paper* on 'The Military Lessons of the Arab-Israeli Conflicts: Past and Future'. Rosemary Hollis looked at 'Tactical Dynamics of the Intafada and Israel's Response' in the winter of 1989 which rounded up a fairly comprehensive coverage of the region – perhaps more could have been published on the Iran-Iraq War in the *Journal* although it was covered in other RUSI publications – before Saddam Hussein launched his invasion of Kuwait in 1990.

Internationalisation

In 1994, Group Captain Bolton retired as director to be replaced by Rear Admiral Richard Cobbold, a frigate captain who had gone on to work as the director of defence concepts at the MoD. One of Bolton's last achievements had been to cope with the increasing reluctance of the Treasury to fund the Institute and to wean it off government grants. Indeed he put the Institute on such a good financial footing that it could afford a much-needed redecoration and upgrade of its facilities which had, over a century of wear and tear, begun to look a little tired. Having set this in motion, he generously left Admiral Cobbold to endure the discomfort of working with the builders for the next two years. When the work was completed it included better acoustics for the lecture theatre, the provision of audio-visual facilities, a newly waterproofed roof and a covered walkway between the editorial offices and the research offices, which had previously been open to the elements. This great leap forward was accompanied by a move into cyberspace when, at the official re-opening on 26 June 1996, the president pressed the start button and launched the RUSI website. Cobbold also, finally, allowed the RAF onto the RUSI badge.

Under Cobbold's direction, the Institute began to take on an increasingly international character. Visiting fellows from places as diverse as Ukraine, Japan, Korea and Taiwan were invited to spend time at the Institute. Links were also developed with the United Services Institute in India, the Swedish War College, the Centre de Recherches et Etudes sur les Strategies et Technologies in Paris and the German Stiftung Wissenschaft und Politik in Eberhausen. In 1996, an annual joint US/Russia/UK naval conference was begun. It became increasingly common to bump into people from all disciplines and every corner of the world around the buffet at the conferences and symposiums. It would not be unheard of, for example, to find a Lebanese filmmaker chatting over a glass of wine in the Library about Middle Eastern arms sales with an African historian, a student from King's College London and a Canadian soldier. This is how international understanding begins. Indeed, it was these methods that the Institute hoped to use when it brought together Greeks and Turks to talk about Cyprus in 1997.

Cobbold also initiated a flagship publication, the annual *RUSI International Security Review*, which by 1998 contained thirty-three chapters broadly grouped into British security issues, the challenges to European security and the wider global view. In December 1997, another step forward saw Don Neese (of Lockheed Martin) and Stephen Henthorne (a longstanding American RUSI member) set up a sister institute, the Defence Studies Foundation in Washington, DC, to improve coverage of transatlantic affairs. This would culminate in the opening of the Institute's first regional office in Washington, DC in 2007, a year that also saw the opening of a further branch in Qatar. Overseas signatories were well represented too, and included figures such as King Michael I of Romania, the Polish and Slovenian foreign ministers in 1997 and the heads of state of Estonia and Latvia in 2000, all of whom would hardly have been considered possible contributors before 1989. In July 2001, the Institute decided that it would now pitch to become an international centre of excellence, moving beyond its late remit of being a mainly British institute.

All this was achieved without neglecting relationships closer to home as the Institute maintained its links with the universities of Oxford and Cambridge, King's College London and the London School of Economics, and expanded its links in 1996 to take in the Consortium of Northern Universities and Cranfield University. The MoD also asked the Institute to co-operate in bringing out its publications on *British Defence Doctrine* in 1997. There was also a new publication launched, focused on defence technology, *World Defence Systems*: a reflection of the director's interest in procurement issues. At the same time, around forty research-led seminars were held each year, in addition to the regular conferences, lectures, book launches and the more discreet lunchtime round table discussions where knowledgeable actors could talk off the record. The *Journal* too continued to attract informed contributions from the leading actors; in 1994, for example, it featured contributions from ten generals (including three Germans), four admirals (one French), four air marshals, three professors, four doctors, six MPs (including the soon-to-be-jailed Jonathan Aitken) and the commissioner of the Metropolitan Police. The range of issues remained impressive too: in 1996, for example, *Journal* articles covered the problems of the Balkans, the Russian navy (two contributions for which were written by Russian \dmirals), China, India's nuclear forces, the Canadian and Japanese armies, Palestinian elections, Bismarck, the Somme, Ernest Hemmingway, a Polish view on NATO enlargement, and homosexuality in the armed forces. The last was provocatively titled 'Rum, Bum and the Lash' and drew a lively correspondence – proof positive that the *Journal* was fulfilling its mission to ensure that all current issues on defence were actively debated in its pages.

In financial terms too, Cobbold made great strides for the Institute so that by the end of the twentieth century, the Institute was financially independent of the government. This was done largely through seeking outside sponsorship, particularly from BAE Systems, but also through hiring out the Institute's facilities and expanding the number of conferences held. Indeed, by the time that the chairman made his Annual Report in 2001, the old battle with the Treasury had been resumed – this time over the size of the rent, 'a process familiar to all members who have bought carpets in the souk'. An exasperated Sir Michael Alexander complained that:

> Many visitors from abroad assume that we are sponsored by the government. There is a certain irony in the reality, which is that we will be supporting the government to the tune of a million pounds or so between now and 2007.

Not satisfied with ensuring the intellectual and financial health of the Institute, Cobbold also initiated a programme guaranteed to strike terror into the heart of any self-respecting academic researcher – the *Team RUSI* marathon runners. Despite the hacking coughs, mumbled excuses and rustling of hastily concealed cigarette packets, two members completed the 1996 London Marathon in under three hours in what Cobbold was pleased to describe as 'a pleasant way of passing a Spring Sunday morning'.[5] It was also a good fundraiser, bringing in around £3,000 in sponsorship each year. He was, however, pushing his luck a little too far when he suggested in 1997 that 'if you can't do it yourself ... volunteer a friend'.

The War on Terror

Ejecting Saddam Hussein from Kuwait was a relatively simple matter, but the failure of the United Nations to authorise his ejection from Baghdad meant that all the efforts of the Coalition forces had been wasted. He was still in power, still in possession of huge oil revenues and still a threat. The only real change in the equation was a result of Yasser Arafat's backing of Iraq, which undermined much of his credibility and forced him to open up negotiations with the Israelis at the 1991 Madrid Conference. However, as Coalition forces were building up in Saudi Arabia in 1990 prior to the liberation of Kuwait, an apocryphal story had begun to circulate around the expatriate communities that a female US soldier had been assaulted with a whip by a *mutawa* – a religious policeman – for wearing shorts, and that she had pulled a pistol on him in return. Whether the story was true or not was beside the point: it was the shocking nature of the clash of cultures that was being illustrated. For fundamentalist Islam, the presence of the infidel on Saudi soil represented a profound violation worse than anything Saddam Hussein might have done, and a loose coalition of virulently anti-Western groups under the general banner of Salafism decided to act. With a base in Afghanistan, veterans of the war against the Russians and sympathisers among Islamic communities throughout the world came together under the leadership of Osama Bin Laden and Al-Qa'ida to wage war against the West. There were a few warning blows, but the 9/11 'spectacular' came, quite literally, out of a clear blue sky in 2001.

At a stroke, the whole nature of 'security' had been changed. Instead of inter-state war or intra-state rebellion, there now existed a curious and lethal hybrid of 'non-state actors' existing in 'ungoverned places', inspiring home-grown amateur jihadist 'franchises' determined to wage 'asymmetric' war both as volunteers in distant parts and within their own societies. There was also the terrifying possibility that they might indeed 'capture' a state and acquire weapons of mass destruction (WMD), which they would have no fear of using, being convinced that the rewards of martyrdom would be theirs in the afterlife. The mad men believing themselves to be sane were back: a wave of revulsion, spine-chilling fear and cries for revenge followed as President George W Bush called for a crusade (a term that was hastily retracted when the connotations for the Islamic world were realised) and Colin Powell, Secretary of State, declared that America was now at war with terrorism.

The Institute decided, however, to keep its head. Coincidentally, the Institute had planned a conference on Gulf security issues for just two days after the attacks and used the opportunity to discuss the implications for the region, and indeed the world, of this new development. It also developed links with Paul Wilkinson, an expert on terrorism at the Oxford Research Group and organised a conference in October 2001 to start people thinking about a proper response. Whatever the heady calls for revenge 'in a media stoked frenzy for immediate action', or the grandstanding of 'ministers whose knowledge of history is on a par with their skill at political management', clear thinking and serious analysis must take precedence in informing policy, argued Professor Michael Howard.[6] With US forces already attacking Al-Qa'ida bases in Afghanistan, Howard warned against over-reacting to the 9/11 attacks by attacking Iraq and pointed out that declaring 'war' accorded Bin Laden a status that he did not deserve. Frenzied attacks were not the best tools to defeat Al-Qa'ida but 'secrecy, intelligence, political sagacity, quiet ruthlessness, covert actions that remain covert [and] above all, patience'.[7] Sir Michael Alexander, chairman of the Institute, saw the disaffection generated by poverty and advertised by globalisation as the root cause of the problem and Bin Laden as merely a symptom. For him, this was a civil war in the global village which could only be won by real transfer of wealth, while the erosion of civil liberties in regard to the ability of government to track and restrict the activities of suspect individuals would have to become a feature of this civil war, if WMD attacks were to be avoided.[8] In June 2002, the *Journal* published a chilling article entitled 'I am Osama Bin Laden', which was firmly in the tradition of Dorkingism, being a fictional attempt to articulate the motivations, aims, methods and prospects for the Salafist programme. 'Think of me as an agenda and inspiration for self-directed action', wrote Bin Laden (in reality, Paul Schule of the MoD). 'We want you out of the Islamic World.... We also want to protect our faith against your endless corrosive images'.

As the prospect of war with Iraq began to grow larger, Rear Admiral Cobbold asked two pertinent questions in his August 2002 comment column. The first was a straightforward enquiry as to whether the capability existed to destroy Iraqi targets without the collateral damage that the media, he felt, were always wanting to 'snaffle up'. The second was more barbed:[9]

> If Saddam Hussein is removed, is the next regime waiting in the wings? ... Are there long-term contingencies all worked out, and we just have not been told about them?

His October 2002 comment posed several other pertinent questions in an imaginary Socratic interchange between 'Hank Hawk', 'Des Dove' and the 'sparky and erudite' average member of the Institute:

> So why bash Saddam? He was a bastard in 1991 and he's still a bastard now, only 11 years older. Why bother?

> When will the hot part of the war end and when will the last British troops leave Baghdad?

The first question was torturing the body politic at the time and was still around when the Iraq War inquiry was announced in 2009. The second question provoked two radically different answers – three months and fifteen years.

When Saddam was overthrown in March 2003, in the aftermath of one of the most divisive debates in recent British political experience and the resignation of Robin Cook, the foreign minister, Cobbold had the protagonists meet again in the June 2003 *Journal* to debate the aftermath, especially as it began to look like the destruction of Saddam's regime had released a Pandora's box of separatist and religious disorder. The war had 'been won well, but the peace [looked] like being a little trickier'; an analysis that hinted at his earlier worries about post-war planning. There was also a growing suspicion that the WMD, on which Prime Minister Tony Blair had misguidedly placed so much emphasis as a reason for the war, did not actually exist – the

US, by contrast, justified the war largely because, as Cobbold had so rightly pointed out, Saddam was a bastard, and a bastard with a WMD programme. Hans Blix's UN weapons inspectors had been right all along, it seemed, and yet it also seemed perfectly clear to all, including the world's intelligence agencies, that Saddam himself had been under the impression that *he had actually possessed them*. To these august bodies was added Neil Partrick, head of the RUSI Middle East/North Africa programme, who was so convinced that both Iran and Iraq had WMD capabilities that he gave a presentation on them to a Gulf security conference in September 2001.

Unsurprisingly, the controversy provoked by the tangled relationship between intelligence and policy in the run-up to the Iraq war meant equal but retrospective castigation in the *Journal*. The first, 'Pre-War Intelligence and Iraq's WMD Threat' by John Hughes Wilson, an experienced ex-Intelligence Corps officer, lambasted the government's decision to change the Joint Intelligence Committee's 2002 report into Saddam's WMD 'for presentational purposes'. Intelligence, he argued, was no longer about cautious assessment and careful balancing of possibilities and probabilities, but because Blair and Alastair Campbell had had direct input into the 'dodgy' dossier, it was now 'a tool of government policy ... [and] public relations'. Even worse, he thundered, was that the intelligence community had allowed itself to be suborned by Blair and Campbell and concluded that, given their reputation for 'spin', the Joint Intelligence Committee should have kept to the motto 'When you sup with the devil, use a long spoon'. In August 2004, Michael Herman gave a more sympathetic verdict on the performance of the intelligence community, preferring to argue that it was subject to a 'group-think' failure rather than any desire to please its political masters on the issue of WMD. IT-savvy members of the Institute were also able to read Sir Paul Lever's comments on the Butler Report in that now-indispensable part of the modern debate, the online forum. In October 2003,

Cobbold had again used his column to assess the prospects for Iraq, emphasising that in the new security environment 'war-fighting, peace support and humanitarian operations' would have to be conducted simultaneously within the same area if insurgents and non-state actors were to be divided from the mass of the population and a breeding ground for Al-Qa'ida denied. And again he pointed to the role of the media as being part of the problem, rather than part of the solution.

The suicide bombings that took place in London in July 2005 were a widely expected event. Although of course, no one knew precisely when, where or how the atrocities would take place, the common view was that Britain 'was next', as Al-Qa'ida franchises exported the war from Iraq and Afghanistan back to the UK. And again the Institute had already made valuable contributions to the study of this problem, with articles on the financing of terrorism and the relationship between governments and their domestic Islamic communities in the *Journal* of June 2003. In November 2006, a major three-day conference was organised to discuss the problem of transnational terrorism, sponsored by the state of Qatar and opened by the British foreign secretary, Margaret Beckett, and her Qatari counterpart Sheikh Hamad Al-Thani. The problem is still with us at the time of writing and the Institute, as might be expected, remains engaged in research and debate on this issue.

The Achilles Heel of Democracy: Media War

Admiral Cobbold's distrust of the role of the media during this period was part of a longstanding debate about the role of a free press in the delicate, sometimes murky actions needed to make defence and foreign policy effective. In 1878, as Britain geared up for war with Russia, a young officer in the intelligence branch of the War Office was given the job of drawing up a policy for dealing with the media. Lieutenant John Ross-of-Bladensburg's analysis of the problem was so prescient that it is electrifying in its relevance today; indeed it could have been written today.[10]

> The presence of Newspaper Correspondents ... is an evil of modern warfare which cannot be avoided. The public will not consent to be shut out from all news of the theatre of war; nor is it wise that they should be. But, on the other hand, the presence of the agents of newspapers, whose sole desire is to gain as much authentic information as they can and who publish it to the whole world without considering the consequences, is most detrimental to the well being of the army.

It was bad enough, he continued, that correspondents spoke *ex cathedra* 'on matters which they do not understand',[11] but what made it worse was that:[12]

> British newspapers would naturally be in our camp, but not that of the enemy ... thus it is probable that the enemy would derive more benefit from the press with our army than we should from that with his.

Ross's analysis identified the key problems facing an army going to war in the company of a free press in a democracy: the need to manage access to sensitive information; to explain military norms and practices to an overwhelmingly civilian media; and to prevent an undemocratic enemy undermining the will to fight by developing a media policy aimed at exploiting the freedoms enjoyed by a democracy. In short, Ross, a member of RUSI and a contributor to the *Journal*, identified the media as, in effect, the Achilles Heel of a democracy at war and opened a long-running debate at the Institute on the issue of media-military relations. The fact that his words feel so fresh today is due to the real tension that emerged between the government and the media during the 1990s, and that came to a head in the bruising encounter between Prime Minister Blair and the BBC over the 2003 Iraq war and the Hutton Report of 2004. It is also the case that the problem of media-military relations has, again at the time of writing, not gone away.[13]

Ross was no doubt drawing on the experience of the Crimea, where a legend of media power had been created in which too many people were inclined to believe too much. Despite repeated claims to the contrary,[14] William Howard Russell's reports on army incompetence from the Crimea did not bring down the government and usher in reform; reform was already underway[15] and most of the supply problems had been solved before the government fell. On the other hand, press distortions created a heroic Florence Nightingale, 'the Lady with the Lamp', rather than reporting a more accurate picture of the well-meaning but amateur nurse whose hospitals were a death trap. Crudely put, Russell missed the big point too – if the British Army was so incompetent, how did they win? In war, incompetence is often relative and what appears to be military blundering is often the result of Treasury parsimony. This was, however, small comfort to those within the military on the receiving end of the reporting and it is fair to say that a general atmosphere of distrust was engendered between soldier and journalist. By the time of the Second Anglo-Boer War, many officers had learned to use the media to their own advantage and were generally welcoming of journalists, but this did not include Lord Kitchener, who after the pillorying he got, did his utmost to keep them away from the Western Front in 1914. Mutual distrust and antagonism lasted, arguably, until the outbreak of the Second World War, when the sense of national solidarity did much to smooth over the differences.[16]

Over the twenty years that followed 1945, however, there was such a change in the culture of the media as to tear away any semblance of trust or mutual respect between the military and journalism. In 1969 Tom Pocock, defence correspondent of the *Evening Standard* and veteran of the Normandy campaign, argued in 'Defence and Public Relations' that this was because the wounded officers who had originally made up the bulk of the press corps were gradually replaced by reporters too eager to gain a scoop. The public relations staff of the armed services, who had tended to work well with the war correspondents, also changed in nature as regular officers with an ingrained dislike of journalists took over – in Jerusalem in 1948 an infantry colonel had virtually the whole of the international press corps arrested for interfering in a cordon and search operation. This was matched by equally unsavoury attempts by service spokesmen to manipulate the media when the MoD centralised public relations during the inter-service bickering that resulted from the cancellation of Skybolt (and thus the possible abolition of the RAF).[17] The resultant centralisation also produced formulaic and uninformative PR churned out by career-minded bureaucrats, whose individuality and creativity had been crushed out by the prospects of secure employment and a pension. Even worse, argued Pocock, during these years:[18]

> [The] essential sanctity of News had been forgotten and public relations debased ... The manipulation of News by journalists to 'make a story' and sell newspapers, or support the personal quirks of a proprietor, have always rightly been regarded as unworthy and unsavoury. But now the Services – or those in the Services anxious to please their political and civil masters – were guilty of manipulating News.

In short:

> The trust that had existed between the MOD and journalists ... has been dissipated ... Journalists no longer seek advice and guidance as they once did. Whitehall still seems tainted with mistrust and intrigue. ... Journalists denied assistance, will look elsewhere for information.

By far and away though, it was the Vietnam War that did the most damage. This is, of course, a controversial point on which both soldiers and journalists are divided; the charge that journalists lost the Vietnam War by deliberately or accidentally undermining support for the war at home is a serious one. It is no less than a charge of treason, and it has been well argued that this is no more than a 'stab in the back' myth.[19] Nevertheless, Robin Day's claim that 'the war was lost on the television screens of America'[20] was widely believed within both the media and the services,[21] especially when commentators as diverse as Jane Fonda and John Pilger passed over from legitimate criticism of military strategy and practices to outright espousal of the cause of the enemy. The failure to prosecute Jane Fonda especially opened the floodgates to a form of journalism that revelled in opposition to all things military and displayed a 'malice and unscrupulousness' hitherto unknown in the coverage of conflict.[22]

Then there was also the age-old question of reliability of reporting through the fog of war. Henry Stanhope, defence correspondent of *The Times* made the point with commendable candour in the *Journal* in 1976 that 'It is arguably impossible to cover a theatre of war so adequately and accurately that [the] work will survive retrospective analysis'.[23] Perhaps more important was the effect of the Vietnam War on the radicalisation of a new generation of young journalists in Britain who were less committed to the straight reporting of 'history as it is made' as in actively pushing a particular political line or who, at the very least, confused a general centre-left perspective with 'objectivity'. As this young talent rose through (mainly) the broadcast media (print tended to lean the other way) during the 1980s and 1990s they created a culture that increasingly saw itself as a more legitimate expression of power than Parliament itself.[24]

The first real clash between the media and the military in Britain came with the Falklands conflict and was partly a result of the completely unexpected nature of the war. There was no planning for a war in the South Atlantic and so there was no planning for media access. There was no head of public relations at the MoD as the previous incumbent had retired and a successor had yet to be appointed; the press were accredited on forms printed for the Suez

Crisis and given only one day's notice to get aboard the Task Force at Southampton. This meant that the journalists who went were the journalists who were available, rather than any particular specialists, and the option to fly out more to be picked up at Ascension was initially denied because the navy did not want the undefended state of the island reported. The inexperience of the journalists was matched by the inexperience of the PR officers too, and by that of the Royal Naval officers who, unlike their army counterparts with experience from Northern Ireland, had little experience of, or time for, the press.

Technical problems also abounded; video had to be sent to Ascension before it could be transmitted, a gap of between nine and twenty-three days, which handed the initial media advantage to the Argentineans who were thus able to get their pictures on TV before those of the embarked journalists. Furthermore, reporters were frustrated that the services always had the final say in any censorship/access dispute because they had exclusive control of the means of transmission. The result was extreme irritation between the various parties involved; the embarked journalists believed that their efforts were being deliberately frustrated while the services felt that the 'lack of magnanimity' shown towards the press officers 'was conspicuous and does them [the journalists] little credit'. The services further accused both the embarked and home-based journalists of behaving 'like critics booking the best seats in a theatre of war' and making petulant complaints that 'at least the Israelis provide telex and telephone trucks'. They accused journalists of a readiness 'to jump to conclusions and look for Machiavellian rather than simple explanations' for inconsistencies in the way information was disseminated, and furthermore 'an exaggerated view' of their own importance in the conflict, and a readiness to 'impute motives to others without properly admitting the motives – competitive by-lines, circulation wars, and professional *amour propre* – which underlay their own activities and attitudes'.[25] Perhaps the most damning condemnation came from Sir Frank Cooper, permanent under-secretary at the MoD (and RUSI member), who complained of journalists that:[26]

> I have not seen or heard a single admission … that any of them got anything wrong or that every single correspondent was not a Knight in shining armour riding a white horse in search of the absolute truth.

This was perhaps unfair. There were indeed those like Michael Nicolson, who revealed the presence of the nuclear attack submarine HMS *Conqueror* after the sinking of the Argentine cruiser *Belgrano* in a flagrant security breach brought on by his irritation at PR staff who he arrogantly dismissed as 'mostly failed journalists rather than ex-journalists' and apparent pique at not being treated with enough respect by naval officers.[27] But there were also those like Brian Hanrahan and Max Hastings who did try to co-operate with the services and report fairly. Nevertheless, the experience had been bruising for both sides and it was a truth rediscovered that led to 'a general feeling on all sides that arrangements for reporting such events could and should be improved before Britain was involved in any future conflict'.[28] The Institute was particularly interested in this issue and in 1984 invited Derrik Mercer, former editor of Channel Four News, then taking part in an MoD-sponsored investigation into media-military relations, to ask the question: 'Is Press Freedom a Threat During National Crises?' This was an article that presciently foretold an international media possessed of its own communications links, and with its own agendas, about to emerge in the very near future. There could be no question of censorship or appealing to national interests to restrain this media and that the power of this media would grow to the point that it would be impossible for a democratic government to sustain a military venture 'against media hostility or ridicule'. The answer, for Mercer, was for the military to trade access for self-censorship on the principle that 'journalists sharing common dangers with servicemen are more likely to identify with their interests'[29] – effectively the adoption in British conflicts of embedded reporters.

By 1990, the international media had indeed developed their own myriad channels of communication and expected to report on a rolling basis whether they had anything meaningful to report or not. The technology also demanded, ludicrously, that journalists pronounce authoritatively on affairs into which they had only recently been parachuted and had little time to research.[30] As the demand for news grew exponentially, the expertise of individual journalists on defence issues shrank at a similar rate as the specialist defence correspondent became something of a rarity – a point made by Mark Laity in 'The Media, the Military and Policy Making: Who's Calling the Shots?' written for the *Journal* in December 2000. This in turn meant that during the First Gulf War leading journalists were completely ignorant of military basics, a fact obvious to the soldiers but utterly missed by their audiences.[31] This was matched during the Second Gulf War by ludicrous predictions of a 'Stalingrad on the Tigris' scenario by leading journalists unable to distinguish between the capabilities of Iraqi ramshackle militia and the professional armies of Britain and the US. Similarly, Lieutenant Ross never considered the possibility that in 1957 Herbert C Matthews would pull off one of the most important journalistic coups ever. By interviewing Fidel Castro in his Cuban hideout he established a new target for journalists – the scoop of interviewing the enemy while engaged in hostilities against him (even though Castro was not technically an enemy of the US yet). Nor would he have imagined that after Peter Arnett of CNN established himself as the only Western journalist left in Baghdad in 1991, it became *de rigeur* for Western journalists to establish themselves in the camp of the enemy in pursuit of a scoop. No doubt he would have been repulsed at the inevitable trade off; being rude about Western foreign policy and military action from the comfort of the MoD press centre is a pretty safe option, but criticising genocidal murderers when under their eye is usually best avoided. When coupled with the pressure to file as many stories as possible the results were predictable. Jeremy Bowen's BBC report on the mistaken destruction of an Iraqi bomb shelter by American aircraft in 1991 handed a perfect propaganda weapon to Saddam in a war that was characterised by a determination to minimise civilian casualties.

Clearly, some form of media management was required. The first response developed in both Britain and the US during the 1980s became known as the 'pool system'. This consisted mainly of journalists being briefed by and accompanied by escort officers whose job was to provide as much information as possible on the understanding that there would need to be security blackouts on certain subjects at certain times. The principle behind this was that:[32]

> [Presumably] viewers and listeners will continue to trust the sources of news they have learned to trust … one cannot see many people getting anything but a good laugh out of some Arab heavy churning out tales of disaster … like the voice over in an advertisement for lavatory cleaner.

There can be little doubt that in the First Gulf War, the media war was won hands down by the Coalition and that the lessons of successful media management were being studied with great interest by the emerging New Labour establishment.

Believing that their demise in the 1980s was in part due to the hostility of the media, the progenitors of New Labour – Tony Blair, Alastair Campbell and Peter Mandelson – developed a hyperactive approach to media management, which ramped up the practice of 'spin' to previously unheard-of heights. When they took office in 1997, Campbell was determined that the plodding PR of the government information services should be replaced by a 'proactive and interventionist news factory aiming to control the news agenda and impose its view of a story on the media',[33] and indeed the MoD's Defence Information Department was given a radical shake up in

October 1997. The routine harassment of journalists unwilling to toe the New Labour line and the favouring of others with stories rapidly became a feature of the new approach to media management. It also produced a huge amount of distrust among journalists and a very great degree of cynicism on both sides. This was important from the defence point of view because the power of a hostile media was about to be displayed when, in 1999, Tony Blair committed Britain to participation in the NATO bombing of Serbia after ethnic cleansing had been attempted in Kosovo. In August 1999, the *Journal* pulled off its very own scoop in persuading Alastair Campbell himself to tell of his battle with the media in 'Communication Lessons for NATO, the Military and the Media' based on his lecture given to the Institute on 9 July. It was a brutal attack on the reporting of the war delivered in his trademark hectoring style, yet it contained much that was true. The media, he argued were apt to complain about the lack of information and then dismiss what was provided as 'spin'; they had given a moral equivalence to the Serbian and NATO positions, 'between ethnic cleansing and a stray bomb that accidentally killed civilians'; they had concentrated on 'NATO blunders' rather than successful operations. 'We had to justify the action, show we had right on our side. And the military action had to be seen to be effective', he argued, exasperated that NATO even had to make a case at all. Accusing journalists inside Kosovo of being only too ready to pass on reports from the Serbian state-controlled media, of being cynical about refugee stories and being determined not to report stories unless there were accompanying pictures – which could only be got from the Serbian media – his judgement was damning on two fronts. Firstly, he argued that 'the media cannot surely dispute that the balance of coverage did not remotely reflect the reality on the ground'. More worryingly, his second judgement went even further.

For the Serbs the information war was a key battlefront. That put a real responsibility on the media to ensure they were not being had. After Iraq and Kosovo, the media needs to reflect whether it has not provided a kind of template to dictatorial regimes in how to use the Western media to their own advantage.

The Institute also managed to get an interview with Oona Muirhead, the MoD's director of information strategy and news, in July 1999 in which she explained the nuts and bolts of running such a strategy and urged journalists to bear in mind that they were indeed of value to an enemy. Tom Laity, late of the BBC, also broadly agreed with Campbell in his December 2000 *Journal* contribution 'The Media, the Military and Policy Making – Who's calling the Shots', lambasting journalists for their 'sloppiness', 'intellectual cowardice', 'instinctive anarchy', 'inconsistency and unconstructiveness' and calling on them to exercise more responsibility in the use of their considerable power.

There could be little doubt that media-military relations were at a low point, but it was unclear whether this was a result of growing media opposition to the New Labour project in general or the military in particular. In February 2000, therefore, the Institute brought together government officials and journalists in a closed, unattributable session to explore whether the media and the MoD were actually 'doomed to be opponents'.[34] From the report that ensued, it seemed that they were indeed so doomed; the military saw the media as usually ignorant of military realities and technicalities, refusing to acknowledge the caveats that went with released information and only willing to accept the pool system if and when it suited them (and not above leaving hotel bills unpaid). The media regarded the MoD as trying to dictate a 'message' for them to convey, guilty of producing propaganda and unreasonably trying to restrict their freedom to report. There was little common ground.

Understandable though Alastair Campbell's frustrations were, they owed something at least to the limitations of his own belief that the media could be managed according to an agenda determined by the government.[35] His obvious pleasure in overcoming media scepticism in Kosovo masked a realisation that 'spin' was becoming more of a hindrance to government policy than a boon, a fact made evident by Jo Moore's callously professional reaction to the Al-Qa'ida attacks on the twin towers 9/11 – 'A good day to bury bad news'.[36] While Campbell had enjoyed enormous success as Blair's campaigning press secretary, it was only a matter of time before the rebelliousness of the journalist culture reasserted itself – a culture now reinforced by a strong dash of the celebrity hubris that allowed John Simpson to claim that 'the BBC liberated Kabul'.[37] Admiral Cobbold judged that at best journalists in a conflict could be expected to be 'sanctimoniously neutral' and 'grossly irritating' even though some of them were, he claimed, his best friends.[38] The subsequent clash between Gilligan and Campbell was an accident waiting to happen as the BBC tried to justify its anti-war stance in the run up to the Second Gulf War, and the government tried to defend the premises on which it had gone to that war. The Hutton Report was a bruising encounter for both sides and the vexed question of whether the media is the Achilles Heel or the guarantor of democracy in a war remains unsatisfactorily answered. The Institute continues to insist, however, that it is debated – in February 2008, Peter Riddell of *The Times* contributed 'Armed Forces, Media and Public: The Current Crisis in Historical and Political Perspective' in which he went a long way to dismiss military complaints as mere 'victim psychology'. However, in the April 2009 member's lecture 'Operation Snakebite: An Inside Story of Britain's Afghanistan War' given by Stephen Grey of the *Sunday Times'* investigations unit, it was still possible to detect the shoehorning in of themes held so dearly by journalists unchanged; lions led by donkeys, Vietnam and, above all, the claim to insights denied to mere soldiers.

Africa and RUSI

> It occurs to me that there must be upon this great continent
> some awful curse, some withering blight, and that to delude
> and to mock at the explorer, the gold-hunter, the merchant,
> the speculator, and even at ministers and monarchs, is its dark
> fortune and desperate fate.
>
> (Lord Randolph Churchill, after visiting Salisbury, 1891)[39]

If the media landscape had changed radically since the end of the
Second World War, it had been more than matched by the changes
in the political and social landscape of the world's poorest continent.
During the sixty years after 1945, Africa presented a series of challenges
that the Institute was keen to investigate and its response to these
problems might be taken as a case study indicative of its response to
other security issues. Sometimes the coverage was excellent; at other
times, for reasons thoroughly understandable, it was patchy; but the
recognition of shortfalls and a determination to address them has
always been part of the Institute's make-up.

Decolonisation had been on the Colonial Office agenda since
the 1930s when it had been realised that the costs of empire in
Africa far outweighed the benefits. There had been several Colonial
Development Acts passed by Parliament both before and during
the Second World War that transformed the Colonial Service into a
development agency with the express purpose of preparing the African
colonies for independence. The 1947 Local Government Despatch
drawn up by Andrew Cohen (head of the African Department) and
the anti-imperialist Colonial Secretary Arthur Creech Jones effectively
committed Britain to decolonisation, especially as Creech-Jones was
personally friendly with many African leaders. He also managed to
persuade the Institute to put on an exhibition showcasing the colonial
contribution to victory in the Second World War. The independence
movements that grew up in Africa during the war were therefore

pushing at an open door as far as Whitehall and the Colonial Office were concerned. This was something that the European settlers in Africa were well aware of and sought increasingly to resist. During the immediate post-war period there had been a wave of European emigration to the East and Southern African colonies and many of these settlers thought that although independence was on its way, it was a lot further off than anyone imagined. The West African colonies of Nigeria and Ghana gained their independence without much controversy, largely because they contained very small settler populations – a point made by Richard Goold-Adams in the 1961 *Journal* article, 'Britain in Africa Today' – but when Harold MacMillan stood in the Cape Parliament in 1960 and gave his 'Winds of Change' address, it dawned on the settlers that majority Black rule would be upon them sooner rather than later. This sent many of them into a panic that contained interwoven intellectual, political, economic and moral threads. For the Afrikaners, White rule was ordained by God while for the more liberal English settlers, Black rule was fine in theory – but just not yet. Both feared the erosion of enviously comfortable lifestyles, economic mismanagement by poorly educated African administrators or the repossession of land taken from African cultivators under dubious circumstances. Otherwise decent people reacted to the question 'Would you let a *kafir* marry your sister?' by answering 'No'; it did not matter whether this was uttered with embarrassment or defiance. Until the settlers could get over their racial attitudes, there really was no hope for successful progress to democracy.

RUSI was ahead of most in considering the problem of decolonisation when it invited Colin Legum, late of the Johannesburg city council and then colonial correspondent of the *Observer* to lecture on South Africa in 1957. Legum was already an opponent of Apartheid and his lecture laid out in stark terms the reality that South Africa had ceased to be a British colony in 1948 when D F Malan and Hendrick Verwoerd's National Party had been elected – Verwoerd had been interned by the British during the war. The touchstone of their policy was 'maintaining, uncorrupted, white supremacy in South Africa', which they saw as essential for 'maintaining Christianity and western civilisation' in South Africa. Legum pointed out that although liberals such as Alan Paton and Trevor Huddleston existed in both the English and Afrikaner communities, they probably appealed to no more than 1 per cent of White South Africans; anyone who objected to Apartheid, which meant approximately 88 per cent of the population, was branded a communist.

This was a harsh judgement: Apartheid was gaining in acceptance in South Africa, but it had been introduced against substantial White opposition. There was also a gleam of hope in the opposition of big business, in the form of Harry Oppenheimer, to the Apartheid policy of shovelling Africans into reserves that lay hours away by bus from their places of work and thus guaranteeing a demotivated workforce. For him, migratory labour and the separation of the migrant worker from his family was both inhumane and inefficient, but most of industry preferred to ignore the rights and wrongs of the situation and get on with making a profit. Legum gave a fair analysis of the developing situation in South Africa, which, even now, stands up well.

But what he failed to convey was the underlying lawless brutality of Apartheid. Sharpeville was still three years away, but, out in the *dorps*, an African could be beaten to death by any thug for any reason (or none) without facing any consequences from the law.[40] When the shootings did occur in 1960, Richard Goold-Adams made the point that the Nationalist government in South Africa was becoming more determined 'with every blast of the wind of change', and that settler intransigence was endangering the tie to Whitehall that most Commonwealth African countries were eager to maintain. For Britain, to South Africa was added the problem of Rhodesia, which, in a bizarre twist, was not wanted in its fellow racist state South Africa, because its racists were English rather than Afrikaans.

Legum returned to the Institute in 1963 with 'British Commitments Overseas: The African Continent' in which he pointed out one of the main reasons for Britain not abandoning South Africa altogether when it became a republic in 1961 – the naval base facilities at Simonstown. This tiny facility was important because it was the only one in southern Africa and therefore important in Cold War terms; an important part of the justification for Apartheid was its role in resisting Soviet communism. Legum argued, however, that the Russians had very little hope of real influence in Africa largely because African leaders preferred non-alignment and were instantly suspicious of anything that looked like neo-colonialism with a Red Star on it. The thrust of his argument was that if the West wanted friendly states in Africa, then they would have to do two things: stay out of internal African affairs and take on South Africa.

The latter was something that Britain was simply not interested in doing – the whole point of decolonisation was to get *out* of Africa and a third Anglo-Boer war was out of the question. What gave the settlers real ammunition for their resistance to democratic rule however was the performance of African leaders themselves in the newly independent countries. It took no time at all for Kwame Nkrumah to lead Ghana to ruin. Independent in 1957, Nkrumah made strikes illegal and introduced detention without charge in 1958, formed his own Presidential Guard exempt from constitutional control, and then ruined the economy with Marxist-inspired folly. He was deposed in a coup in 1966. The disintegration of the Congo in 1960 and the massacres in Katanga seemed to prove to settlers that Africans were not capable of governing themselves, and added to fears of African savagery that had been raised by the Kenyan Mau Mau rebellion 1953–56. In 1964, there were massacres of Arabs and Asians in Zanzibar, military mutinies in Tanzania and Uganda, ethnic violence in Rwanda and an increasing Soviet presence in the newly independent countries.

However bad White or colonial rule was, argued the settlers, Black rule could be proven to be worse. This attitude was given an airing at the Institute by John Connell, biographer of Field Marshal Auchinleck, in 'The Future of Southern Africa' in February 1964. According to him, Rhodesia was about to be pressured by 'force, fear or fraud into a black-dominated one-party dictatorship' like the rest of the 'corrupt, economically precarious, tyrannies manipulated and exploited by the communists' in Africa; the settlers throughout southern and eastern Africa were regarded as 'expendable' by Whitehall, 'hostages held in a large pink-grey paw'; African nationalism was in the hands of Chinese Communists, and Zanzibar a Chinese outpost, with Tanzania, Uganda and Kenya shortly to follow; Africans in general were 'manic-depressive' ready to switch to 'resentment, hysteria and neurotic violence'; Nyerere, Obote and Kenyatta were compared to Kerensky, but propped up by British bayonets; racial prejudice was as common among Black people as it was among Whites; race war was not just on its way, but here already. Against all this stood the bastion (or potential settler Dunkirk) of South Africa, which, if not entirely perfect, was at least worth supporting as the least worst option. Patrick Wall MP, a member of the newly formed group of right-wing Conservatives, the Monday Club, gave strong support to Connell. In the discussion that followed, the chairman (depressingly) could find no one to challenge the views expressed.

When Rhodesia made the Unilateral Declaration of Independence in 1965 rather than face democratic rule, the talking stopped. There would be intermittent talks, but the fate of southern Africa would be decided on the battlefield and not in the way that anyone expected. The truth was that most of the informed opinion in the Western world had no answer to the question of apartheid. In a situation where vital economic resources could only be had from South Africa – it accounted for 95 per cent of platinum, 90 per cent of chrome, 75 per cent of gold and 30 per cent of uranium in the non-communist world according to the *Journal* in 1977[41] – and where substantial

British, American and European investments still existed, there was a strong economic motive to prevent a meltdown in South Africa. This was not driven solely by the demands of big business as the various anti-Apartheid campaigners claimed, but by a very great realisation that millions of Africans would not be well served by unemployment or economic mismanagement. Nevertheless, the repulsion felt against Apartheid still existed and disinvestment began to happen from the mid-1970s onwards as business came increasingly to regard the future of South Africa as a bad business bet; racism was bad for business (and it is worthwhile noting that South African supermarkets were never segregated).

War in Southern Africa

The Rhodesian War began in April 1966 when a group of Zambian-based, Chinese-trained, Zimbabwe African National Union (ZANU) insurgents were ambushed by Rhodesian security forces at Sinoia and wiped out. Zimbabwe African People's Union (ZAPU) and African National Congress (ANC) insurgents joined in with similar lack of success, taking a further sixteen months before killing their first Rhodesian soldier, and it was not until 1972 that the *Chimurenga* [Liberation War] began to bite. In the meantime, South Africa temporarily overcame its disdain for English settlers and sent forces in to Rhodesia to aid in counter-insurgency. In 1974, however, the situation was revolutionised by the Portuguese decision to pull out of its African colonies and end the war with the Mozambican opposition FRELIMO – this despite the incredibly optimistic report of Portuguese successes given by Brigadier Calvert to the Institute in 'Counter-Insurgency in Mozambique'.[42]

At a stroke, Rhodesian forces now had to cover a hostile border that was twice as long as the existing hostile border with Zambia and which presented endless opportunities for the infiltration of guerrilla units. In 1975, South Africa pulled its forces out of Rhodesia in the hope of building a *détente* with Mozambique and from that point on, it was only a matter of time before weight of numbers defeated the Rhodesians. By 1979, despite the tremendous efficiency, daring and ability to improvise of the Rhodesian security forces, everyone knew the game was up.[43] Thomas Arbuckle, a journalist with extensive experience of bush wars in South East Asia, made the point in 1978 that despite a 6:1 kill rate in favour of the Rhodesian Security Forces, this did not 'validate the Rhodesian military claims that the guerrillas are being defeated'.[44] The basic problem was that the Rhodesians were using a version of 'search and destroy', which consisted of covert teams, such as the Selous Scouts, calling in a 'Fireforce' to destroy likely targets. However effective this was against sizeable targets, it did not deal with the underlying ability of the guerrilla to move unseen among the people and garner popular allegiance. Nor did the greater efficiency of the Rhodesian soldier matter in the long run:[45]

> The real problem is that the Rhodesian military have misunderstood the nature of the war that they are fighting. They have failed to realise that the war is essentially political rather than military and that the guerrillas have no immediate need to be militarily efficient.

This was an excellent analysis, which effectively condemned the Rhodesians to defeat because they had no political strategy and therefore no counter-insurgency strategy at all. In 1986, Roger Marston underscored these lessons when he argued that the Rhodesian military were actually quite aware of the need for a political strategy; Putterill, Walls and Hickman, successive commanders of the Rhodesian army, were followers of Templer, while the last two had actually served in Malaya. Defeat was due to the political and social culture of Rhodesians who lived in a version of England 'pickled' in the imperialism of the 1890s and who believed themselves to be the intellectual and physical superiors of Africans. The settlement of Rhodesia by Rhodes' Pioneers was compared to the voyage of the *Mayflower* when in fact it was nothing more than a freebooting expedition gone wrong. Nevertheless, argued Marston, Rhodesians believed themselves to be good masters who had brought many benefits to the Africans and thus could justify their dominance over them. The irony of this was that most Rhodesians were not 'Rhodesians' – in 1961 only 35 per cent could claim to have been born there and there was a constant exchange as British or South African White people moved in and out of the country. In short, Marston argued, loyalty to Rhodesia was conditional indeed and this contributed to the creation of a 'White Island' mentality, which prevented any meaningful political offer being made to the African majority. This was at the centre of Mugabe's success in 1980. Iain Smith, the Rhodesian prime minister, claimed betrayal by Britain for his defeat, but in reality he had only his Social Darwinism to blame.[46]

The interest in the Rhodesian war was important because many regarded it as a dress rehearsal for what was to come in South Africa. Indeed, when British military training teams went out to Zimbabwe to aid in the integration of the army with guerrilla forces, the guerrillas asked to be schooled in battlegroup training to enable them to take on South African armour. Needless to say, they were persuaded otherwise.[47] In South Africa, the beginning of the armed struggle during the early 1960s had as little success as the insurgents had enjoyed in Rhodesia. Nelson Mandela was caught in 1962 and the ANC's armed wing, Umkhonto we Sizwe (MK – 'Spear of the Nation'), had little to show in the way of success. The South African Defence Forces (SADF) and the Bureau of State Security outclassed them completely, while the strong, almost self-sufficient economy allowed the South African government to wage bush wars against the neighbouring 'front-line states' aimed at convincing them that South Africa was best left alone. Mozambique was neutered through poverty and support for the RENAMO rebels; Botswana was too small to prose any threat; Mugabe kept Zimbabwe out in order to concentrate on consolidating his grip on power. That left the SWAPO bases in Angola from 1975 onwards to deal with, which were partially neutralised by alliance with another rebel group, UNITA.

Yet the South African government still had to deal with the reality that 88 per cent of its population had little reason to support the state while significant portions of the White remainder had only a tenuous loyalty (at best). By the mid 1980s, demonstrations by White students were a regular feature on university campuses while the faculty staff of many departments of the Universities of Cape Town and Natal had gone over to the ANC almost in their entirety. By 1976, the director of RUSI, A E Younger, was arguing that in the interests of all parties in South Africa, and also the strategic security of the oil route to the west, that a settlement was needed and that the best way to influence this was through a policy of engagement. 'In this process', he argued, 'time is of the essence, as it has often been shown that early concessions are best and that delay raises the stakes'.[48] Colonel Norman Dodd wrote on developments and capabilities of the SADF and its associated arms industry in 1974 and again in 1980 when he noted that the government itself was being driven into violating its apartheid principles in order to keep the armed forces staffed; the officers and men of the Durban naval base were 90 per cent of Indian extraction, while significant numbers of Black African and 'Cape coloured' men were being recruited for service in Namibia. The presence of Black soldiers fighting for Afrikanerdom in a wide range of units was an uncomfortable reality for many anti-Apartheid campaigners; the issue was at bottom, Black and White, but this did not negate the fact that there were many complexities at work too. There was also the fact, not quite self-evident yet in 1980, that 'even though some of the internal policies of the Republic may be repugnant to those living in more liberal surroundings ... the loss ... of South Africa to the Communists would be a complete disaster to the whole of NATO'.[49]

Was the strategic security of the West a justification for supporting Apartheid, as many on both sides of the argument claimed?

Christopher Coker thought not when he argued that South Africa was dependent on the West rather than vice versa because it needed Western markets, investment and technology to oppose Soviet-backed forces there. Neither was the old argument about the security of the Cape route relevant anymore, he argued – if Russia wanted to interdict oil supplies it would be far easier to do this at Hormuz. Furthermore, if the Russian navy, present in the Indian Ocean after 1968, did decide to attack South Africa (a dubious concept), South Africa would have to appeal for Western help especially after Britain pulled out of the Simonstown Agreement in 1974. What was more, Africans understood this reality more completely than either Europeans or the Soviets and knew that they had to work to persuade the US to apply pressure on South Africa. Here then were the seeds of a solution to ending Apartheid *and* ensuring strategic security. The only danger, argued Coker, was that a mass exodus of White skills would undermine the whole basis of a strong pro-US South Africa.[50] On the whole, however, even the emergence of a non-aligned Black Africa would be no bad thing for the West.[51]

That the Institute was giving a platform to someone with a workable solution to the South African problem at a time when the popular debate was both heated and simplistic was very much to its credit. There were 60,000 Cuban troops in Angola during the 1980s and the defeat of the SADF there would open up all sorts of possibilities to the Soviets.[52] This was something that the South Africans fully understood when in late 1987 they attacked the combined Cuban/Angolan forces at Cuito Cuanavale and defeated them in that rare thing, a tank battle fought south of the Sahara. Castro responded by pouring in more troops to Angola than the SADF could ever hope to defeat, thus upping the ante to the point at which the South Africans were forced to the negotiating table. From May 1988, it was clear that Namibian independence was on its way. Military victory had only presaged political defeat. Cuito Cuanavale is not a well-known battle. Physically isolated and difficult to get to even now, Greg Mills (shortly to begin a strong RUSI connection) and his fellow researchers were unable to visit the site of the battle for his 2006 book, *Seven Battles that Shaped South Africa*, and most contemporary reportage was based on official claims and denials. South Africans who fought there are often surprised that people in Britain have even heard of it – whereupon they may discreetly reveal the Cape Buffalo tattoo that marks them out as members of the mixed-race elite 32 Battalion – yet it was one of the most important battles of the late twentieth century. It is to the credit of RUSI that it had a hand in bringing knowledge of it to a wider audience through its book review columns. Two years later, in February 1990, when Mandela walked out of jail, Apartheid itself was defeated and it is a moot point as to whether it was this battle, rather than sanctions and protests, that ultimately brought down the apartheid state.

Africa in the New World Order

'Nothing is so bad in Africa that things can't get worse' goes the proverb, and the 1990s in Africa held plenty of examples to prove its truth. Indeed, so bad did things get, that the Institute took the decision to open up a new programme devoted to African issues led by Knox Chitiyo in April 2007 and develop an important link with the Johannesburg-based Brenthurst Foundation, whose leading light was Greg Mills. Indeed, it is fair to say that the Institute was not at its best in reporting African issues during the 1990s, concerned as it was with the more pressing, from Britain's perspective, crises in the Balkans and the Middle East. The failure of the UN in Somalia was not covered in the *Journal* until piracy began to make itself felt increasingly in the waters off the Horn of Africa, a tendency noted in the *Journal* as early as June 1997,[53] but it was not until April 2005 that the *Journal* turned its attention to the problems of Somalia in an article contributed by Kurt Shillinger of the South African Institute of International Affairs. This was largely as a result of fears that such a 'failed state' could be exploited by Al-Qa'ida franchises.

For many in Africa and around the world, the experience of Somalia seemed to hold three main lessons. Firstly, the notion grew that the US would always run away from a fight because American public opinion would not tolerate casualties in foreign wars that did not directly threaten its security. This was widely held to be true of other Western nations, too. Secondly, warlords, militias and organised criminals could defy the international community with impunity and that this was thus a viable way to do business. They believed that the UN would never back its own peacekeepers and could thus be ignored. Thirdly, many in the West believed that the UN was incompetent, corrupt and not to be trusted. This was problematic as the conflict over whether the UN should have the last say on legitimising a conflict such as the occupation of Iraq in 2003 was powerfully affected by its poor record in Africa during the 1990s. Many also began to suspect that the aid agencies were also incompetent and, increasingly, that they were part of Africa's problem not its solution.

In Angola, the government drew another conclusion. After a disputed election in 1991, lacking confidence in both its own army and the ability of the UN to do anything meaningful against Jonas Savimbi's UNITA rebels, it hired the mercenary outfit, Executive Outcomes. This force, consisting mainly of demobilised South African special forces, and their equally demobilised MK opponents, led the Angolan army into battle and quickly defeated the UNITA forces. The employment of mercenaries sent the UN into a panic – mercenaries in Africa have not enjoyed a good reputation and they had been outlawed by the UN in 1980 – and great pressure was put on the Angolan government to sack them. Seeing that they were now winning, the Angolan government preferred to keep Executive Outcomes fighting than settle for anything the UN could do. In the end it took the combined efforts of the US and the UN to have Executive Outcomes removed in 1995 – but by then they had already left and the private military company had been born.

This was a lesson not lost on Sierra Leone when in March 1991, the Revolutionary United Front (RUF) led by Foday Sankoh and financed by a criminal warlord from neighbouring Liberia, Charles Taylor, invaded the country. In fact, the RUF had no ideology whatsoever and was simply aiming to grab the diamond fields by whatever means possible – the more brutal the better. Sankoh's troops of choice were children captured, indoctrinated, taught to kill and rewarded with drugs and alcohol. There is no description that can possibly convey the horrors that these children inflicted. The adult troops were also given free rein to rape, murder and steal at will; no restraint was exercised. By 1995, the RUF was in virtual control of the country and Sankoh was poised to attack Freetown itself. President Valentine Strasser (an army captain who seized power as the head of the National Provisional Ruling Council in a 1992 coup) took a leaf out of the Angolan book and hired Executive Outcomes. Within a week they had beaten the rebels back from Freetown and by August 1995 had driven the RUF off the diamond fields.

In January 1996, Strasser was deposed and elections were held, which brought Ahmad Tejan Kabbah to power. Unfortunately, as a condition of receiving development aid from the IMF, Kabbah was told to sack Executive Outcomes. This meant that fourteen months later in May 1997, he was deposed by another coup by the army – forming the Armed Forces Revolutionary Council – that then went on the rampage in Freetown committing all sorts of atrocities. The new leader, Johnny Paul Koroma, did a deal with the RUF that allowed their fighters to walk into Freetown. The Nigerian Army intervened and for the next year, Freetown became a battleground before the RUF was expelled in March 1998 and Kabbah returned as president. Kabbah and the Nigerians had only survived because a British mercenary company called Sandline had trained Sierra Leonean forces loyal to Kabbah. In January 1999, the RUF launched 'Operation No Living Thing', a campaign that lived up to its name and began another advance on Freetown. They captured the city, pillaging and massacring 6,000 people before retreating with thousands of children destined to become child soldiers and sex slaves. In July, Kabbah gave in and entered a power-sharing arrangement with Foday Sankoh and the RUF; Sankoh got control of the diamonds in return for a promise to disarm. A UN force came in to supervise the disarmament but when it attempted to move into the diamond fields, the RUF captured the 500 Kenyan and Zambian peacekeepers. It looked like Freetown would be attacked again. This time, the British intervened in 2000 with a properly armed force with a clear mission. Amid rejoicing from the people of Freetown, Sankoh was captured and British officials took over the running of the government. Once stability was restored, the UN then came back with 18,000 troops and the RUF fell apart. In 2002, Kabbah declared that the war was over. 50,000 people had died, 20,000 had been mutilated and 75 per cent of the two million Sierra Leoneans had been turned into refugees.

Neither the conflicts in Angola, Sierra Leone or Liberia were well covered by the *Journal* for very good reasons; it was simply too dangerous to go there. Indeed, between 1994–96 there were no articles on Africa. However, the Institute was by now painfully aware of this lacunae as there was a growing realisation that those who exercised power in these areas resembled organised crime rather than any legitimate government and that the way in which the UN was dealing with them was completely inappropriate. John Mackinlay, then about to finish his PhD at King's College London before joining its War Studies Group, published 'War Lords' in the April 1998 *Journal*, which began to trace the aims and methods of men like Charles Taylor and criticised the international community for creating 'an alternative version of the crisis which is politically more comfortable' – treating them like insurgents with a political programme. What was needed was 'the resolve to commit the necessary forces'. In December 2001, Paul Eavis backed up this argument by baldly stating the dangers posed by organised crime in 'The Hidden Security Threat: Transnational Organised Criminal Activity' in which he pointed out that most of the weapons that had poured into Africa originated with criminal networks in the former Soviet Bloc.

The Rwandan Genocide

Ethnic violence had been rumbling on for some time between Tutsi and Hutu in Rwanda and in August 1993 the UN brokered the Arusha Peace Accords, which aimed to end the war and set up a government of national unity with the aid of a UN mission. Almost immediately, however, the UN began to receive reports that the Hutu dominated government, supported by elements within the Presidential Guard and a militia called the *Interahamwe*, were targeting Tutsi people with massacre, murder, rape and intimidation. Against this declining situation the UN decided to deploy a peacekeeping force – UNAMIR – led by French Canadian Brigadier Romeo Dallaire, which consisted of some excellent Belgian commandoes, some good Ghanaian and Tunisian troops, and an ineffective Bangladeshi battalion. On arrival Dallaire asked the UN for permission to disarm the *Interahamwe*, who were little more than armed Hutu mobs as often as not drunk or high. The UN HQ never responded and thus set a pattern of incompetence, which continued until all the worst fears of Dallaire had been realised. By the end of April 1994, some 200,000 people had been massacred. By the middle of May it was 500,000 and the credibility of the UN was completely exhausted – the Hutu government actually sat on the Security Council at the time. Paul Kagame and the rebel Rwandan Popular Front (RPF) demanded that the UN mount an operation against the Rwandan government rather than attempt any peacekeeping measures as it was the Rwandan government that was effectively carrying out the genocide. When this was not forthcoming, the RPF began to advance southwards at the beginning of May 1994. On 4 July, Kagame and the RPF took the capital Kigali and 2 million Hutus fled over the border into

Zaire. The UN declared this to be a humanitarian disaster and the aid agencies delivered assistance to the camps full of Hutus under the effective control of the *Interahamwe*. On 18 July 1994, Kagame declared the war over; in 100 days, 800,000 people had been killed.

Again, lessons were drawn about Africa and the UN from the genocide. The reputation of the UN was severely dented in the eyes of both Westerners and Africans, especially when it began to leak out that while Dallaire was kept desperately short of supplies, the UN personnel under Jacques-Roger Booh-Booh, head of the mission, appeared to have been living in some luxury. Booh-Booh himself did not start work until 10am, took long lunches and finished at the office at 4pm – and left orders that he was not to be disturbed at the weekend. Dallaire himself commented that the UN HQ in Addis Ababa, Ethiopia, had 'more Mercedes in the parking lot than I had ever seen in my life … The UN staff waltzed around in expensive tailored suits … as if they were in downtown Geneva rather than the middle of the Third World'.[54] Dallaire had a nervous breakdown at the end of his mission. The UN itself issued a report blaming Dallaire and 'the international community' as the root cause of the UN failure.

The Rwandan genocide was one of the driving forces behind the Institute's decision to expand its coverage of Africa and John Mackinlay took the opportunity to review Dallaire's book, *Shake Hands With the Devil*, for the *Journal* in August 2004, while in August 2005, Admiral Cobbold was able to interview Dallaire himself at the Institute. Not surprisingly, Dallaire was a bitter man and spread the blame for the genocide widely (including himself; selfless but completely unnecessary), but he singled out the UN Secretary-General Boutros Boutros-Ghali as the man who 'totally abdicated his responsibilities'. He also made it clear that outside NATO, there were few countries who could provide adequately trained forces for a humanitarian intervention or peace-support operation and that the UN should only be allowed in as a 'follow on' force. In October

2006, Paul Kagame himself was invited to deliver the first Nelson Mandela lecture on International Security and Development at the Institute.

The appalling experiences of many Africans during the 1990s led to a renewed determination to improve the lot of the continent and the Institute was only too willing to get involved. In 2004, it joined in co-hosting the Tswalu Dialogue, an annual event sponsored by the Oppenheimers and the South African Institute of International Affairs, aimed at looking for African solutions to African problems. There was a new maturity in thinking about Africa as Cold War attitudes were shrugged off and the rhetoric of anti-colonialism began to give way to something more thoughtful. The 2004 dialogue looked at bridging divides between the perceptions of Africans and the West while in 2005 the intertwined strands of trade, development and security were discussed. The new Brenthurst Foundation, another Oppenheimer organisation that aimed to find ways to promote economic growth in Africa, became a co-host for the 2005 dialogue. In 2006, the Institute inaugurated a Nelson Mandela Essay Prize competition in conjunction with the Brenthurst Foundation, whose first winner, David Chuter, fired a broadside at what he argued was the main flaw in the approach to Africa: Africa needed peace and security more than it needed aid and the Western attitude to giving aid was more about *feeling good* than *getting better*. If Africa was to get better, he argued, building decent police forces and armies was the real way forward, not celebrity-inspired anti-poverty campaigns. In 2007, Nicky Oppenheimer appeared at RUSI to deliver a paper entitled 'Why Africa Will Succeed', which represented a new optimism towards African security and development that the Institute had helped to foster, even if it had come a little late to the subject. Greg Mills, director of the Brenthurst Foundation, also opened up the debate on how to react to the crisis in Zimbabwe: he contributed a view on how the descent into chaos might be avoided in 'Turning Zimbabwe From a Failed State to a Functional State' in June 2003 and an address to the US House Committee on International Affairs to the *Journal* of June 2005. Knox Chitiyo, being Zimbabwean himself, organised the 'Zimbabwe: Crisis, Reconstruction and Security' conference in February 2008, which brought together academics, businessmen and politicians from both sides of the divide to debate the future of that beautiful but troubled land. At the end of the conference Dr Chitiyo made the point that such a debate could not have happened in Zimbabwe itself; RUSI could congratulate itself on bringing together opposition, government and members of the diaspora for a frank discussion on the future of their country.

New Horizons

RUSI had always hosted major figures from the defence world both in the *Journal* and through its lecture programme. However, it is probably fair to say that the Institute tended to attract the contributions of officers on their way up and who became rather more reticent with age, experience and political acumen. Hackett, we should recall, used retired officers to write his *Third World War*, but during the 1980s this began to change. Most of the Conservative Party defence ministers took the opportunity to speak at RUSI, which was enough to rouse suspicions in the minds of the left of the Labour Party that the Institute was a hotbed of right-wing reactionaries. Chris Mullin, in his 1982 novel *A Very British Coup*, held out the serious proposition that the defence and security establishment would carry out a coup if a left-wing prime minister were elected – and he was concerned enough about RUSI being part of it that he asked questions in the house about its financing.[55] Despite this, during the 1990s, it became almost *de rigeur* for any politician with an interest in defence, security and foreign policy to appear at the Institute. In April 1997, Menzies Campbell of the Liberal Democrats and John Reid of the Labour Party contributed articles to the *Journal*, while June saw Michael Portillo give the Conservative view. George Robertson, the incoming Labour defence secretary, presented his views on the 'Strategic Defence Review' and Geoff Hoon spoke on Kosovo in April 2000.

In April 2001, Margaret Thatcher was honoured by the Institute with the Chesney Gold Medal, whose terms of reference had been revised (one suspects, specially) to allow the award to be made to someone other than a military author, who had contributed generally to defence issues. She answered with a typically combative speech of acceptance. Her sometime foreign minister, Douglas Hurd, wrote for the *Journal* in February 2003 and often chaired debates in the following years. In August 2001, Admiral Cobbold organised a hustings of the three main parties to showcase and debate their respective defence policies, with Geoff Hoon, Iain Duncan-Smith and Menzies Campbell on the platform. Malcolm Rifkind and George Roberson wrote for the June 2002 *Journal*. In November 2003, George W Bush spoke to an audience of mainly RUSI members at the Banqueting House while Tony Blair spoke on the HMS *Albion* in January 2007, which necessitated the Institute moving wholesale to Plymouth for the day. Gordon Brown, reputed never to have been inside the MoD building, made history by being the first Chancellor of the Exchequer to speak at the Institute in February 2006. It was a lacklustre performance that attracted not a single question from the audience, but did produce more than a few sighs of despair at his risible but headline-grabbing declaration that more cadet forces would be set up in state schools. From 2000 onwards, the chief of the Defence Staff gave a lecture annually with General Sir Charles Guthrie being the first, an event that as often as not coincided with the subdued bacchanalia of the Institute Christmas party.

RUSI was by now the British – and very often the *international* – podium of choice for leading policy-makers and practitioners in all areas of defence and security policy. In September 2007, General David Petraeus, who was charged with formulating and overseeing a new American policy for Iraq, spoke at RUSI with Ryan Crocker, the US Ambassador to Iraq. Their presentation to RUSI presaged a further step-change for the United States as it seemed to be dealing successfully with an apparently insurmountable insurgency in Iraq. Their presentation at RUSI was in recognition of RUSI's existing research in current counter-insurgency operations. Through its flagship publication, the *RUSI Journal*, RUSI had commissioned a series of leading thinkers to offer policy options to the new insurgency issues of our time. John Nagl, the US colonel charged with redrafting the US field manual on counter-insurgency together with Alexander Alderson, his British counterpart, have both defined their take on counter-insurgency through RUSI's publications. In the matter of attracting leading policy-makers and making RUSI the centre of defence debate, the Institute could hardly have done better.

However, a feature of RUSI has always been to shape the debate rather than simply provide a platform for it, and this was especially the case when in 2009 the collapse of the US sub-prime real estate market precipitated a banking crisis in the UK which, coupled with what many felt were unrealistically high levels of public expenditure, brought Britain to the brink of financial collapse. The crisis was averted by the then-prime minister, Gordon Brown, by effectively nationalising the threatened banks with money raised on the increasingly shaky security of future tax receipts. The resulting necessity to meet the demands of its creditors now meant that Britain would have to introduce major cuts to the public expenditure budget. When New Labour was finally voted out of office in 2010, the situation was summed up succinctly by Liam Byrne, Chief Secretary to the Treasury, in a note left on his desk: 'I'm afraid to tell you there's no money left'.[56]

RUSI had seen what was coming already. Whichever party won the election, the armed forces budget would be raided as it always had been, and so RUSI embarked on a project to at least inform the policy-makers about the pros and cons of what they were about to do. Beginning in June 2009, a series of Future Defence Review Working Papers attempted to point the government in the direction of properly matching ends to means within an overall strategic concept.

Taking as their starting point the 1998 Defence Review when Blair, gifted a strong economy and a full treasury, had laid out his concept of expeditionary warfare in support of 'liberal interventionism', Professor Malcolm Chalmers and RUSI Director of Military Sciences Michael Codner laid out the bare facts of the situation.

Their view was that the armed forces really were the Cinderella of the New Labour spending spree: if the actual spend on defence had increased by 19 per cent to meet the demands of war in Sierra Leone, Kosovo, Iraq and Afghanistan, it paled in significance when compared with the 85 per cent increase in health spending, 63 per cent increase in education and 50 per cent increase in Social Security. If Byrne's comment was true, then a cut of 15 per cent in real terms would be heading for the MoD.[57]

This situation was made worse by inefficient and costly MoD procurement processes which had been exposed by Brigadier Bill Kincaid, then editor of *RUSI Defence Systems*, in his 2008 book, *Changing the Dinosaur's Spots: The Battle to Reform UK Defence Acquisition*, published by the Institute.[58] The accuracy of his findings could be inferred from the robustness of the denials issued by the New Labour press machine, the commissioning of a review by the then defence secretary, John Hutton, and the admission by the Under-Secretary Quentin Davies at a RUSI conference that the UK would now consider buying its armoured vehicles off-the-shelf from overseas rather than trust to the MoD. Kincaid's regular 'RUSI Acquisition Focus' discussion series and *RUSI Defence Systems* feature was also used as the basis for the House of Commons Defence Committee's scrutiny of the MoD in November 2008. In July 2009, the *Future Defence Review Working Papers* initiative paid off when the government announced at a RUSI conference that a defence Green Paper would precede a full strategic defence review after the 2010 election. The MoD then named RUSI as its principal source of 'outside' viewpoints and invited Professorial Research Fellow Malcolm Chalmers and ex-head of MI6, John Scarlett, to sit on the National Security Council and the Cabinet

Office Working Group on the Strategic Defence and Security Review. This was a major success for the RUSI mission to give expert advice to the policy-makers: how far those policy-makers would be able to resist the depredations of the Treasury was, however, a moot point.

The autumn of 2010 saw the Institute develop further with the launch of RUSI International, a new virtual platform for geopolitical and strategic thinking designed to link up major analysts from around the world in both public and private meetings. The brain child of RUSI's first civilian director, Professor Michael Clarke, appointed in 2007, the idea was to go beyond the work of the Institute's overseas offices to use unconventional platforms to bring people who might not otherwise discuss world affairs together. Led by RUSI Vice-Presidents Dr Alexander Mirtchev and Sir John Scarlett, RUSI International quickly made links with the Atlantic Council, the Eisenhower, Kissinger and American Enterprise Institutes and persuaded Judge William Webster, ex-director of both the CIA and the FBI to take part. The United Services Institute in Delhi – a Raj-era RUSI foundation – and the Gulf Centre for Strategic Studies took the initiative east of Suez, while a new relationship with the Japan Institute for Strategic Studies pushed it further into the Far East. There was also an ambassador-at-large appointed – Georgette Mosbacher, CEO of Borghese Inc, a senior Republican and cosmetics manufacturer.

Professor Clarke's other influence on RUSI was to turn it into an organisation that was much more responsive to the media than before, while retaining and expanding its academic edge. A conscious effort was made to make the Institute the first stop for journalists who needed fast, accurate briefings on areas that they had little personal experience or expertise in. This began with a *Journal* article in December 2007 that discussed drug abuse in the British armed forces and argued that the cost – the equivalent of one battalion per year – was greater than the casualty rolls from Afghanistan and Iraq.[59] In February 2008, a further *Journal* issue published the consensus view of a wide array of prominent defence intellectuals that the UK was a soft touch when it came to terror attacks.[60] Both articles generated mainstream press and TV interest and from that point on a steady stream of print and broadcast journalists regarded RUSI as the one-stop shop for authoritative comment on defence and security issues. Moving defence out of the messes and into the popular arena has been a feature of the Institute since its foundation, but Clarke did well to reshape and sharpen up the RUSI response to a new media environment and to move RUSI more comprehensively into the virtual world, the blogosphere and even onto that coolest of twenty-first century communication devices – the social networking website.

RUSI Today

What then could a first-time visitor to the Institute expect to meet with in 2011? The first difficulty presenting such a visitor is actually finding the Institute, because the main building occupies a frontage of only 57 feet of Whitehall, sandwiched in between the Banqueting House and the Wales Office. Academics wandering up and down Whitehall with bewildered looks on their faces are therefore not an uncommon sight and the visitor cannot fail to be surprised at the discreet doorway with the small brass plaque, having imagined something perhaps a little grander. Entering the building, the visitor is immediately seized by its light and spacious foyer and stepping through towards the Duke of Wellington lecture theatre, amazed at its breadth, depth and height. The architects, Sir Aston Webb and Ingriss Bell, pulled off a real triumph back in 1895 when the large bay was erected at the rear of the building. The ornate ceiling is worth the visit alone.

Going up to the first floor to the Library, there are the paintings on military and naval subjects as one would expect, with a large portrait of Earl Roberts by Adrian Jones (1914) on guard on the first-floor landing. The Library itself was relaunched in July 2009 as the RUSI Library of Military History by Major General the Duke of Westminster, who contributes an annual medal for writings on military history. Adorned with bronzes, shelving that requires a certain amount of mountaineering ability to reach the top volumes and comfortable leather chairs, it retains the air of an Edwardian house or officer's mess. The collection is very good and contains many rarities that would be difficult to source together in one place, but also contemporary works from a wide range of authors. The Institute has always been proud of its Library; one can often find volunteers cleaning and maintaining the volumes. There is also a gallery connected by a spiral stair, concealed like a secret passage, in one corner. Up here are many of the older collections and one may find a particularly dedicated researcher on his or her knees under the writing desks in search of the *Minutes of the Royal Artillery Institute* or other hidden gems.

During conferences, the Library will often be used for the lunchtime buffet, which allows those vitally important informal contacts to be made. The visitor may see an American civilian identified by his lapel badge as a 'Planner' earnestly persuading a PhD student, recently returned from an attachment with Pakistan's ISI, to talk to his associates; a professor of naval history discussing the defeat of the *Graf Spee* with a German film-maker; a couple of BBC researchers looking glum at having to wear the lapel badges that immediately put people on their guard when talking to the media; there is a photographer recently back from Darfur and another singing the praises of Gandamack Lodge, Kabul's first decent hotel; three students from the War Studies Department at King's College London are hungrily devouring large helpings of coronation chicken; four RAF officers debating the ground war in Helmand with an infantry colonel from the Defence Academy writing on counter-insurgency; there are several conversations going on in unfamiliar accents and languages yet to be learned. Informing informed opinion is RUSI's mission. A well-attended conference will see the crowd spill over into the reception room opposite, which has excellent views of Whitehall and display cases containing such things as the sword of General Sir Aylmer Hardane, a warrior who saw action in India in the 1890s, South Africa during the Boer War, France during the First World War, and retired in 1925 as Governor of Mesopotamia. The walls throughout the Institute carry portraits and also a large bust of Blücher from an old barracks in Jena, the nose of which was broken by a Russian rifle butt in 1945. Downstairs there is another bust with a broken nose, but here it was a busy waitress (certainly not tipsy) who was to blame, and Nelson has since been restored.

The next floor up is reserved for members. On the right is the entrance to the Library gallery and next to it the librarian's office, crowded floor to ceiling with books to be catalogued. On the left is a large office full of researchers staring intently into computer screens; this is where the serious business of research goes on. There are also a couple of narrow staircases here which lead up and across the roof to the upper offices where more staff are kept, like a collection of Mrs Rochesters. It is a little cramped up here, but typical of the Whitehall warren. There are around 100 staff members in total, including Visiting and Associate Fellows, but usually there are no more than thirty or forty visible at any one time. The work in progress will include projects on climate change and security, resilience, emergency management, European and international security as well as military and naval subjects. Its worth has also been recognised by its peers; in 2008 RUSI won the *Prospect* magazine Think Tank of the Year Award, and was then honoured again with its Foreign Policy Think Tank of the Year Award in 2009. Whatever the visitor chooses, he or she will go away with new ideas; some difficult, some challenging, but all worthy of consideration. And he or she will definitely be back for more.

Between Peace and War

From the time of its founding in 1831, RUSI has been remarkably consistent in its advocacy of the need for defence debates, but its methodology has been both flexible and responsive to the changing circumstances that it has witnessed.

The first step in accomplishing its mission was the establishment of the Museum and Library in 1833 at a time when museums were much more about speculating on the future than repositories of the past. The publication of the *Journal* after the Crimean War in 1857 marked the second major response by appealing to both a wider audience and calling for a wider range of voices to respond to the changing circumstances of the mid-nineteenth century.

The stimulation of debate brought on by the publication of the *Battle of Dorking* and the related arguments about imperial defence brought RUSI to a prominence that surprised many – and dismayed not a few of the many British anti-imperialists at the time – but it did not lead the Institute to become intoxicated with the wilder ideas of an ever-expanding empire. The Institute was interested in *defence* not imperialism per se, or any other particular programme or ideology. This was made clear with its sober approach to the emerging threat from Germany before 1914 alongside its determination to ensure that the growing demands for a welfare state enunciated by Lloyd George and the Liberals did not eclipse the need for adequate defences.

After the First World War, the Institute recognised that economics and international relations were more immediately relevant to security than previously, and tailored its interests in the *Journal* to engage with them. It was also hugely to its credit that RUSI did not succumb to the dreams of League idealists, Nazi militarists or Bolshevik ideologues, as so many others across Europe did, but held on to the moderate values of Britain that at times looked dangerously like a candle in the wind.

The decline of British power after 1945 was also faced squarely by the Institute as was the loss of the Banqueting House; again, it is to the Institute's credit that faith in its mission to push forward the cause of adequate defences survived both the post-war shock and the eviction. It also managed to keep a clear view through the purple haze of the anti-establishment 1960s and 1970s, a clear view which saw the need for a re-statement of *The Battle of Dorking* in Hackett's *Third World War*.

The end of the Cold War and the slow return to a multi-polar world, akin to nineteenth-century European great power politics and the 'small wars' that went with it, also saw the Institute respond to changing situations, not least in recognising the rising power of the media[61] in a fast-paced and ever more fluid international environment. The complications to that environment introduced by jihadism and organised crime were also quickly responded to – the Institute had never bothered with the Fenian outrages of the 1860s and the anarchist disturbances of the late nineteenth century, but the New York and Washington 9/11, London 7/7 and 2008 Mumbai outrages meant that this threat could not be similarly treated.

It also recognised that in a globalised world, there was nowhere that could be safely ignored; groups as disparate as South American drug cartels, Somali pirates and Pakistani Swat Valley radicals all needed to be studied. Nor did the Institute forget the need to peer into the future; in 2009 RUSI was invited by a collection of South American governments to assess the security implications for them of climate change, warned against a resurgent threat from a Russia rediscovering its imperial instincts, and in 2007, RUSI encouraged Professor Noel Starkey to speculate on the possibility of an international robotic arms race that would replace suicide bombers as the main terrorist threat.

It is safe to assume, therefore, that in 2011, the Institute is still true to its aim of being 'strictly a scientific and professional society, not a club' to further 'the promotion and advancement of Naval and Military Science and Literature'. But, it has also undoubtedly grown; first into a British institute for defence studies and now a major international centre for defence and security studies. It is a repository of analysis and advice, and a centre for the essential free discussion, forward thinking and careful reflection that will be needed until the mad men who think themselves to be sane decide that a ploughshare is a better use for metal than a sword. Long may it be so.

NOTES AND REFERENCES

I. Origins: 1829–60, pp. 1–20.

1. See Walter Thornbury, *Old and New London, A Narrative of its History, its People and its Places. Illustrated with Numerous Engravings from the Most Authentic Sources*, Vol. 4 (London: Cassell Petter & Galpin), p. 155.

2. In its early years, RUSI went through several changes of name. For simplicity, the term 'Institute' is used unless otherwise stated.

3. Forerunners may have included the General Military Club and the Navy Club formed in 1816, but this is uncertain. The entry in the National Maritime Museum catalogue states the formation of these institutions as beginning in 1916, but this is probably a typo.

4. Hew Strachan, *Wellington's Legacy: The Reform of the British Army 1830–54* (Manchester: Manchester University Press, 1984), p. 110. Much of this section is drawn from this work.

5. E Altham, 'The Royal United Services Institute, 1831–1931', *RUSI Journal* (Vol. 76, No. 502, 1931). See also RUSI annual report, 1853.

6. *Ibid.*

7. Then converted into the HMS *Black Joke*, tasked with hunting slavers.

8. Papers relating to the origin and progress of the United Services Museum, collected by J Ford Late of the 79th Regt, Report of the Committee 1 August 1831, RUSI Library.

9. Hardinge was at that time Chief Secretary for Ireland, a fact which might have encouraged the Lord Lieutenant in his membership.

10. Prospectus of the United Service Museum, Commander Henry Downes RN, Secretary.

11. Altham, *op. cit.*; Papers relating to the Origin and Progress of the United Services Museum, collected by J Ford Late of the 79th Regiment, Report of the Committee 1 August 1831.

12. *The Times*, Letters to the Editor, 28 and 30 December 1831.

13. RUSI annual report, 1832.

14. Papers relating to the Origin and Progress of the United Services Museum, collected by J. Ford Late of the 79th Regt., Report of the Committee, 1 August 1831.

15. *The Times*, 7 July 1831.

16. 'One asks the watermen hard by Where may the Poet's Palace lie? Another of the Thames inquires If he has seen its gilded spires. At length they in the rubbish spy A thing resembling a goose pye'. Jonathan Swift, 'Vanbrug's House', 1703.

17. Proceedings of the 2nd Anniversary Meeting.

18. Altham, *op. cit.*

19. *Ibid.*

20. Strachan, *op. cit.*, p. 131.

21. RUSI annual report, 1849.

22. United Services Museum Minutes, June 1856.

23. United Services Museum Minutes, September 1856.

24. RUSI annual report, 1840.

25. RUSI annual report, 1858.

26. Now available at the National Maritime Museum.

27. G F Crutchley, *Crutchley's London in 1865: A handbook for strangers showing where to go, how to get there, and what to look at* (London: 1865).

28. *The Times*, 12 March 1858.

29. Report of the Committee, 1831.

30. *Daily Telegraph*, 'Wellington's Second Waterloo', 23 March 2004.

31. *The Times*, 7 June 1893. *The Times* said £2,000 but this is probably a misprint; *The Times*, 10 July 1850.

32. RUSI annual reports, 1869, 1873.

33. Altham, *op. cit.*

34. United Services Museum minutes, 7 April 1856.

35. RUSI annual report, 1858.

36. RUSI annual report, 1841.

37. RUSI annual report, 1855.

38. Strachan, *op. cit.*, pp. 21–26.

39. Michael D Welch, *Science and the British Officer: The Early days of the RUSI for Defence Studies (1829-1869)*, Whitehall Paper No. 44 (London: RUSI, 1998), p. 28.

40. See, for example, Peter Burroughs, 'Defence and Imperial Disunity', in Andrew Porter (ed.), *Oxford History of the British Empire: Vol. III, The Nineteenth Century* (Oxford: Oxford University Press, 1999).

41. David Gillard, *The Struggle for Asia 1828–1914: A Study in British and Russian Imperialism* (London: Meuthen and Co, 1977), pp. 96, 103.

42. For a description of the technical character of officers, see 'British Officers in 1878' by Miles, Letters to the Editor, *The Times*, 25 January 1878.

43. Colonel Lindsay, 'Supply – Army Estimates', *Hansard* HC Vol. 141, Cols. 185–209 (14 March 1856).

44. United Services Museum minutes, 2 February 1857.

45. George Tyler, in *Hansard, op. cit.*

46. *The Times*, 12 March 1858.

47. RUSI annual report, 1860, p.5.

48. Welch, *op. cit.*, p. 53.

49. 29th Annual Report of the Council, 1860, p.5.

II. Demanding Security in a Great Power Age: 1860–90, pp. 21–80.

1. Lord Robert Cecil, *Quarterly Review* (July, 1864).

2. John N Westwood, *Endurance and Endeavour: Russian History 1812–1986* (Oxford: Oxford University Press, 1988), p. 96.

3. David Stone, *First Reich: The German Army in the Franco-Prussian War 1870–1871* (London: Brassey's, 2002), p. 296.

4. Barbara Messamore, 'Diplomacy or Duplicity? Lord Lisgar, John A Macdonald, and the Treaty of Washington, 1871', *Journal of Imperial & Commonwealth History* (Vol. 21, No. 2, May 2004).

5. RUSI annual report, 1860.

6. Hew Strachan, *Wellington's Legacy: The Reform of the British Army 1830–54* (Machester: Manchester University Press, 1984).

7. George Chesney, 'The Battle of Dorking: Reminiscences of a Volunteer', *Blackwood's Magazine* (May 1871).

8. The story begins with an outright condemnation of Parliament for neglecting its duties out of a desire to pander to the Radicals. Then follows an avalanche of misfortune as the USA threatens Canada, the Fenians threaten a revolt in Ireland and India rises in rebellion again. With the fleet divided to protect Vancouver from the Americans and Constantinople from the Russians, what was left is destroyed by 'fatal engines' when it puts to sea to halt the German invasion armada. The defence is left to an enthusiastic but untrained Volunteer movement which is quickly dispersed by the clockwork German army disembarking at Worthing, marching up to the decisive battle at Dorking and then on into Wimbledon. The government, in thrall to newspapers demanding resistance one moment and spreading defeatism the next, has no choice but to surrender. The empire is divided up between Germany and Russia, the fleet disarmed, Ireland detached and the Treasury raided for an indemnity. George Tomkyns Chesney, *The Battle of Dorking: Reminiscences of a Volunteer* (London: Lippincott, Grambon and Co, 1871).

9. I F Clarke, *Voices Prophesying War, 1763–1984* (Oxford: Oxford University Press, 1966).

10. Quoted in *Ibid.*, p. 39.

11. Hew Strachan, *The First World War: A New History* (Free Press, 2006), p. 224.

12. George Peden, 'The Treasury and Defence of Empire 1856–1956', Paper presented to Joint Services Command and Staff College, 7 December 2007.

13. The author is grateful to Stephen Badsey for this point.

14. USM Minutes, 1871.

15. *Ibid.*

16. Sir John Hay's Question, *Hansard* HC Vol. 174, Col. 182 (17 March 1864).

17. *Hansard* HC Vol. 209, Cols. 7–40 (6 February 1872).

18. *The Times*, 5 March 1877.

19. See for example Sir Garnet Wolseley's comments in the debate following Major T Hutton, 'Mounted Infantry', *RUSI Journal* (Vol. 30, No. 135, 1886/87).

20. Michael D Welch, *Science and the British Officer: The Early Days of the RUSI for Defence Studies (1829–1869)*, RUSI Whitehall Paper No. 44 (London: RUSI, 1998), p. 60.

21. P H Colomb, 'Lessons From Lissa', *RUSI Journal* (Vol. 11, 1867).

22. Stephen Badsey, 'The Anglo–Zulu War and British Defence Policy', paper presented to the 130th Anniversary Anglo–Zulu War Conference, Dundee, South Africa 2009.

23. T Symes Prideaux, 'On Economy of Fuel in Ships of War', *RUSI Journal* (Vol. 16, 1873). See also R S Lowrey, 'On Coaling Ships or Squadrons on the Open Sea', *RUSI Journal* (Vol. 27, 1884).

24. ADM 1/8869, p. 28. See also PRO CAB 7/3, 'Second Report of the Royal Commissioners appointed to inquire into the defence of British Possessions and Commerce Abroad. Part I: The Duties of the Navy', Carnarvon Commission, March 1882.

25. T Brassey, 'The Mercantile Marine considered as an Auxiliary to the Royal Navy', *RUSI Journal* (Vol. 20, 1877).

26. PRO CAB 7/2.

27. J C R Colomb, *The Defence of Great and Greater Britain: Sketches of its Naval, Military and Political Aspects: Annotated with Extracts from the Discussions they have called Forth in the Press of Greater Britain* (London: Edward Stanford, 1880) pp. 75–81.

28. *Ibid.*, p. 58.

29. WO 33/19, 'General Report of Director of Ordnance 1866–7'. See also CAB11/81, 'Report on the General Scheme of coast defence for India', November 1879.

30. CAB 11/81, 'Report on the General Scheme of Coast Defence for India', November 1879.

31. PRO 30/6/122, 'Defence of Commercial Harbours and Coaling Stations', Defence Committee Meeting, 18 May 1877. See also, 'Acts of Defence Committee and Memoranda with reference to the defence of

Commercial harbours and Coaling stations', J L A Simmons Inspector-General of Fortifications report, 1877. See also J C R Colomb, *op. cit.*, p. 58.

32. PRO 30/6/33, 'Frere to Carnarvon', 24 August, 1877. See also ADM 1/8869, pp. 31–33; CAB 11/81, 'Report on the General Scheme of coast defence for India', November 1879; PRO 30/6/122, 'Defence of Commercial Harbours and Coaling Stations'.

33. 'Frere to Hicks-Beach', 30 April 1878. Reproduced in W B Worsfold, *Sir Bartle Frere* (London: Butterworth Ltd., 1923), pp. 72–74. See also PRO 30/6/122.

34. John Francis Beeler, *British Naval Policy in the Gladstone-Disraeli Era* (Stanford: Stanford University Press), p. 17.

35. Mabel V Jackson Haight, *European Powers and South East Africa 1796–1856* (London: Routledge, 1967), p. 111. See also J C R Colomb, *op. cit.*, pp. 146–47.

36. Merchant shipping that was nominally civilian but in practice under naval command.

37. ADM 1/26721, 'General Instructions for guidance of Officers in command of H M Ships on East Indies Station, to meet the emergency of the sudden outbreak of war with France or Russia', 3 March 1883.

38. PRO CAB 7/4, 'Third and Final Report into the Defence of British Possessions and Commerce Abroad', Carnarvon Commission, 1882.

39. PRO CAB 7/2, 'First Report of the Royal Commissioners appointed to inquire into the Defence of British Possessions and Commerce Abroad', Carnarvon Commission, 8 September 1879.

40. Commodore Schufeldt, commanding USS Ticonderoga, to R W Thomson, Secretary of the Navy. Quoted in Kenneth J Hagan, *American Gunboat Diplomacy and the Old Navy 1877–1889* (Connecticut: Greenwood Press, 1973), p. 104.

41. J R Hamilton, 'The American Navy; its organisation, ships, armament, and recent experiences', *RUSI Journal* (Vol. 12, 1869).

42. G Noel, 'Naval Prize Essay 1876', *RUSI Journal* (Vol. 20, 1877).

43. Dictionary of National Biography.

44. G A Ballard, 'The Protection of Commerce during War', *RUSI Journal* (Vol. 42, 1898).

45. D P O'Connor, 'Defending Australia: Imperial Expansion and Local Defence', *Journal of Australian Naval History* (Vol. 6 No. 1, March 2009).

46. T Brassey, 'The Mercantile Marine considered as an Auxilliary to the Royal Navy', *RUSI Journal* (Vol. 20, 1877).

47. H L Hoskins, *British Routes to India* (New York, Longmans, Green and Company, 1928), p. 370.

48. ADM 1/8869, 'General Outline of Possible Naval Operations against Russia', 14 March 1885.

49. 'If you wish for peace, prepare for war'. See, for example, R Scott, 'The Maritime Defence of England, including Offensive and Defensive Warfare', *RUSI Journal* (Vol. 27, 1884); Sir John Coode, 'On Military (or Strategic) and Refuge Harbours', *RUSI Journal* (Vol. 19, 1876); R S Lowrey, 'On Coaling ships or squadrons on the open sea', *RUSI Journal* (Vol. 27, 1884).

50. Dictionary of National Biography.

51. Dictionary of National Biography.

52. The Topographical department was the forerunner to the Intelligence Branch. See 'Topographical Department', *The Times*, 14 April 1865.

53. PRO 30/40 Box 1, Ardagh Papers.

54. *The Times*, 4 March 1889.

55. For example, T Symes Prideaux, 'Economy of Fuel in Steam Ships', *INA Transactions* (Vol. XIII 1872).

56. C Brackenbury, 'The Intelligence Duties of the Staff Abroad and at Home', *RUSI Journal* (Vol. 19, 1879).

57. J A S Colquhoun, 'Essay on the Formation of an Intelligence Department for India', *USI Journal* (Vol. IV, 1874).

58. WO 147/17, 'Rules for the Conduct of the War Game', 1872. See also WO106/1, 'Turkey'.

59. Dictionary of National Biography. Also see, for example, OIOC MSS EUR F.75/7, 'Frere to Jacob', 15 May 1857.

60. OIOC IOR L/MIL/17/17/15/1, 'Official Journal of the Reconnoitring Party of the British Force in Abyssinia'.

61. Adrian Preston, 'Sir Charles Macgregor and the Defence of India, 1857–1887', *The Historical Journal* (Vol. 12, No. 1, 1969).

62. The Royal Geographical Society was behind the decision to create a Readership in Geography at Oxford in 1887. Its first holder was Halford Mackinder. It is unprovable, but highly probable, that he met Frere at the RGS during this period and may have been influenced by him. See Brian Blouet, 'The Imperial Vision of Halford Mackinder', *Geographical Journal* (Vol. 170, No. 4, December 2004) and F Emery, 'Geography and Imperialism: The Role of Sir Bartle Frere (1815–84)', *The Geographical Journal* (Vol. 150, No. 3, November 1984). It has also been argued that the RGS was formed as a vehicle for imperialism. See Rachel Woodward, 'From Military Geography to militarism's geographies: disciplinary engagements with the geographies of militarism and military activities', *Progress in Human Geography* (Vol. 29, Issue 6, December 2005).

63. See for example, 'The Turks in Persia and the Caucasus', *The Asiatic Quarterly Review* (Vol. I, Jan/April 1886); O T Burne, 'The Empress of India' (Vol. III, Jan/April 1887); Colonel Malleson, 'The Sea Route to India' (Vol. V, January/April 1888).

64. OIOC IOR, L/MIL/17/17/16/1, 'Confidential Papers Connected with the Abyssinian Expedition', First Series.

65. Damian P O'Connor, 'In Praise of the Tail: The Land Transport Corps in Abyssinia 1867–8', *RUSI Journal* (Vol. 151, No. 1, 2006).

66. OIOC IOR MSS EUR/PHOTO/EUR/319, 'Captain Augustus Arthur Currie's experiences on the march'.

67. See, for example, G A Furse, 'Studies on Military Transport; Home and Indian Transport and Steps Taken to Provide a Transport Corps in Some of our Former Wars', *USI Journal* (Vol. VII, No. 53, 1878); J C Graves, 'How a Horse Transport Ship should be Ventilated and Remarks as to the Fittings for the Same', *USI Journal* (Vol. II, No. 16, 1874).

68. O'Connor, *op. cit.* in note 65.

69. WO 33/32, 'Reports and Memoranda 1878', October 1878. See also Thomas G Fergusson, *British Military Intelligence* (Frederick, MD: University Publications of America, 1984), p. 59; J A S Colquhoun, 'Essay on the formation of an Intelligence Department for India', *USI Journal* (Vol. IV, 1874).

70. Fergusson, *op. cit.*, p. 63.

71. CO 885/4/156, 'India Office to Colonial Office, Correspondence respecting the Defences of the Colonies Colonial Office', 1878.

72. Colonel Sir Harry Green, *The Defence of the North West Frontier of India, with reference to the advance of Russia in Central Asia* (London, 1873).

73. Sir F Goldsmid, *Central Asia and its Question* (London: 1873) and *Eastern Persia* (London: 1876).

74. WO 33/32, 'Reports and Memoranda 1878'. See also E B Hamley, 'The Strategical Conditions of our Indian North West Frontier', speech given at RUSI, 13 December 1878. Rawlinson was in the Chair.

75. WO 106/174, 'Russian Advances in Asia', 1873.

76. Bartle Frere, *Afghanistan and South Africa. Letters to the Right Hon. W.E. Gladstone, M.P. regarding portions of his Midlothian Speeches, and a letter to the late Sir John Kaye and other papers* (London: 1881).

77. Angus Ross, *New Zealand Aspirations in the Pacific in the Nineteenth Century* (Oxford: Clarendon Press, 1964), p. 132. See also R Dalziel, 'Southern Islands: New Zealand and Polynesia', in A Porter (ed), *Oxford History of the British Empire Vol. III, The Nineteenth Century* (Oxford: Oxford University Press, 1999), p. 591.

78. RUSI annual report, 1869.

79. RUSI annual report, 1873.

80. USM minutes, 7 March 1872.

81. RUSI annual report, 1878.

82. See, for example, J C R Colomb, 'General Principles of Naval Organisation', *RUSI Journal* (Vol. 15, 1872) and 'The Naval and Military resources of the Colonies', *RUSI Journal* (Vol. 23, 1880). Also 'Naval Intelligence and the Protection of Commerce in War', *RUSI Journal* (Vol. 25, 1882).

83. See, for example, R Scott, 'The Maritime Defence of England, including Offensive and Defensive Warfare', *RUSI Journal* (Vol. 20, 1877) and G Noel, 'Naval Prize Essay 1876', *RUSI Journal* (Vol. 20, 1877).

84. CO 854/15, Colonial Office Circulars 1874.

85. Add. Mss. 607968, Holland to Carnarvon, 20 August 1874, Carnarvon Papers.

86. Dictionary of National Biography.

87. CO 882/3/4, Clarke to Carnarvon, 5 November 1874.

88. BL Add, Mss 60812, Carnarvon Papers, C Gavan Duffy to Carnarvon 16 September 1874, 'Memorandum on the organization of the Colonial Empire'.

89. D M Schurman, *Imperial Defence 1868–1887* (London: Frank Cass, 2000), pp. 32–35.

90. CO 882/3/6, Carnarvon to Jervois, 25 November 1875.

91. CO 882/3/6, Jervois to Carnarvon, 14 December 1875.

92. PRO 30/6/115, Memorandum on Russo–Turkish War, Wolseley to Carnarvon 7 May 1877, Carnarvon Papers. See also OIOC IOR C141, Memorandum by Maj–General Sir Garnet Wolseley 20 March 1878.

93. ADM1/26721. See also LQV I, Beaconsfield to Queen Victoria, Secret Memorandum No. 2, 23 April 1877, p. 530.

94. PRO 30/6/115, Simmons to Hardy 19 April 1877 and 2 May 1877, Carnarvon Papers.

95. David Gillard, *The Struggle for Asia* (London: Methuen and Co, 1977), pp. 63–64, 79.

96. Dictionary of National Biography.

97. FO 358/1, Reports and Memoranda relative to Defence of Constantinople and other positions in Turkey also on routes in Roumelia, 1877, Simmons Papers.

98. FO 358/1, Instructions to Major and Brevet Lieutenant Colonel Home, Simmons Papers.

99. WO106/1, E Baring, 'The Russo–Turkish War 1877–78', November 27 1870. See also E Baring, 'Turkey'.

100. FO 385/1, Memorandum, 2 December 1876, Simmonds papers.

101. FO 385/1, Further Memorandum, 4 December 1876, Simmonds papers.

102. *Ibid.*

103. FO 358/2, Memorandums from Simmons to Mr Hardy, SOS for War.

104. *Ibid.* See also Memorandum on the Forces and Probable Operations in Asia Minor, 17 April 1877.

105. FO 358/3, Simmons to Hardy 23 April 1877, Simmons Papers.

106. *Ibid.*

107. *Ibid.*

108. WO 163/2, War Office Council Meetings 1874–79.

109. FO 358/1, Very Confidential Memorandum, 8 July 1878, Simmons Papers.

110. Peter Hopkirk, *The Great Game* (London: John Murray, 1990), pp. 301, 308, 353.

111. Adrian Preston, 'Sir Charles Macgregor and the Defence of India, 1857–1887', *The Historical Journal* (Vol. 12, No. 1, 1969).

112. Frere, *op. cit.* in note 76. The letter was privately printed for circulation among Indian Council members.

113. Baker was found guilty of sexually assaulting a woman in a railway carriage. He was fined, spent a year in jail and was cashiered after offering no defence.

114. Betty Balfour, *The History of Lord Lytton's Indian Administration, 1876 to 1880* (London: Longman's, Green and Co., 1899), p. 45.

115. Brian Robson, *The Road to Kabul: The Second Afghan War 1878–1881* (London: Staplehurst, 2003), pp. 74–79.

116. Byron Farwell, *Eminent Victorian Soldiers: Seekers of Glory* (New York: W. W. Norton Company, 1988), pp. 164–5.

117. Robson, *op. cit.*, p. 118.

118. Bartle Frere, 'The Eastern Question', *Quarterly Review* (October 1876), pp. 504–05, 544–46.

119. Damian P O'Connor, *The Zulu and the Raj: The Life of Sir Bartle Frere* (London: Able Publications, 2002). The issue of Frere's disobedience is hotly debated.

120. For a fuller exposition of this point, see D P O'Connor, 'Imperial Strategy and the Anglo–Zulu War of 1879', *The Historian* (Vol. 68, No. 2, 2006).

121. F Thesiger, 'Is a Radical Change in the Tactical Formation of our Infantry Really Necessary?', *USI Journal* (Vol. II, No. 10, 1873).

122. J L Sturgis, *John Bright and the Empire* (London: Athlone Press, 1969), pp. 13, 83.

123. Richard Shannon, *The Crisis of Imperialism 1865–1915* (London: Paladin: 1974), p. 20.

124. For its influence on the Labour Party see Sturgis, *op. cit.*, p.185.

125. J Bright, 'Foreign Policy, October 29th, 1858' in *Selected Speeches of the Rt. Hon. John Bright on Public Questions* (London, J.M. Dent & Co., 1907), p. 220 and also entry 18 July 1882. See also Sturgis, *op. cit.*

126. Bright, *op. cit.* in note 122.

127. See also Sturgis, *op. cit.*, p. 179.

128. J Bright, 'General Politics, November 5th, 1868' in *Speeches, op. cit.* in note 125, p. 118. See also W F Monypenny and G E Buckle, *The Life of Benjamin Disraeli, Earl of Beaconsfield: Vol II 1860–1881* (London: John Murray, 1929), p. 29.

129. J Bright, 'General Politics, November 5th, 1868', in Bright, *op. cit.* in note 122, p. 204.

130. *Ibid.* See also Sturgis, *op. cit.*, p. 107.

131. J Bright, 'General Politics, November 5th, 1868' in Bright, *op. cit.* in note 122, p. 119.

132. Sturgis, *op. cit.*, p. 83.

133. P M Kennedy, *The Rise of the Anglo–German Antagonism 1860–1914* (London, 1980) p. 61.

134. Entry 2 March 1867 KJ. A Hawkins and J Powell, *The Journal of John Wodehouse First Earl of Kimberley for 1862-1902* (London: 1997).

135. Shannon, *op. cit.* in note 123, p. 47.

136. C Dilke, 'Greater Britain', reproduced in Peter Cain (ed.), *Empire and Imperialism: The Debate of the 1870s* (Little Bend, IN: St Augustines Press, 1999), p. 20.

137. *Ibid*, p. 24.

138. R A Lowe, 'Value of the Foreign Dominions of the Crown', reproduced in Cain, *op. cit.*, p. 118.

139. *Ibid.*, p.109.

140. Frederic Rogers, Lord Blatchford, 'The Integrity of the British Empire', reproduced in Cain, *op. cit.*, p. 121.

141. William E Gladstone, 'Aggression on Egypt and Freedom in the East', reproduced in Cain, *op. cit.*, p.188.

142. WO 106/272, 'Digest of History of Somaliland Camel Corps KAR 1912', p. 2.

143. E Dicey, 'Our Route to India' (1877) reproduced in Cain, *op. cit.* p. 163.

144. Gladstone, *op. cit.*, p. 200.

145. J Morley, *The Life of William Ewert Gladstone: Vol. II* (London: Edward Lloyd, 1908), pp. 67–69.

146. Richard Shannon, *Gladstone: Heroic Minister 1865–1898* (London: Allen Lane, 1999) p. 86.

147. See Gladstone to Childers 21 December 1884, published in *The Gladstone Diaries* (Oxford: Oxford University Press, 1994).

148. D A Farnie, East and West of Suez. The Suez Canal in History 1854-1956 (Oxford: 1969), p. 263.

149. William E Gladstone, 'England's Mission' (1878) reproduced in Cain, *op. cit.*, p. 236.

150. Dicey, *op. cit.*, p. 184.

151. Gladstone, *op. cit.* in note 149, p. 240.

152. *Ibid.*, p. 235.

153. E Dicey, 'Mr. Gladstone and Our Empire' (1877) reproduced in Cain, *op. cit.*, p. 222.

154. Adrian Preston, 'Sir Charles Macgregor and the Defence of India, 1857–1887', *The Historical Journal* (Vol. 12, No. 1, 1969).

155. Frederic Seebohm, 'Imperialism and Socialism' (1880) reproduced in Cain, *op. cit.*, p. 298.

156. R A Lowe, 'Imperialism' (1878) reproduced in Cain, *op. cit.*, p. 268.

157. *Ibid.*, p. 270.

158. *Ibid.*, p. 273.

159. J Morris, *Heaven's Command: Imperial Progress* (London: Faber & Faber, 1973), p. 441. According to legend there is a row of peach trees marking the spot where the dead soldiers were buried with the peaches they were eating in their pockets. The author could not find them, however; the graves were moved to make way for a new road. The battle is now marked only by a small pillar situated between an enormous Buddhist pagoda and a *slaghuis*. Author's visit, August 2004.

160. Entry 20 June 1882, published in *Gladstone Diaries, op. cit.*

161. See for example, Northbrook to Baring, 27 September 1882. Quoted in B Mallet, *Thomas George, Earl of Northbrook G. C. S. I.: A Memoir* (London: Longmans, 1908), p. 168.

162. I Hamilton, 'Naval bombardment of the coastal defences at Alexandria (1882) and the Dardanelles (1914–15): lessons and consequences', paper presented to the US Naval Academy, Annapolis, USA, September 2007.

163. *Ibid.*

164. OIOC IOR Mss Eur D604/10, Childers to Hartington 19 June 1881, Hartington Papers.

165. WO 147/17, E Baring, Rules for the Conduct of the War Game, 1872. See also WO106/1, 'Turkey' by E Baring 1870.

166. IOR L/MIL/17/17/44, Edwin Collen, Memorandum on the Employment of an Indian Force in Egypt, First Assistant Mil Sec, India. Intelligence Branch, QMG's Dept 18th January 1878, Horse Guards.

167. WO33/41 Papers 1883 Part 2. 0931 TO 0948, Papers in connection with the Egyptian Campaign of 1882.

168. On one occasion, Hartington and Gladstone appeared to have come close to fisticuffs. Entry 20 June 1882, Gladstone Diaries, *op. cit.*

169. J C R Colomb, *The Defence of Great and Greater Britain: Sketches of its Naval, Military and Political Aspects: Annotated with Extracts from the Discussions they have called Forth in the Press of Greater Britain* (London: Edward Stanford, 1880).

170. Schurman, *op. cit.*, pp. 90–93.

171. See Entry 24 May 1884 in J Vincent (ed.), *The Diaries of Edward Henry Stanley, 15th Earl of Derby (1826–93), Between 1878 and 1893* (Oxford: Leopard's Head Press, 2003).

172. Schurman, *op. cit.*, p. 131.

173. *The Times*, 20 November 1884.

174. BL.Add.60777, Carnarvon to Stead, Carnarvon Papers, 12 October 1884.

175. Schurman, *op.cit.*, p. 134.

176. P Jackson, *The Last of the Whigs* (London: Associated University Presses, 1994), pp. 282–83. See also F A Johnson, *Defence by Committee: The British Committee of Imperial Defence, 1885–1959* (Oxford: Oxford University Press, 1960), p. 27.

177. J C R Colomb, 'Imperial Federation', *RUSI Journal* (Vol. 30, 1886).

178. See, for example, H O Arnold–Forster, 'Our Position as a Naval Power', *The Nineteenth Century* (Vol. 13, January–July 1883).

179. Mr Howard Vincent, 'Imperial Federation, Naval and Military— Captain Colomb's Lecture', *Hansard*, HC Vol. 306, Col. 1015 (4 June 1886).

180. William E Gladstone, 'Imperial Federation, Naval and Military— Captain Colomb's Lecture', *Hansard*, HC Vol. 306, Col. 1015 (4 June 1886).

181. Discussions after presentation of Colomb, *op. cit.* in note 177.

182. Sir Charles Hugent, 'Imperial Federation', *RUSI Journal* (Vol. 30, 1886).

183. R K Ensor, *England 1870–1914* (Oxford: Clarendon Press, 1936), p. 178.

184. Entry 16 February 1885 in Vincent, *op. cit.*

185. Entry 11 January 1884, in *ibid.*

186. Comments by Sir Charles Dilke following Colonel Sir Howard Vincent, 'Lessons of the war in South Africa', *RUSI Journal* (Vol. 94, 1900).

187. Gladstone to Lord Acton, 11 February 1885, in *Gladstone Diaries, op. cit.*

188. Damian P O'Connor, 'Who Killed Cetshwayo? A Case Study of Ethical Foreign Policy', *RUSI Journal* (Vol. 149, No. 5, October 2004).

189. *Hansard*, HL Vol. 326, Cols. 91–110 (14 May 1888).

190. John Charmley, *Splendid Isolation? Britain and the Balance of Power 1874–1914* (London: Hodder and Stoughton, 1999), p. 224.

III. La Belle Époque: 1890–1914, pp. 81–132.

1. RUSI annual report, 1897.

2. Michael D Welch, *Science and the British Officer: The Early Days of the RUSI for Defence Studies (1829–1869)*, RUSI Whitehall Paper 44 (London: RUSI, 1998), p. 70.

3. Hew Strachan, *The First World War: A New History* (Free Press, 2006), pp. 10–15.

4. Albert T Lauterbach, 'Militarism in the Western World: A Comparative Study', *Journal of the History of Ideas* (Vol. 5, No. 4, October 1944), pp. 446–78.

5. Colonel Malleson, 'The Sea Route to India', *The Asiatic Quarterly Review* (Vol. 5, January–April 1888).

6. See, for example, BL 44629 Vol. DXLIV, 'Memorandum for HM Plenipotentiary in Egypt, C. Gordon', Gladstone Papers, 22 January 1884. See also BL 44147 Vol. LXII, 'Hartington to Gladstone 15 January 1884', Gladstone Papers, for Gordon's contradictoriness.

7. Charles E Callwell, 'Notes on the Tactics of our Small Wars', *Minutes of the Proceedings of the Royal Artillery Institution* (Vol. XII, 1884).

8. See for example, Peter Cain (ed.), *Empire and Imperialism: The Debate of the 1870s* (Little Bend, IN: St Augustines Press, 1999).

9. *Ibid.*

10. Dennis E Showalter, 'Information Capabilities and Military Revolutions; The Nineteenth Century Experience', *Journal of Strategic Studies* (Vol. 27, No. 2, 2004).

11. *The Times,* 'The Operations of War', 1 November 1869.

12. *The Times*, 'Colonel Chesney on Prussian Tactics', 10 January 1871.

13. *The Times*, 'Editorial', 27 July 1881.

14. See for example, *The Times*, 'The Cinque Ports and Imperial Defence', 8 September 1898.

15. Dictionary of National Biography.

16. A N Porter, 'Sir Alfred Milner and the Press, 1897-1899', *The Historical Journal* (Vol. 16, No. 2, 1973).

17. Paul M Kennedy, *The Rise of the Anglo-German Antagonism 1860–1914* (London: G Allen & Unwin, 1980), p. 150.

18. *Ibid.* pp. 87–89.

19. David Brown, 'Compelling but not Controlling? Palmerston and the Press, 1846-1855', *History* (Vol. 86, No. 281, January 2001).

20. *Ibid.*

21. Porter, *op. cit.* See also Mark Hampton, 'Journalists and the "Professional Ideal" in Britain: the Institute of Journalists, 1884–1907', *Historical Research* (Vol. 72, No. 178, June 1997).

22. KJ 28 July 1875 in A Hawkins and J Powell, *The Journal of John Wodehouse First Earl of Kimberley for 1862–1902* (London: 1997).

23. DD 11 January 1884 in J Vincent (ed), *The Diaries of Edward Henry Stanley, 15th Earl of Derby (1826-93), Between 1878 and 1893* (Oxford: 2003).

24. Dictionary of National Biography.

25. G A Henty, *Through the Sikh War* (London: Blackie & Son, 1894).

26. In this case, a particularly unpleasant Latin master sacked for being 'blind drunk ... screwed as an owl'.

27. Ian Beckett, *The Victorians at War* (London: Hambledon Continuum, 2003), pp. 172–73.

28. Now hung in the National Portrait Gallery.

29. Bernard Porter, *The Lion's Share: A Short History of British Imperialism 1850–1983* (London: Longman, 1984), p. 117.

30. George Chesney, 'Value of India to England' (1878), reproduced in Cain, *op. cit.*

31. Henry de Worms, 'Egypt – The Suez Canal', *Hansard*, HC Vol. 271, Cols. 412–14 (26 June 1882).

32. John Hay, 'Mercantile Marine – Signalling at Sea', *Hansard*, HC Vol.

278, Cols. 65–66 (12 April 1883); John Heaton, 'Army (Ordnance Department) – Small Arms – The Martini Breech-Block', *Hansard*, HC Vol. 307, Cols. 257–78 (24 June 1886).

33. Henry Labouchere, 'Departmental Statement', *Hansard*, HC Vol. 286, Col. 137 (17 March 1884).

34. Francis Charteris, 'Motion for a Paper', *Hansard*, HL Vol. 317, Cols. 1743–51 (22 July 1887).

35. Charles Dilke, 'Cyprus – Grant in Aid', *Hansard*, HC Vol. 31., Cols. 683–98 (8 March 1895).

36. *The Times*, 4 March 1889.

37. J L Sturgis, *John Bright and the Empire* (London: Athlone Press, 1969), p. 105.

38. Gladstone to Madame O Novikov, 8 August 1883, H.C.G. Matthew, The Gladstone Diaries Vol.X, XI (Oxford, 1990)

39. Gladstone to Harcourt, 19 January 1885, in Gladstone Diaries, *op. cit.*

40. Gladstone to Harcourt, 19 January 1885; Gladstone to Lord Acton, 11 February 1885; Gladstone to Rev M MacColl 30 January 1884, Gladstone to E A Freeman 14 February 1884, in Gladstone Diaries, *op. cit*

41. KJ 9 December 1878; see also KJ 1 May 1879 in Hawkins and Powell, *op. cit.*

42. DD 18 July 1882 in Vincent, *op. cit.*

43. DD 18 July 1882; DD 6 June 1884 in Vincent, *op. cit.*

44. John Nolan, 'Supply – Army Estimates', *Hansard*, HC Vol. 348, Col. 414 (9 August 1890).

45. *Ibid.*

46. Parl. Debs. (series 3) vol. 348, cols. 74-76 (7 Aug. 1890). Viscount Sidmouth.

47. *The Times*, 23 July 1889.

48. *Ibid.*

49. RUSI annual report, 1890.

50. E Stanhope, 'Supply – Army Estimates', *Hansard*, HC Vol. 348, Cols. 367–425 (9 August 1890).

51. *The Times*, 4 November 1890.

52. Mr James (Gateshead), Parliamentary Debates, *Hansard*, HC Vol. 349, Cols. 1276–77 (29 January 1891).

53. *The Times*, 9 March 1891.

54. *The Times*, 28 June 1892.

55. John Hibbert, 'The United Service Institution', *Hansard*, HC Vol. 13, Col. 509 (8 June 1893).

56. *The Times*, 31 August 1892.

57. 'The Laying of the Memorial Stone of the New Wing by HRH The Prince of Wales KG', *RUSI Journal* (Vol. 37, No. 185, July 1863).

58. *The Times*, 7 June 1893.

59. RUSI annual report, 1896.

60. Earl of Wemyss, Parliamentary Debates, *Hansard* (Series 4) Vol. 75, Col. 1433 (4 August 1899).

61. *Ibid.*

62. Gwendolen Cecil, *Life of Robert Marquis of Salisbury, Vol. 1: 1830–68* (London: Hodder & Stoughton, 1971), p. 218.

63. *New York Times*, 27 November 1898.

64. John Charmley, *Splendid Isolation? Britain and the Balance of Power 1874-1914* (London: Hodder & Stoughton, 1999), p. 234.

65. Daniel H Wicks, 'The First Cruise of the Squadron of Evolution', *Military Affairs* (Vol. 44, No. 2, April 1980), pp. 64–69.

66. Paul M Kennedy, *The Rise and Fall of British Naval Mastery* (London: Allen Lane, 1976), p. 250.

67. 'Naval Notes', *RUSI Journal* (Vol. 46, No. 292, 1902).

68. WO 106/40, 'Defence Plans pre-1914'.

69. Charmley, *op. cit.,* p. 228.

70. I am grateful to Dr Stephen Badsey for this point.

71. Anonymous, 'Ein Sommernachtstraum' (English translation in *United Service Magazine,* 1890).

72. R Home, *A Precis of Modern tactics* (London: The Stationery Office, 1882), quoted in F W Sweet, 'Evolution of Infantry Assault Tactics 1850-1918', unpublished thesis (American Military University, 1997).

73. Donald M Schurman, *Imperial Defence 1868–1887* (London: Frank Cass, 2000), p. 32.

74. CO 885/4/14, 'Correspondence concerning the Defences of the Colonies Colonial Office', June 1878. See also Schurman, *op. cit.,* pp. 62–63.

75. This was before the CDC of 1885 was established. Peter Burroughs, 'Defence and Imperial Disunity', in Andrew Porter (ed.), *Oxford History of the British Empire Vol. III, The Nineteenth Century* (Oxford: Oxford University Press, 1999).

76. CO 885/4/14. Also see Schurman, *op. cit.,* p. 63.

77. Schurman, *op. cit.,* p. 83.

78. Captain Colomb applied for, but was refused, a place on the Commission, and as a result published his book, *The Defence of Great and Greater Britain: Sketches of its Naval, Military and Political Aspects: Annotated with Extracts from the Discussions they have called Forth in the Press of Greater Britain* (London: Edward Stanford, 1880). See also CO 885/4/18, 'Colomb to Hicks-Beach, 13 September 1879', 'Hicks-Beach to Colomb, 25 September 1879', 'Correspondence respecting the Defences of the Colonies Colonial Office, July 1879.

79. Schurman, *op. cit.,* p.89.

80. J C R Colomb, 'Naval Intelligence and Protection of Commerce in War', *RUSI Journal* (Vol. 25, No. 112, 1882), p. 582.

81. OIOC IOR Mss EUR D604/63, 'Kimberley to Hartington', Hartington Papers, 5 December 1881.

82. Schurman, *op. cit.,* p. 129. See also OIOC IOR Mss EUR D604/63, 'Summary of Recommendations of the Inspector-General of Fortifications. Approved by HRH George', Hartington Papers.

83. Gladstone to Hartington, 10 March 1884 in Gladstone Diaries, *op. cit.*

84. Schurman, *op. cit.,* p. 134.

85. Viscount Esher, 'The Co-ordination of the Naval and Military Services', *RUSI Journal* (Vol. 56, No. 4, 1912).

86. PRO 30/40/18, Ardagh Papers, 'Wolseley to Ardagh', 14 September 1895.

87. Now housed in The Royal Army Medical Corps Historical Museum.

88. F James Mouat, 'A Visit to Some of the Battle Fields and Ambulances of the North of France', *RUSI Journal* (Vol. 15, No. 64, 1871).

89. David Rattray used this phrase often in his tours of Rorke's Drift. He was murdered tragically in 2007.

90. I am grateful for much of this to Martin Everett of the South Wales Borders Museum, Brecon.

91. W H James, 'The Necessity for an Army as well as a Navy for the Maintenance of the Empire', *RUSI Journal* (Vol. 40, No. 219, 1869).

92. H Elsdale, 'The Defence of London and of England', *RUSI Journal* (Vol. 30, No. 135, 1886).

93. *The Times*, 5 March 1877.

94. He gave him a reference in his application for the Intelligence Bureau. See Collinson to Ardagh 11 Jan 1875, *The Ardagh Papers*, Public Record Office 30/40 Box 18.

95. 'The Dutch in the Medway', first published in C R L Fletcher and Rudyard Kipling, *A School History of England* (Oxford: Clarendon Press, 1911).

96. William Le Queux, *The Invasion of 1910 with a Full Account of the Siege of London* (London: E Nash, 1906).

97. National Archives, WO 138/7, Lieutenant Colonel Charles à Court-Repington, Personal Files.

98. Theodore Ropp, 'Conscription in Great Britain, 1900–1914: A Failure in Civil-Military Communications?', *Military Affairs* (Vol. 20, No. 2, Summer 1956), pp. 71–76.

99. Le Queux, *op. cit.*, p. 168.

100. F S Roberts, 'Rough Notes on Formation, Equipment, and Despatch of a Force from India for Service in China, Egypt, or Elsewhere beyond the Sea', *USI Journal* (Vol. 1, No. 1, 1871).

101. Beckett, *op. cit.*, p. 129.

102. National Archives, WO 106/6188, 'Handbook for the London Defence Positions', 1903.

103. National Archives, WO 106/47 Box ID/8 (Invasion), 1908.

104. Colonel George Tomkyns, 'The Defeat of the Navy in the Battle of

Dorking', *Colbourn's United Service Magazine* (Part II, 1871).

105. C Campbell, 'Concentration of a Force to Resist Raids or Invasion, Training, Organisation and Rapid Deployment', *RUSI Journal* (Vol. 52, No. 370, 1908).

106. Christopher Andrew, *The Defence of the Realm: The Authorised History of MI5* (London: Penguin Books, 2009), p. 8. Much of this section is drawn from this source.

107. Paul M Kennedy, *The Rise and Fall of British Naval Mastery* (London: Macmillan, 1983), p. 275.

108. Kennedy, *ibid.*, p. 272.

109. Parl. Debs. (series 4) vol. 156 col. 394 (1 May. 1906). Mr Bellairs (Lynn Regis).

110. Kennedy, *op. cit.* in note 66, p. 279.

111. Quoted in Ropp, *op. cit.*

112. RUSI annual report, 1908.

113. J K Laughton, 'The Study of Naval History', *RUSI Journal* (Vol. 40, No. 7, 1896).

114. RUSI Annual Report, 1910.

115. Robin Higham, 'The Dangerously Neglected: The British Military Intellectuals, 1918-1939', *Military Affairs* (Vol. 29, No. 2, Summer 1965), pp. 73-87.

116. Niall Ferguson, *The War of the World: Twentieth-Century Conflict and the Descent of the West* (London: Penguin Books, 2006), p. 106.

117. Beckett, *op. cit.*, p. 176.

118. PRO 30/40/18, Ardagh Papers, 'Wolseley to Ardagh', 19 July 1892.

IV. The Crucible: 1914–45, pp. 133–90.

1. K P Smith, 'The National Will to War', *RUSI Journal* (Vol. 83, 1938).

2. John MacDonald, 'The Knife in Trench Warfare', *RUSI Journal* (Vol. 62, No. 445, 1917).

3. RUSI annual report, 1919.

4. Gordon Corrigan, *Mud, Blood and Poppycock* (London: Cassell Military Paperbacks, 2003), p. 189.

5. Michael D Welch, *Science and the British Officer: The Early Days of the RUSI for Defence Studies (1829–1869)*, RUSI Whitehall Paper No. 44 (London: RUSI, 1998).

6. Dictionary of National Biography.

7. William Hill, RUSI annual report, 1919.

8. Anne Applebaum, 'Now We Know', *anneapplebaum.com*, 17 June 2009, <http://www.anneapplebaum.com/2009/05/31/now-we-know/>.

9. Eustace Percy, 'The League of Nations', *RUSI Journal* (Vol. 64, No. 456, 1919).

10. See 'Discussion' in *ibid*.

11. *Ibid*.

12. Colonel John Ward, 'Labour in its Relations to the Army', *RUSI Journal* (Vol. 66, No. 461, 1921).

13. C J Mackay, 'The Influence in the Future of Aircraft upon problems of Imperial Defence', *RUSI Journal* (Vol. 67, No. 466, 1922).

14. See the debate in Peter Silverman, 'The Ten Year Rule', *RUSI Journal* (Vol. 116, No. 661, 1971) and K Booth, 'The Ten-Year Rule – An Unfinished Debate', *RUSI Journal* (Vol. 116, No. 661, 1971).

15. 'Secretary's Notes', *RUSI Journal* (Vol. 73, 1928).

16. 'Secretary's Notes', *RUSI Journal* (Vol. 70, 1925).

17. 'Secretary's Notes', *RUSI Journal* (Vol. 68, 1923).

18. 'Secretary's Notes', *RUSI Journal* (Vol. 69, 1924).

19. 'Secretary's Notes', *RUSI Journal* (Vol. 83, 1939).

20. 'Secretary's Notes', *RUSI Journal* (Vols. 72, 1927 and 73, 1928).

21. *The Times*, 20 May 1920, 30 December 1924, 13 November 1929, 22 November 1938.

22. *Hansard*, HC Vol. 348, Cols. 2482–3 (22 June 1939).

23. *The Times*, 20 March 1936.

24. Council minutes, 20 December 1938 and 7 February 1939.

25. Council minutes, 4 February 1930 and 4 February 1936.

26. R Gibson, 'Royal United Services Institution (Exhibition)', *Hansard*, HC Vol. 332, Cols. 1895–6 (9 March 1938).

27. *The Times*, 23 March 1936.

28. Secretary's Notes, *RUSI Journal* (Vol. 71, 1926).

29. *Ibid.*

30. *Ibid.*

31. RUSI annual report 1923.

32. *The Times,* 3 June 1935.

33. J Dundas, 'Gold Medal (Naval) Prize Essay for 1925: The Communications across the Oceans of the World being essential to the Empire, how best can they be safeguarded?' *RUSI Journal* (Vol. 71, No. 482, 1926).

34. R J Wilkinson, 'Singapore', *RUSI Journal* (Vol. 69, No. 476, 1924).

35. Mackay, *op. cit.*

36. J L Vachell, 'A Flight to Abyssinia', *RUSI Journal* (Vol. 77, No. 506, 1932).

37. See, for example, R D Pearce, *The Turning Point in Africa: British Colonial Policy 1938–48* (London: Taylor and Francis, 1982).

38. *The Times,* 3 June 1935.

39. Lieutenant Colonel Poudret, 'An Essay on the Employment of Cavalry', *RUSI Journal* (Vol. 64, No. 456, 1919).

40. E R Macpherson, 'The Maintenance of Mechanized Formations', *RUSI Journal* (Vol. 77, No. 506, 1932).

41. J F C Fuller, 'The War on Land: The Application of Recent Developments in the Mechanics and Other Scientific Knowledge to Preparation and Training for Future War on Land', *RUSI Journal* (Vol. 65, No. 458, 1920).

42. J F C Fuller, 'Progress in the Mechanicalisation of Modern Armies', *RUSI Journal* (Vol. 70, No. 477, 1925).

43. R McLeod, 'Some Reflections on Modern Military Tactics', *RUSI Journal* (Vol. 77, No. 505, 1932).

44. J K Edwards, 'The Functions of Tanks', *RUSI Journal* (Vol. 80, No. 517, 1935).

45. See Gordon Beckles, *Tanks Advance* (London: Cassell, 1942).

46. Heinz Guderian, *Panzer Leader* (London: Cassell, 1952) p. 24.

47. Commandant Andriot, 'Infantry and Tanks in the Spanish Civil War', *RUSI Journal* (Vol. 84, No. 533, 1939).

48. Lieutenant Warringa, 'Tanks in the Attack: French and German Tactical Theories', *RUSI Journal* (Vol. 83, No. 532, 1938).

49. B T Wilson, 'Modern War and its Maze of Machines', *RUSI Journal* (Vol. 83, No. 530, 1938).

50. Guderian, *op. cit.*, p. 25.

51. Alistair Horne, *To Lose a Battle: France 1940* (London: Cassell, 1999) p. 93.

52. Lieutenant Colonel Hilton, 'Anti-Tank Tactics', *RUSI Journal* (Vol. 84, No. 535, 1939).

53. 'Review of J M Spaight, *An International Air Force*', *RUSI Journal* (Vol. 77, No. 507, 1932).

54. Malcolm Smith, 'A Matter of Faith: British Strategic Air Doctrine before 1939', *Journal of Contemporary History* (Vol. 15, No. 3, July 1980), pp. 423–42.

55. P Landon, 'Aerial Bombardment & International Law', *RUSI Journal* (Vol. 77, No. 505, 1932).

56. J B S Haldane, 'Science and Future Warfare', *RUSI* Journal (Vol. 82, No. 528, 1937).

57. Authored anonymously by General Armengaud, Inspector-General of the French Airforce and Member of the Conseil Superieure de la Defense, 'The Offensive in Future Warfare: A French View', *RUSI Journal* (Vol. 78, No. 511, 1933).

58. Brigadier B T Wilson, *op. cit.*

59. Robin Higham, 'The Dangerously Neglected: The British Military Intellectuals, 1918–1939', *Military Affairs* (Vol. 29, No. 2, Summer 1965), pp. 73–87.

60. M H C Young RN, 'Aircraft Attacks or Gunfire against Warships', *RUSI Journal* (Vol. 81, No. 522, 1936).

61. Higham, *op. cit.*, pp. 73–87.

62. Smith, *op. cit.*, pp. 423–42.

63. Wilson, *op. cit.*.

64. J P D Dunbabin, 'British Rearmament in the 1930s: A Chronology and Review', *The Historical Journal* (Vol. 18, No. 3. September 1975), pp. 587–609.

65. Much of this section is drawn from *ibid.*

66. B T Reynolds, 'Germany of To-day', *RUSI Journal* (Vol. 77, No. 505, 1932).

67. 'The International Situation: France and Germany', *RUSI Journal* (Vol. 79, 1934).

68. Anon, 'German Aviation', *RUSI Journal* (Vol. 79, 1934).

69. J K Dunlop, 'The Territorial Army', *RUSI Journal* (Vol. 80, No. 518, 1935).

70. General Service Notes quoting from 'Statement relating to defence', 4 March 1935.

71. Editor, 'The International Situation: The Aftermath of the Italian Conquest of Abyssinia', *RUSI Journal* (Vol. 81, 1936).

72. Dunbabin, *op. cit.*

73. Smith, *op. cit.*

74. D L Raymond, 'The Royal Navy', *RUSI Journal* (Vol. 81, No. 523, 1936).

75. A G Armstrong, 'The Army of Today', *RUSI Journal* (Vol. 81, No. 523, 1936).

76. A G Armstrong, 'The Army's new weapons and equipment', *RUSI Journal* (Vol. 84, No. 534, 1939).

77. FFG, 'The Royal Air Force', *RUSI Journal* (Vol. 81, No. 523, 1936).

78. Council minutes, 7 July 1936.

79. Council minutes, 3 October 1939.

80. Ernst Woermann, 'Germany of To-day', *RUSI Journal* (Vol. 83, No. 531, 1938).

81. RUSI did forgive Fuller after the war, awarding him and Liddell-Hart the Gold Medal in 1963.

82. *The Times,* 1 September 1945.

83. Secretary's Notes, *RUSI Journal* (Vol. 86, 1941).

84. Martin S Alexander, *The Republic in Danger: General Maurice Gamelin and the politics of French Defence* (Cambridge: Cambridge University Press, 1992).

85. R Macleod and D Kelly (eds), *Time Unguarded: The Ironside Diaries 1937–1940* (London: Constable & Co, 1962), pp. 115, 132.

86. *RUSI Journal*, 'Germany's Oil Supplies' (Vol. 86, No. 543, 1941).
87. *RUSI Journal*, 'The Higher Commander: General Wavell's Views' (Vol. 86, No. 541, 1941); originally printed as A P Wavell, 'The Higher Commander', *RUSI Journal* (Vol. 81, No. 521, 1936).

88. Twas grillig and the Congreelites,
    Did barge and shoblbe in the swope
    All jinsy were the Pskastanites
    And the spruft Sikhs outstrop.

89. Russell W Glenn, 'Earning the thanks of Harry and Jack: The Journal of the Royal United Service Institution and World War Generalship', *RUSI Journal* (Vol. 142, No. 1, 1997).
90. Council Minutes 2 February 1943 and 4 May 1943.
91. Laurence Bergreen, 'Irving Berlin: This Is the Army, Part 4', in *Prologue Magazine*, US National Archives (Vol. 28, No. 2, Summer 1996).
92. H Rowan-Robinson, 'The Buckler of the New Order', *RUSI Journal* (Vol. 88, No. 550, 1943).

V. Cold War, Decline and Revival: 1945–1989, pp. 191–240.

1. D W Brogan, 'The American Attitude towards International Affairs', *RUSI Journal* (Vol. 95, No. 577, 1950).
2. *Ibid.*
3. Editor's Notes, *RUSI Journal*, May 1962.
4. A Shenfield, 'The Impact of Reductions of Defence Requirements on British Industry', *RUSI Journal* (Vol. 104, 1959).
5. Charles Stevenson, 'Labour's Defence Policy: Promises and Performance', *RUSI Journal* (Vol. 111, 1966).
6. Editor's Notes, *RUSI Journal* (Vol. 112, August 1967).
7. Editor's Notes, *RUSI Journal* (Vol. 113, May 1968).
8. Editor's Notes, *RUSI Journal* (Vo. 113, February 1968).
9. Editor's Notes, *RUSI Journal* (Vol. 113, February 1968).
10. A Gwynne Jones, 'The Nature of the Communist Threat', *RUSI Journal* (Vol. 103, 1958).
11. 'Permission to Speak, Sir?', *RUSI Journal* (Vol. 119, No. 2, 1974).

12. Reginald Plunkett-Ernle-Erle-Drax, 'A Ten-Year Forecast 1960–70', *RUSI Journal* (Vol. 105, 1960). Drax also wrote 'WWIII: Some Pros and Cons', *RUSI Journal* (Vol. 100, 1955).

13. Editor's Notes, *RUSI Journal* (Vol. 106, February 1961).

14. Richard Kelly, 'Not as Daft as You Thought', *New Statesman*, 2 June 2003.

15. William Burr (ed), 'US Planning for War in Europe 1963–64', National Security Archive Electronic Briefing Book No. 31, 24 May 2000, Document One: U.S. National Security Council, Net Evaluation Subcommittee, The Management and Termination of War With the Soviet Union, 15 November 1963.

16. J M Spaight, 'The Pattern of Future War', *RUSI Journal* (Vol. 95, 1950).

17. Editor's Notes, *RUSI Journal* (Vol. 109, August 1964).

18. Michael Howard, 'Strategy in the Nuclear Age', *RUSI Journal* (Vol. 102, November 1957).

19. TNA, CAB 120/69.

20. Giffard Martel, 'Tank Policy', *RUSI Journal* (Vol. 96, 1951).

21. F W von Mellenthin, *Panzer Battles* (London, Ballantine Books, 1955), p. 362.

22. Spaight, *op cit.*

23. Lieutenant Colonel Carver, 'Tanks and Infantry: The Need for Speed', *RUSI Journal* (Vol. 96, 1951).

24. G G R Williams, 'Atomic Weapons and Army Training', *RUSI Journal* (Vol. 99, November 1954).

25. J Erickson, '"Shield-72": Warsaw Pact Military Exercises', *RUSI Journal* (Vol. 117, No. 669, December 1972).

26. *The Times*, 22 October 1954.

27. Viscount Montgomery, 'A Look Through a Window at World War III', *RUSI Journal* (Vol. 99, No. 596, 1954)

28. P Pelly, 'The Pattern of a Future War', *RUSI Journal* (Vol. 95, 1950).

29. Editor's Notes, *RUSI Journal* (Vol. 110. November 1965).

30. L B Oatts, 'Guerrilla Warfare', *RUSI Journal* (Vol. 94, 1949).

31. F Mellersh, 'The Campaign against the Terrorists in Malaya', *RUSI Journal* (Vol. 96, 1951), pp. 401–15.

32. Marion C Dalby, 'Operations in Vietnam', *RUSI Journal* (Vol. 11, 1966).

33. Donald Cameron Watt, 'Lessons of the American Defeat in Vietnam', *RUSI Journal* (Vol. 118, June 1973).

34. David Starkey, *Six Wives: The Queens of Henry VIII* (London: Vintage, 2004), p. 680.

35. Council Minutes, 2 July 1946.

36. Council Minutes, 4 December 1951.

37. Council Minutes, 6 February 1945.

38. Council Minutes, 8 May 1951.

39. *The Times,* 17 July 1954.

40. *The Times,* 9 December 1959.

41. Special Meeting of the Council Minutes, 19 July 1960.

42. 'The Future of the Museum if the B-H is taken over by Government', RUSI files, box 3.

43. 'A Note on the closure of the Museum', RUSI files, box 2, August 1964.

44. *Guardian*, '"Headless men" in sex scandal finally named', 10 August 2000.

45. 'Charity Commissioners Bundle', RUSI files, box 1, November 1962–August 1963.

46. 'A Note on the closure of the Museum', *op cit.*

47. *The Times*, 3 April 1970.

48. Council Minutes, 5 March 1963.

49. *The Times*, 28 March 1964.

50. Editor's Notes, August 1964.

51. 'Britain looks at defence Analysis Methods in the US', *The Times*, 13 August 1963.

52. Editor's Notes, November 1968.

53. Neil Cameron, K Hunt and Captain Le Bailey, 'A National Institute of Strategic Affairs', Letters to the Editor, *RUSI Journal*, 11 July 1963.

54. Council Minutes, 3 March 1964.

55. 'D W Ward to Brigadier Stephenson', RUSI files, box 1, 28 January 1966.

56. 'The Future of the RUSI: Joint RUSI–MOD Working Party', RUSI files, box 1, 24 May 1966.

57. Marked 'restricted'. 'Notes of Discussion between Secretary of State for Defence and Representatives of the RUSI', RUSI files, box 1, 9 Feb 1967.

58. 'The Future of the RUSI: Report by a Joint RUSI/MOD Study Group', RUSI files, box 1, 9 May 1967.

59. 'Hugh Hanning: The lessons of war taught him to love peace', *The Guardian*, 27 May 2000.

60. Editor's Notes, November 1968.

61. Editor's Notes, November 1968.

62. Editor's Notes, November 1968.

63. Editor's Notes, September 1969.

64. Obituary, *RUSI Journal*.

65. 'Why the General is re-Fighting World War III', *The Times,* 19 June 1982.

66. Diary, *The Times*, 8 October 1981.

67. P H Vigor, 'Doubts and Difficulties Confronting a Would-be Soviet Attacker', *RUSI Journal* (Vol. 125, 1980).

68. Steve Smith, 'The Myth of the Soviet threat', *RUSI Journal* (Vol. 127, No. 2, 1982).

69. Professor Ronald Mason and D P Hall, 'Emerging Technology in Defence: Real Gain or False Economy?' *RUSI Journal* (Vol. 129, 1984).

70. Editorial, 'Soviet Military Power', *RUSI Journal* (Vol. 128, No. 3, 1983).

71. Editorial, 'Four More Years', *RUSI Journal* (Vol. 129, No. 4, Dec 1984).

72. E P Thompson, 'Dr Popov's Missile Misfires', *The Times,* 17 November 1982.

73. Letters, *The Times*, 16 December 1982.

74. 'Stand Up and Start Counting', Editorial, *RUSI Journal*, March 1981.

75. *Ibid.*

76. *Hansard*, HC Vol. 34, Col. 536 (22 December 1982).

77. *The Times,* 4 September 1982.

78. Mungo Melvin, 'Exercise United Shield 2008', *RUSI Journal* (Vol. 154, June 2009).

79. John L Romjue, 'The Evolution of the Airland Battle Concept', *Air University Review*, May – June 1984, <http://www.airpower.maxwell. af.mil/airchronicles/aureview/1984/may-jun/romjue.html> last accessed 17 April 2011.

80. *Hansard*, HC Vol. 69, Col. 273 (6 December 1984).

81. J P Riley , 'MCV-80 and Beyond: Implications for the Infantry', *RUSI Journal* (Vol. 131, No. 3, 1986).

82. Charles J Dick, 'The Goodwood Concept: Situating the Appreciation', *RUSI Journal* (Vol. 127, March 1982).

83. Interview with Sir Clive Rose by Virginia Crowe, 30 August 2003, <www.chu.cam.ac.uk/archives/collections/BDOHP/Rose.pdf> last accessed 17 April 2011.

84. Editor's Notes, 1985.

85. Field Marshal Sir John Stanier, council chairman, RUSI Annual Report 1986.

86. RUSI Annual Report 1986.

87. Review article, *RUSI Journal* (Vol. 130, December 1985).

88. Editorial, 'The End of an Era, the Beginning of a New', *RUSI Journal* (Vol. 132, March 1987).

89. RUSI Annual Report 1990.

VI. The New World Order: 1990–2010, pp. 241–92.

1. RUSI annual report, 1990.

2. *Ibid.*

3. Daniel Yergin, *The Prize: The Epic Quest for Oil, Money and Power* (London: Simon and Schuster, 1993).

4. *Ibid.*, pp. 565–56.

5. 'Director's Column', *RUSI Journal* (Vol. 141, No. 5, October 1996).

6. Michael Howard, 'Mistake to Call this a "War"', *RUSI Journal* (Vol. 146, No. 6, December 2001).

7. *Ibid.*

8. Michael Alexander, 'A Global Civil War', *RUSI Journal* (Vol. 146, No. 6, December 2001).

9. 'Director's Column', *RUSI Journal* (Vol. 147, No. 4, August 2002).

10. National Archives WO 33/32 Newspaper Correspondents with an Army in the Field, and Military Attaches of Foreign Powers at Head-Quarters. Lt. John Ross of Bladensburg, Coldstream Guards Intelligence Branch 28th Feb 1878.

11. *Ibid.*

12. *Ibid.*

13. The most recent examples in the *RUSI Journal* of the continuing debate are 'Book Reviews: War Reportage' (Vol. 156, No. 1, February 2011) and Neville Bolt, 'The Leak before the Storm: What WikiLeaks Tells us About Modern Communication' (Vol. 155, No. 4, August 2010).

14. For example see Andrew Marr, *My Trade: A Short History of British Journalism* (London: Macmillan, 2004), p. 76.

15. See Hew Strachan, *Wellington's Legacy: The Reform of the British Army 1830–54* (Manchester: Manchester University Press, 1984). See also Stephen Badsey, 'The Media War' in John Pimlott and Stephen Badsey (eds) *The Gulf War Assessed* (London: Arms and Armour Press, 1992).

16. See Tom Pocock, 'Defence and Public Relations', *RUSI Journal* (Vol. 104, No. 655, September 1969).

17. *Ibid.*

18. *Ibid.*

19. Badsey, *op. cit.*

20. Quoted in *ibid.*

21. House of Commons, First Report of the Defence Committee Session 1982–3, *The Handling of Press and Public Information during the Falklands Conflict* Vol. 1 (London: The Stationery Office, 1983), p. xiv.

22. Donald Cameron Watt, 'Lessons of the American defeat in Vietnam', *RUSI Journal* (Vol. 118, No. 2, June 1973).

23. Henry Stanhope, 'War Mis-Reporting', *RUSI Journal* (Vol. 121, No. 2, June 1976).

24. Bernard Ingham, *The Wages of Spin: A Clear Case of Communications Gone Wrong* (London: John Murray, 2003), p. 151.

25. House of Commons, *op. cit.*

26. *Ibid.*, p. lii.

27. House of Commons, First Report of the Defence Committee Session 1982–3; *The handling of Press and Public information during the Falklands Conflict* Vol. 2, Minutes of Evidence (London: The Stationery Office, 1983).

28. *Ibid.*

29. Dereck Mercer, 'Is Press Freedom a Threat During National Crises?', *RUSI Journal* (Vol. 129, No. 3, July 1984).

30. Marr, *op. cit.*, p. 341.

31. Pimlott and Badsey *op. cit.*, p. 222.

32. Badsey, *op. cit.* in note 15.

33. Ingram, *op. cit.*, p.181.

34. Jonathan Eyal, 'The Media and the Military: Continuing the Dialogue after Kosovo', *RUSI Journal* (Vol. 145, No. 2, April 2000).

35. Ingram, *op. cit.*, p. 181.

36. Andrew Sparrow, 'Sept 11: "a good day to bury bad news"', *Daily Telegraph*, 10 October 2001.

37. John Simpson later claimed, unconvincingly, that this was a joke. See John Simpson, *News from No Man's Land: Reporting the World* (London: Pan, 2002), p. 12.

38. 'Director's Column', *RUSI Journal* (Vol. 147, No. 5, October 2002).

39. Quoted in Arthur Keppel-Jones, *Rhodes and Rhodesia: The White Conquest of Zimbabwe 1884–1902* (Montreal: McGill-Queen's University Press, 1983), p. 297.

40. Pietro Giannone, *Dorp Days* (forthcoming). Pietro Giannone grew up in Boksburg, East Rand, and witnessed countless acts of mindless violence against Africans.

41. Dennis Chaplin, 'Cape of Good Hope?', *RUSI Journal* (Vol. 122, No. 3, 1977).

42. Michael Calvert, 'Counter Insurgency in Mozambique', *RUSI Journal* (Vol. 118, No. 1, 1973).

43. See Paul Moorcraft and Peter McLaughlin, *The Rhodesian War: A Military History* (Barnsley: Pen and Sword, 2008).

44. Thomas Arbuckle, 'Rhodesian Bush War Strategies and Tactics: An Assessment', *RUSI Journal* (Vol. 124, No. 4, 1979).

45. *Ibid.*

46. Roger Marston '"Not ordinary White people": The Origins of Rhodesian COIN Theory and Practice', *RUSI Journal* (Vol. 131, No. 4, August 1986).

47. The author is grateful to Lieutenant Colonel Peter Knox, who served in Rhodesia-Zimbabwe during this period.

48. A E Younger, 'The Strategic Position of South Africa', *RUSI Journal* (Vol. 121, No. 3, 1976).

49. Norman L Dodd 'The South African Defence Force', *RUSI Journal* (Vol. 125, No. 1, 1980).

50. Christopher Coker, 'South Africa's Strategic Importance: A Reassessment', *RUSI Journal* (Vol. 124, No. 4, 1979).

51. Christopher Coker, 'South Africa and the Western Alliance 1949–81: A History of Illusions', *RUSI Journal* (Vol. 127, No. 2, 1982).

52. Fidel Castro to Erich Honecker, quoted in Greg Mills and David Williams, *Seven Battles that Shaped South Africa* (Cape Town: Tafelberg, 2006), p. 171.

53. Geoffrey Till, 'Security Concerns in the Indian Ocean: Making Waves?', *RUSI Journal* (Vol. 142, No. 3, June 1997).

54. Romeo Dallaire, *Shake Hands with the Devil: The Failure of Humanity in Rwanda* (London: Arrow, 2004).

55. Chris Mullin, 'When the threat of a coup seemed more than fiction', *Guardian*, 7 March 2006. On the Parliamentary question, see *Hansard*, HC Vol. 177, Col. 922 (18 October 1990):

    Mr. Mullin

    To ask the Secretary of State for Defence if he will give details of Government funding for the Royal United Services Institute and describe the Royal United Services Institute's relationship with his Department.

    Mr. Archie Hamilton

    The Royal United Services Institute (RUSI) is an independent academic institute with charitable status. It is the professional association of the armed forces and one of many academic institutes with which the Ministry of Defence maintains contacts.

For the current financial year we expect MOD funding for RUSI to be around £130,000. The sum of £10,000 is a grant in aid towards expenses of the institute in support of its academic activities. The remainder is a contribution towards the cost of rental and maintenance of its accommodation.

56. Paul Owen, 'Ex-Treasury secretary Liam Byrne's note to his successor: there's no money left', *Guardian*, 17 May 2010.
57. Malcolm Chalmers, 'Preparing for the Lean Years', RUSI Future Defence Review Working Paper No. 1, July 2009.
58. Bill Kincaid, *Changing the Dinosaur's Spots: The Battle to Reform UK Defence Acquisition* (London: RUSI, 2008).
59. Sheila M Bird, 'Compulsory Drugs Testing in the British Army: Assessing the Data', *RUSI Journal* (Vol. 152, No. 6, December 2007).
60. Gwyn Prins and Robert Salisbury, 'Risk, Threat and Security: The Case of the United Kingdom', *RUSI Journal* (Vol. 153, No. 1, February 2008). The article, based on the authors' own views, was nevertheless based on a private seminar series that included Sir Mark Allen, Vice Admiral Sir Jeremy Blackham, Chris Donnelly, Field Marshal the Lord Inge, Tom Kremer, Lord Leach, Baroness Park of Monmouth, Douglas Slater, General Sir Rupert Smith and Professor Hew Strachan.
61. Damian P O'Connor, 'Putting a Kevlar Boot over the Achilles heel of Democracy' (unpublished) was runner-up in the RUSI Trench-Gascoigne Essay Competition in 2006. It was a call for more responsibility from the British media in its war reporting.

APPENDIX
RUSI Governance, 1831 and 2011

RUSI Committee, 1 August 1831

Patron

The King [HM William IV]

Vice-Patron

The Duke of Wellington KG, GCB,GCH

Presidents

Right Hon Sir James Graham, Bart, MP, First Lord of the Admiralty
Admiral Sir J Saumarez, Bart, GCB, Vice Admiral of Great Britain
Admiral Sir Sidney Smith, KCB, General of Marines
General Lord Hill, GCB, GCH, Commander of the Forces
Lieut-Gen Sir J Kempt, GCB, GCH, Master-Gen of the Ordnance
Marquis of Anglesey, KG, KSP, GCB, GCH

Vice-Presidents

Admiral Hon Sir R Stopford, GCB
Gen the Earl of Rosslyn, GCB
Admiral Sir Charles Hamilton, Bart
Gen Lord W Bentinck, GCB, GCH
Adm Sir Thomas B Martin, GCB, MP
Gen Hon Sir Edward Paget, GCB

Vice-Admiral Right Hon Sir George Cockburn, GCB, MP
Gen Lord Viscount Combermere, GCB, GCH
Vice-Adm Sir H W Bayntun, KCB
Gen Lord Viscount Beresford GCB, GCH
Vice-Adm Sir Edward G Colpoys, KCB
Gen Hon Sir A Hope, GCB, MP
Vice-Adm Hon Charles E Fleming
Lieut-Gen Sir Rufane Shaw Donkin, KCB, GCH
Vice-Ad the Hon Sir H Hotham, KCB
Lieut-Gen Right Hon Sir George Murray, GCB, GCH, MP
Vice-Adm Sir Josias Rowley, Bart, KCB
Lieut-Gen Sir Thomas M Brisbane, GCB, GCH
Vice-Admiral Sir E Codrington, GCB
Lieut-Gen Sir Herbert Taylor, GCH
Vice-Admiral Sir Henry Blackwood, Bart, KCB
Lieut-Gen Sir R Hussey Vivan, Bart, KCB and GCH
Vice-Admiral Sir John Poo Beresford, Bart, KCB
Maj-Gen Sir Howard Douglas, Bart, CB
Major-Gen J Macdonald, Adj-Gen
Rear-Admiral Sir Thomas Masterman Hardy, Bart, KCB
Major-Gen Sir Alexander Bryce, CB, KCH
Rear-Admiral Hon Lord James O'Bryen
Major-Gen F W Mulcaster
Major-Gen Right Hon Sir Henry Hardinge, KCB, MP
Director-General Sir James M'Grigor, Knt, MD
Col A H Holdsworth, MP Yeo
Sir William Burnett, Knt, MD RN

Committee for the Present Year
Major-Gen Sir Howard Douglas, Bart, CB, Chairman
Capt F Beaumont, RN
Capt Francis Brace, RN
Capt Norman Campbell,CB, RN

Major T H S Clarke, Staff
Capt Sir Francis Collier, CB, RN
Major the Hon W L F De Roos
Colonel Sir Alexander Dickson, RA, KCB and KCH
Commander W Dickson, RN
Lieut Thomas Drummond, RE
Capt the Hon Henry Duncan, CB, RN
Capt Right Hon Lord Adolphus Fitz Clareence, RN
Colonel C R Fox, Grenadier Guards
Major John Garvock, Assist-Adj-Gen
Capt Basil Hall, RN
Lieut-Colonel Henry Hanmer RH, Guards
Colonel I T Jones, CB, RE
Lieut-Colonel Henry Le Blanc
Capt Edward Lloyd RN
Col W G MacGregor, IFO, Rec Dist
Capt Frederick Marryatt, CB, RN
Col the Right Hon the Earl of Munster
Roderick Impey Murchison, HP, 7th D
Capt G R Sartorius,RN
Capt W H Smyth, RN, St F and M
Capt Hector Straith, HP
Colonel Walter Tremenheere, RM
Capt Sir Thomas Troubridge, Bart, RN, MP
Colonel Sir Charles Broke Vere, KCB
Col Wood, Royal East Middlesex Militia, MP

Secretaries
Com Henry Downes, RN
Lieut W S Hall HP Royal Irish

Treasurer
Charles Downes, Esq, No 8, Regent Street

RUSI governance structure, 1 May 2011

Mr Stephen Phipson CBE
Lt Gen Jonathon Riley CB DSO
Dr Kathryn Vagneur
Mr Ian Willis

Advisory Council
The Rt Hon James Arbuthnot MP
Ms Jane Attwood
Mr Tim Banfield
Mr Stephen R Ball
Rt Hon Sir Menzies Campbell MP
Lord Dobbs of Wylye
Mr Nik Gowing
Mr Robert Hannigan
Mr Bob Keen
Mr Michael M Kurth
Dr Jamie MacIntosh
Dr Greg Mills
Mr Richard Norton-Taylor
Sir Peter Ricketts, GCMG
Professor Mark Welland, FRS, FREng